JOURNAL OF
A SOON-TO-BE
FIRST-TIME DAD

TOM KREFFER

Charlie Cat Books
Kemp House, 160 City Road
London, EC1V 2NX

CCB

First published in Great Britain in 2020 by Charlie Cat Books

Cover Design and layout by TJM Cover Designs
A CIP catalogue record for this book is available from the British Library,
ISBN 978-1-8382225-1-2

To Rebecca
For the introduction of a lifetime

And to midwives
The front-line saviours of humanity

Contents

Before we get started …   1

March   3

April   25

May   55

June   84

July   108

August   134

September   157

October   188

November   207

Acknowledgements   243

A Note From the Author   245

About Tom Kreffer   246

Say Hello!   247

Want More?   248

Before we get started ...

I never meant for this to be a book. And then, when I did, I never meant for it to be published – I initially saw it as a personal project for me and my family, and as a tool to help me process what I was up against.

I woke up one day and found myself facing the emotionally complex realisation that, in eight months' time, I would be responsible for the upbringing of a brand-new member of humanity.

That's one mindfuck I wasn't expecting to land on my doorstop – not when doctors had told me it was all but impossible for my partner to fall pregnant without medical intervention (IVF). I was now standing in the middle of an uncharted landscape, one I found daunting and disorientating. And so I turned to writing to help me plot a course – a pen and paper lighting the way forward (actually, I mainly used my laptop) as I inched towards first-time fatherhood.

I sought guidance in books. Some helped; others didn't. And none (that I read, at least) tapped into what I was looking for – the answers to many questions. How do I prepare for the responsibility of a lifetime? Why does my partner get offended when I walk into the room? Who am I right now? And who do I have to become to be worthy of the title 'parent'?

I've since come to realise how difficult it is to capture the answers to those questions, let alone put them into words. Nevertheless, this is my attempt, and it is why (with my partner's blessing) I have decided to share our story. It is my hope that you will find something to relate to, something to make you smile, or an invitation to reminisce about that time when you or your

1

partner took a pregnancy test and you found out that you were going to be a Mummy or a Daddy.

You are likely to read a lot of incorrect assumptions about pregnancy. You're reading this from my perspective – as I experienced it. This has not been written as a guidebook: it is an insight into the experiences of a first-time father bumbling his way towards parenthood while trying to avoid having his eyes torn out by his hormonal partner.

To any woman reading this who has been pregnant – my intention is not to offend, but test-reader feedback suggests I should offer no guarantees. (God help you if you are currently pregnant and reading this.) You have to understand how crazy this whole child-growing business is from a soon-to-be father's perspective as well. I get it: you do all the work, and you deserve all the praise (and more) – but an unprovoked hormonal attack is no ice cream sundae in the sun.

Know that I have the deepest respect for any woman who carries a child. I can say without hesitation that women are fucking awesome and, on behalf of the human race, you have my gratitude for allowing us to continue existing. You won't find a stronger definition of strength and love than watching a woman give birth.

Finally, I always assumed the pregnancy journey was one that only Mummies took. I got that wrong.

March

Saturday, 16 March 2019 – My Day Of Discovery

I never wake up in the morning anxious about going to the bathroom, but today is an exception, which is stupid, because I'm anxious about something that professionals have told me won't happen.

Still.

I'm also pissed off, because this particular form of anxiety is something I promised myself I wouldn't succumb to, and it's something I've warned the woman lying asleep next to me about as well, so now I'm a pissed-off, anxious hypocrite.

She's wearing Frosties pyjamas, the woman next to me – as in Frosties, the Kellogg's breakfast cereal. Tony the Tiger smiles at me as if to say, 'You never know, mate, even the pros get it wrong sometimes.'

In my head, I instruct Tony to go and fuck himself.

Back to the woman lying next to me. She's the only thirty-something woman I know who occasionally still gets ID'd for alcohol. She looks the same this morning as she did last night, apart from the odd bit of dribble (which I love).

She stirs and then opens her eyes and smiles. After four and a half years, that smile still shatters me.

But then she remembers what we have to do this morning, and I can tell from her facial expression that anxiety has hit her as well. 'Shall we go to the bathroom?' she says.

I nod, but not without trying to invoke a thread of my Don't Be Anxious campaign. 'What must we remember?' I say without a hint of shame.

'Not to get our hopes up,' she says. 'I'm not … don't worry.'

At least I'm not the only liar in our relationship this morning.

We shuffle to the bathroom. The woman sits on the toilet and begins peeing on a stick. Tony the Tiger is still smiling. I want to slap him in the face, but that would result in me slapping the woman I love on the right tit, which would be awfully bad timing on my part, because she's been complaining of pain in that area recently.

Which brings us to now. It's been almost two years without success. The woman peeing on the stick has some body parts that aren't working correctly, body parts that are critical to the thing we're trying to accomplish, parts that doctors want to remove surgically. Pregnancy will not happen naturally, they said. That's why they have also put us on a waiting list for IVF.

And yet she's peeing on a stick because she doesn't 'feel right'.

But with the odds overwhelmingly stacked against us, it's pointless to get our hopes up, which is why I began the Don't Be Anxious campaign in the first place. Oh, I should add that we tried the pee-on-a-stick game yesterday and the results were not what we wanted.

Not everything's in the 'Nope' column, though. The woman's boobs have been hurting her recently, and she's been in a shitty mood; so much so that I've reconsidered slapping Tony, after all.

There could be dozens of reasons why she's experiencing pain; might one of them be the one we want? Another item to add in the 'Not-Nope' column is that we have a difference of opinion about the validity of yesterday's results. I'm adamant it was one line, while she thinks there might have been the briefest-of-brief, faintest-of-faint appearances of the much-coveted second line. It would hardly be the first time that I've been wrong about something and she's been right (not that I would ever be stupid enough to admit that). I wonder …

Fuck, I've done it again. I can't help it. Hope is lethally effective at breaching my defences, no matter how many barriers I plant in its way.

I compromise: I tell myself that it's not going to be the news I want, and I believe that. But in case I'm wrong, I snap a quick picture of the woman peeing on a stick. Tony the bellend Tiger still smiles, telling me that his bowl of Frosties is half-full, not half-empty.

And now we wait sixty seconds for the results to reveal themselves.

I have everything crossed – my campaign is officially dead in the water.

We're back in bed. It's 7.28 a.m. I've turned the stick over so we can both read the results. I'm looking at two very distinct blue lines.

And just like that, I discover I'm going to be a Daddy.

Fuck.

'You're pregnant,' I say, never imagining I'd be uttering those words this morning (or possibly ever). 'I'm going to be a Daddy, and you're going to be a Mummy.' Saying it aloud feels – let's start with wonderful, but one three-syllable word doesn't begin to do it justice: every single one of my 86 billion neurons is alert and firing more powerfully than ever before and my head is a neurological explosion of pure energy and electricity.

What a feeling!

Unless the test results are wrong. They boast a ninety-eight per cent success rate, so it's unlikely, and even if it were only five per cent accurate, in my heart I would still know that it's true: I am going to be a Daddy for the first time to … you, my unborn child. And the woman next to me is going to be your Mummy.

My emotional framework has begun a period of terraforming.

Fuck, fuck and fuck!

How does anyone process these feelings? Chemicals are flooding my nervous system. I'm shocked and surprised, and beyond elation. I'm feeling a hundred per cent pure happiness; not a fraction less. It hasn't been cut with any other emotions, it doesn't contain additives and no synthetic processes were used to manufacture this product. It's pure, organically produced happiness.

It's rare for me to exhibit such an outward display of emotion, but I'm crying. Having said that, I cried when Stallone reprised Rocky in *Creed*.

I wonder if you'll ever see me as a role model like Rocky. Doubtful. Is it normal to have these thoughts right after you find out you're going to be a Daddy for the first time?

It doesn't matter. Regardless of what you think of me or how you see me,

I'll still be there for you. One day, you'll start calling me 'Daddy'.

––––––––

Your Mummy has deployed me on a mission to secure breakfast. I don't feel ready for a field assignment; in fact, I'm so preoccupied with the news that I'm going to be a Daddy that, coming out of a junction, I almost drive into another car. On paper, it was arguably my fault. In reality, absolutely my fault. *Oopsie.* Regardless, I call the other driver a shiny wankstain and go about my day – my amazing day.

I'm at the store, and I've bought Mummy a unicorn Easter egg. Mummy loves unicorns – what 34-year-old doesn't? It comes with a unicorn soft toy. That's for you. I've heard that it's bad luck to buy anything for the baby before the twelve-week scan.

Fuck it. I buy the damn thing and I head home.

The unicorn's red punk-style hair is questionable, and it has eyes that I don't immediately trust. But I do approve of the unicorn's choice of companion (you). I don't know the sex of the unicorn, just as I don't know if you'll be a baby boy or a baby girl. Even you don't know that yet; you won't make that decision until you're seven weeks into your development (I've just looked that up). Mummy and I have decided not to find out your gender until the day we meet you. It's our first parental decision. Unlike a million others that we'll make, this one requires no compromise.

We do need something to refer to you as, though. We can't use 'it', 'thing', 'the baby' or 'fill in the blank'. My preference is 'Thunder Strikeforce', but it's a no from Mummy, so it's back to the drawing board.

It's just occurred to me that your Mummy has over ten years' experience working in a nursery. When it comes to infants, she already holds a number of qualifications. Surely that gives us a leg-up? I, on the other hand, have little childcare experience – but I guess that's about to change. Whenever life presents me with a new subject, my default move is to read as much about it as possible, so I've purchased a bunch of books on babies and pregnancy. Thank God for Amazon Prime. I wonder if Amazon Prime will still be around when you read this.

––––––––

It's later on in the day, and I'm with friends (but without Mummy). I'm not paying attention to what anyone is saying or doing. It's surreal. It's as if the efficiency of all my senses has reduced. I can see lips moving and I can hear noise, but it sounds like background conversation in an almost-empty restaurant. I can't seem to focus on anything. I've spent the day in a higher state of consciousness and it doesn't look like I'm leaving it any time soon.

I had originally planned to spend the night with these friends, but I want to get back home and be with you and Mummy. It's not every day you find out you're both going to be parents for the first time.

————

I'm lying in bed wide awake. I wish I had the skills to accurately transfer from mind to paper the emotional journey I've been on today. It's hard to explain how I feel, because how I feel changes every few seconds. My thoughts and emotions are unstable; they're without order; they're racing around. It's like watching a Grand Prix motor race on the TV with the fast-forward button pressed up to maximum.

I am going to be a Daddy, and your Mummy is going to be a Mummy. It's something we've wanted for years. Right now, the canvas of your life is blank. But soon that canvas will begin to teem with colour and beauty as you grow and reveal yourself.

We can be a part of that process. We can watch it, and we can influence it. We get to decide (partly) how you're exposed to the world. We can help shepherd you through childhood into adulthood and try to share with you the greatest lessons life has taught us. We will equip you with everything we possess to help you along on your path: this is a gift that has no price tag. You will be loved unconditionally and parenting you will be our greatest privilege. A challenge, yes, but a privilege – and a joy.

But then comes fear. You might have instantly become our most valued possession, but you're also our most vulnerable one. At this moment in time, you're a tiny ball of cells – a million things need to go right for you to be born healthy. And then what? Even if you make it safely into the world, there will be dangers all around you. As parents charged with your care, we'll do whatever we can to protect you from these dangers, but we can't protect you from everything. So much exists outside our control:

disease, natural disasters, freak accidents, crime (some of it hideous) and any number of unforeseen variables that could hurt you. Parents aren't privy to every possible outcome when making decisions for their children. How do we cope with this? Does this feeling ever go away? Does it last forever? I ask the questions even though I already know the answers – despite being new to the game.

No matter what happens, no one will ever be able to take away from me the feeling of finding out I'm going to be a Daddy – a beautiful, beautiful moment. I will remember this day for the rest of my life – my day of discovery.

Sleep well, my beautiful ball of cells. Daddy loves you.

Sunday, 17 March 2019 – Am I Dreaming?

I've woken up with my mental state resembling a zombie invasion. Every zombie represents an idea, a feeling or a question. It's crazy and chaotic. I take a deep breath and attempt to bring order to the chaos.

First question: am I dreaming? No, I'm not. I am going to be a Daddy. Good. Next question: is Mummy OK? I turn over to make sure. *Whack.* Fuck, I've just elbowed Mummy in the head; she's not OK. Red alert – I repeat, not OK. I make all the right noises, apologising to the mother of my child: 'I'm sorry, baby, that was my bad.'

It's not my bad – she's occupying seventy per cent of my side of the bed. Well, she was, until I took accidental action. At least now I can get back to eliminating this fast-approaching mental breakdown.

Questions. I have so many questions. How can we be sure you're developing OK? What foods can Mummy eat? What foods can't she eat? What if you develop into more than one foetus? How do we become good parents? How do we not fuck up your life?

Yesterday I was the happiest man alive, but now realisation is setting in, and I'm a different person.

What if something goes wrong with your development and we have to weigh up your quality of life and decide if you should be terminated or not? What if you are born with disabilities? How absurdly terrifying is this? I can't help it; my internal wiring is forcing me to consider every conceivable scenario that could hurt you over the next eight months. I need to go through this process so I can implement as many risk-reduction strategies as possible.

Except I've remembered – I've gone through this exercise already, last night. And I have already arrived at the truth: I can't control everything. I can barely control anything.

There's no use denying that we have a long road ahead of us. Right now, all I can think about is looking after you and Mummy and getting the three of us to the twelve-week scan. At least, when it comes to babies being born healthy, statistics are on our side. Actually, the more I think about it, statistics are very much on our side, and I'd be stupid not to take comfort in that.

It's settled then. I will live my life with the belief that you will be born a healthy boy or girl and that you will grow up to have a life full of meaning and purpose. Until something happens to suggest anything outside that belief, I will keep hold of it, treasure it and nurture it as if it's my favourite childhood soft toy. My favourite childhood soft toy is a black cat called Charlie. He's still knocking around, so I'll introduce you to him someday.

––––––––––

Not to blow our own trumpets, but your Mummy and I are nailing parenting. We've made another decision that we both agreed on without any argument. The same cannot be said for what colours we want the walls painted in our living room, but let's not talk about Mummy's poor taste in colours. Let's talk about you. We've decided that your nursery will be Pixar themed. Mummy loves anything remotely related to Disney, and I love film; Pixar ranks as one of my all-time favourite studios. It might seem silly to you as I doubt you'll ever remember your nursery, apart from when you see pictures of it. However, building you a nursery while you're gearing up to hatch is the thing we're most looking forward to. We will pour all our love and energy into getting it just right for you – and for us as well.

Monday, 18 March 2019 – Are You Fucking Kidding Me?

Our first job this morning is getting Mummy a doctor's appointment. I imagine this will happen quickly; the doctors and midwives will want to see Mummy immediately. After all, we have precious cargo. We're not carrying any baby; we're carrying *our* baby. And because *our* baby is not any baby, then surely we jump ahead of any critically ill patients in the queue for appointments. They'll probably send an ambulance. It will all be rather exciting. I know NHS funding is restricted and, technically speaking, ambulances should only be deployed in emergencies and not for a routine check-up at the start of a pregnancy, but as I've already stated, you're not anyone's baby, you're our baby.

I ring through to the surgery and find myself positioned number sixteen in the queue. *What the fuck?*

Five minutes pass and we've only progressed to number fourteen.

This morning started well but it's now turned a little bit ball-achey – how much longer?

As it turns out – another twenty minutes. Twenty minutes to get through to the most nonchalant of receptionists: a real 'Casual Carol'. You'd have thought we'd misdialled the local bowling alley. Still, Mummy maintains absolute decorum.

'I need to book an appointment with the midwife; I'm pregnant.'

Excellent. Polite, short and to the point.

'Would you like to come in in three weeks?' Casual Carol says.

What the fuckery…? First, I think you've forgotten to say congratulations, and in answer to your dumb fucking question – no, Carol, my dear, we wouldn't. Did you not hear us? We're having a baby! Arranging an appointment for us is your number one priority. You need to get off your arse and divert all resources to our current situation.

Now, where do you plan to land the helicopter?

Absolutely nothing from Carol except to say, 'Well, we are quite busy at the moment.'

Thanks for fucking nothing, Carol. See you in three weeks.

Tuesday, 19 March 2019 – The Baby Daddy Dance

The doctors told us it would be 'extremely unlikely' for us to conceive naturally, which I took to mean that it was almost an absolute certainty we wouldn't, for two reasons: I didn't think the doctors wanted to commit to any absolutes in case they were wrong (I know I wouldn't); and they found several internal defects with Mummy's reproductive organs that suggested a pretty grim outlook for making babies, as far as I could see.

Here's a section taken from the medical notes following a failed procedure that Mummy underwent to try and establish what was interfering with our family goals:

On scan today the uterus is anteverted. There is a small polyp on the fundus; it doesn't look like a fibroid. On the right side, the ovary looks normal and mobile. The left ovary shows collapsing corpus luteum; however, there is a fluid collection which could be due to peritoneal fluid adhesion as she has Crohn's; the other possibility is hydrosalpinx. Unfortunately, the HyCoSy tube was pushed out by the uterus, she was in quite a lot of pain and it was in the cervix, therefore we abandoned the procedure.

Rolls off the tongue, right? I still don't know what any of it means, but the general drift is that Mummy has one set of problems on the right side and a different set of problems on the left. That's the simplified version as described by the doctor, anyway. I used the doctor's abridged explanation plus a bit of maths to calculate my optimism of us conceiving – it was never high!

The outcome was that Mummy landed herself on a waiting list for surgery that included removing at least one of her fallopian tubes. And, to reinforce how unlikely the doctor thought our chances were, he referred us for IVF on the NHS (which we never started).

This was a big blow to our plans and our emotions, so you can imagine our surprise when we read the test results. I don't know what the doctor did when he tried to examine Mummy, but he must have inadvertently shuffled something around.

Rather than question our good fortune, I've decided instead to celebrate through the medium of dance. Now, when it comes to dancing, I'm something of an outlier. But instead of featuring in the top one per cent, I operate all the way over at the other end of the spectrum. The bottom one per cent. Actually, it's more like the bottom one per cent of the bottom one per cent. In short, I cannot dance, not for love nor money. However, that doesn't stop me trying.

And if God loves a trier then he's head over heels for Daddy this evening. I've invented a cute little number for your Mummy. It's called 'The Baby Daddy Dance'. My approach is minimalist in terms of how I've engineered the steps in the routine, opting more for understated elegance as opposed to high-octane adrenalin.

It goes something like this: I fist-pump the air at perfectly timed intervals, yelling 'Baby Daddy' in a slurred tone akin to a football stadium fan-chant.

If you're not welling up with pride already, you will be when I tell you that your old man was naked; except, of course, for Mummy's pink bunny-eared headband.

Wednesday, 20 March 2019 – Your Pre-Birth Name

Your Mummy is not feeling well today. She's tired, she's sore and she's getting cramps in her tummy. This isn't anything out of the ordinary. Doctors think Mummy suffers from this rubbish thing called Crohn's disease. It means she has trouble digesting certain foods and she's used to having her tummy cramp up – to the extent that she occasionally lands herself in hospital on morphine for a week.

But here's the kicker: what we would previously dismiss as 'Crohn's tummy' is now analysed as a potential threat to your development; a threat that we need to eliminate. But we have no idea of how, so we do ourselves no favours and begin researching on the internet. One website we check says that severe cramps in your stomach could be a sign of a miscarriage or placental abruption. Mummy doesn't think they're severe enough for either of those but, still, this evening isn't as much fun as winning a game of Monopoly against people you dislike. And how do you determine how severe a cramp is, anyway? I doubt there's a cramp-pain index to refer to.

After an adult discussion (the third one of our relationship) about the road ahead and how we approach the many periods of uncertainty, we agree to take it one day at a time.

In the film *Finding Nemo*, the character Dory has a catchphrase: 'Just keep swimming, just keep swimming.' It's a wonderful metaphor for moving forward in life despite the many obstacles that we come up against. That's what we'll do – just keep swimming. Every day, the three of us will keep at it.

At least I know what to call you now.

Your pre-birth name is Dory.

Thursday, 21 March 2019 – Pregnant-Woman Road Rage

Let's talk about Mummy's roadside manner. Since I've known her, road rage has formed an integral part of her daily routine. Like breathing, it's a naturally occurring activity. It's strangely endearing how she's able to seamlessly edit in a spot of road rage while having a deep and thoughtful conversation about life.

But this is a personality trait that is at odds with her character. Your Mummy is a carefree, smiley, happy woman, who would give her left big toe to help a stranger in need. And yet, if you piss her off on the road (which isn't hard), she will verbally fuck you up into next Tuesday.

So, it came as no surprise to me when we were in the car this morning that Mummy affectionately referred to the little old man driving his equally little old Fiat as 'a dithering old cunt' because he was driving half a mile per hour below the speed limit. Naturally, she followed this up with a demand for his licence to be revoked and his life to end. That's par for the course.

But rather than return to her normal, happy self, she's remained in angry-road-user mode. What's more, she's dialled it up to unimaginable levels. Her face is contorted into pure rage: a bulging green vein appears on her forehead, and red streaks flash across her eyes like lightning in the sky. She's frothing at the mouth, accelerating aggressively to beat the lights and yelling at young, innocent schoolchildren to 'mind out the fucking way'. (Disclaimer – they're walking on the pavement with no intention of crossing the road.)

I'm about to ask her if she's OK, but then I remember that I want to live, so I keep my mouth shut and my body still – so much so that ten minutes later my musical-statues ranking has shot up into the global top ten. If I were an anger-management therapist and my choice of client that morning was either Mummy or Darth Vader, I'd pick Darth.

Who is this monster, Dory, and what has it done with your Mummy? I've heard people joke about pregnant women becoming hormonal, and I've also heard that it's an unwritten rule that you don't anger a pregnant woman. But how can you not anger a pregnant woman who hulks out over someone driving half a mile per hour below the speed limit on a road that's experiencing heavy traffic? (Oh, I forgot to mention the traffic.)

I don't like this, Dory. I don't like this at all.

Friday, 22 March 2019 – What To Do, What To Do?

We've not told anyone of your existence yet because we're still a way off from the twelve-week scan. This is when most expecting parents begin sharing their news. At the moment, it's the three of us that know (which I love), but we don't think it can remain that way for much longer.

Mummy is both emotionally and geographically close to her parents, Granny Feeder (Mummy's Mummy) and Grandad Tools (Mummy's Daddy). Granny Feeder and Grandad Tools are from Ireland, but they came to England when they were both in their teens.

Granny Feeder gets her name on account of her unrivalled hospitality skills. A look in her food cupboards reveals a magnificent pantry, stocked floor to ceiling with culinary solutions for even the most hard-to-please taste buds. She has some adorable personality traits. One of them is to make stuff up. If it were any other person, they'd be labelled a liar, but your Granny has a certain panache when she bullshits, which gives her diplomatic immunity. Her daughters affectionately refer to these instances as 'hashtag-Mum-facts', or #MumFacts.

I'll give you an example: she's very good at understanding exactly what toys and books your cousin likes. On the surface of it, it's not unusual for a grandmother to get to know her grandchildren. But your cousin is three months old and she can barely see properly.

Grandad Tools is one of my favourite people in the world. If you take all the stereotypical features of a grandad and multiply them by ten, you're on the green. He's extraordinarily accomplished with tools. I've seen him whip up a stud wall in less time than it takes me to eat a packet of crisps.

He's also rather skilled at bargain hunting. So skilled, in fact, that the bargains find him, usually in the afternoon, down at his local pub. I don't know how he does it, but a whole consortium of independent retailers visit Grandad Tools to offer him discounted goods. It's amazing; they give him up to eighty per cent off the RRP. The only thing they ask for in return is to conduct their business away from CCTV cameras. Bloody nice blokes, looking after your Grandad Tools with the best-value deals.

When I say Mummy is geographically close to her parents, I mean so close that we're all under the same roof – we're living with them. And we have been for the past eight months while we've been renovating our own house (it's been a big project).

It's hard to avoid suspicion when we're broadcasting real-time updates of our daily lives. Granny Feeder is highly observant (particularly of her children), and she likes to inquire, often with a frown, about the mundane, with questions such as 'Why is Mummy tired all the time?' and 'Does she need a glass of bubbles?' Fortunately, right now it's Lent, and for the first time in her life Mummy has given up alcohol for it.

We have a few other cards that we can play to defuse any suspicion. First, Mummy has her go-to trusty Crohn's card, which she can lay down reasonably often, although not every day. Second, Granny Feeder knows we were experiencing problems in the baby-making department. Perhaps that knowledge alone will divert suspicion. Finally, we also have the excuse that we're renovating our house – a project we've each been hands-on with.

That can account for some of Mummy's burnout.

But as good as these excuses are, I don't know if they can fool a mother's intuition about her own daughter. Remember: we've been living with Granny Feeder for eight months already, so she's all too aware of our routines and schedules. And if she knows more about the neighbours living eight doors down than they know about themselves, picking up on the nuances and micro-adjustments in Mummy's behaviour will be child's play to the master enquirer.

So, the dilemma we're facing is when to tell Granny Feeder and the rest of the immediate family. We have earmarked a particular weekend, but it's not for another four weeks.

We won't last until then.

As a result, we've decided to target Mother's Day (eight days from now) to tell Mummy's parents and your Auntie Lisa (Mummy's sister).

The other person we'll be telling is my Mummy, your other Granny. You can call her 'Granny Smurf', on account of her Smurf-shaded blue hair. We won't be able to tell Granny Smurf in person as she lives down in Kent (we live in Northampton), but we'll video call her. After all, we daren't wait too much longer, as Inspector Granny Feeder will have upped her frown game when processing her daughter's answers to her questions.

Saturday, 23 March 2019 – Tilegate

We've come to the hardware store to look at tile prices. This is a quick in-and-out mission. We know what tiles we want; we decided on this weeks ago. We have pictures of the room layout that show where the tiles are going, along with the rest of the colours in the room. Easy peasy.

Transcript of events:

11.32 a.m. Dory's Mummy and Daddy enter the hardware store, approach the tile section and quickly find the tiles they're interested in.

11.33 a.m. Daddy: These white tiles are cheaper than anywhere else we've seen.

11.33 a.m. Mummy: Yes, but we're not going with white tiles otherwise they'll clash with the white ceiling.

11.33 a.m. Daddy: I thought we had decided lovingly together on a blue ceiling, my little rose-petal pumpkin.

11.33 a.m. Mummy: No, the ceiling was white. Let me show you a picture as you're clearly an idiot.

11.33 a.m. The Mummy gets out her phone and begins searching through a photo album.

11.34 a.m. The Mummy seems to be at a loss for words.

11.34 a.m. Daddy: What's up, sweetie, can't you find the picture?

11.34 a.m. Mummy: I've found it.

11.34 a.m. Daddy: Excellent stuff.

11.34 a.m. The validity of Daddy's enthusiasm is questionable.

11.35 a.m. Daddy: Well, is it a white ceiling?

11.35 a.m. Mummy: It's blue.

11.35 a.m. Daddy: No!

11.35 a.m. The Daddy appears shocked, but it's ninety-nine per cent certain that this reaction is disingenuous.

End of transcript.

Sunday, 24 March 2019 – Ice Cream To The Rescue

Tilegate continues. We've parked up outside the hardware shop, but we're already facing an obstacle before leaving the vehicle. Mummy has taken the keys out of the ignition with a little more force than usual and hit herself in the face.

Let's pause for a second. There exists no parallel universe in which this isn't a little bit amusing. But Mummy's hormones are wreaking extinction-level havoc with her body, and I have learnt that you can't even make jokes about the mundane, let alone an accidental smack in the face.

Fortunately, I am able to pacify her with an ice cream.

On a more productive note, we complete the tile purchase.

Monday, 25 March 2019 – The Nightmare

Last night I had a dream that Mummy had a miscarriage. My relief and gratitude were off the charts when I woke up and realised it was only a dream.

I daren't tell Mummy. I spare a thought for all the other parents out there who don't get to wake up from the dream; because it's not a dream, it's a reality. The thought is tragic.

Again, this boils down to a serious lack of control. Other than ensuring Mummy eats well and tries to avoid any stress, there is nothing we can do. You're in the hands of science now.

Dory, you may not have developed your hearing yet, but I need you to find a way to listen to me. Listen to your Daddy. Please be OK. Remember the motto – just keep swimming. You've swum so much already to get to this point. Your life began as the ultimate swimming race: one where fifty per cent of your genetic makeup competed against and beat tens of millions of rivals, so I know you can do it. But I need you to keep doing it, and Mummy needs you to keep doing it as well.

In six days' time, it will be Mother's Day, and we're going to tell your grandparents the news, so just keep swimming.

In fifteen days, we have our first appointment with the midwife, so please, please, please, just keep swimming.

Soon after that, it will be the twelve-week scan.

Then we'll be in the second trimester and then the third, and finally we'll be together – and then you can stop swimming.

But in reality, the swimming won't stop. It will never stop. You will always need to keep swimming, but you won't have to swim alone. Mummy and Daddy will be there. When you're tired, we'll cheer you on; when you can't see clearly and lose your way, we'll help steer you back into your swim lane; and if you feel like you can't do it any more, then we'll be there for you with a life jacket and a cuddle until you're ready to continue.

Please find a way to listen to Daddy. Just keep swimming.

Tuesday, 26 March 2019 – I'm Already Carrying Something!

We're at the hardware store, and Mummy states that she can't possibly carry anything as she's already carrying my child. How the fuckety, fuck, fuck do I disagree with that one? God damn it, Mummy will be dining out on that for the rest of the pregnancy.

Mummy is supposed to be on a hen do this weekend, but she's had to drop out. That's because there is no scenario on the planet that involves Mummy not drinking, other than that she is pregnant. Even if she turned up with a tear to one of her major arteries and it was spouting freshly oxygenated blood twelve feet in the air – she'd still smash a couple of ciders. She's such a sociable creature; it's one of the many reasons she's so likeable.

Giving up alcohol for Lent won't wash either, not on a hen do. Mummy has a reputation for being the life and soul of the party, and everyone knows it. If she didn't drink, the assumption would be that she was pregnant, and she wouldn't be able to hide it. Once again, she calls on her trusty Crohn's alibi as an excuse not to go.

I guess this must be common for expecting couples in the early stages. We don't want anyone knowing, so that means a few social sacrifices on Mummy's part. She's gutted, she was looking forward to it – plus she's already paid for the weekend.

Wednesday, 27 March 2019 – Writing Mother's Day Cards

Today I write three Mother's Day cards. The first is to Granny Feeder, who has done a sterling job of looking after me while I've been living in her house for the last eight months. She hasn't even charged me rent. You can relate to that, Dory, can't you – being fed and sheltered and not having to pay rent?

Thank you, Granny Feeder, for providing me with warmth, shelter, food and a comfortable breeding ground for your second grandchild.

The second card is to Granny Smurf and with it come strict instructions not to open it until Mother's Day.

The last one is for your Mummy, and it's my favourite; it's the first of many Mother's Day cards that I'll write from you to her. I'm not sure how many exactly, as I don't know at what age you'll be able to write them yourself. For now, though, I've got your back. This has been the absolute highlight of my day. By the way, you owe me £1.75 for the card.

Thursday, 28 March 2019 – Wowzers, Where Did They Come From?

I think Mummy's taking localised steroids on the sly. Why localised and why on the sly, you ask? I'll tell you, Dory. I suspect they're localised because I've only noticed one part of her body that's grown – seemingly overnight. It's just above where you live, in between her shoulders and below her neck. I imagine you might view this place one day as a branch of McDonald's. The reason she's doing this on the sly is because she absolutely will not let me near her for a closer inspection. I don't know, Dory; something's not quite right.

Truth be told, Dory, the situation is horseshit. Imagine owning a PlayStation 5 (which you love) and then coming home to find it's morphed into a PlayStation 10 (WOWZERS). But it sits behind an impenetrable, see-through barrier, in sight but out of reach. I'm not blaming you; Daddy would never do that. It just sucks a bit, you know? You understand, Dory, don't you? When life sucks?

Friday, 29 March 2019 – Hate Is Such A Strong Word

I've been reading one of the pregnancy books for dads, and I've stumbled upon an enchanting little story where one dad said that he struggled with his partner's mood through the first trimester, and had to remind himself that she didn't hate him …

Does this mean this poor chap's partner told him how much she hated him while carrying his child? Is this what I can expect?

Mummy assures me this will not happen, but in case it does, she's recorded a little voice note that I'm to play to her whenever she feels a bout of hatred invading her emotional control console. Her voice note says this: 'If I am ever mean to you, I don't mean to be; I still love you, but you may be annoying me at one moment in time. But I always love you, and it's probably Dory's fault, anyway.'

If you ask me, I don't think that would hold up in court.

Saturday, 30 March 2019 – Really?

We're at a 1-year-old's birthday party and the parents, Sean and Rebecca, are close friends of mine and Mummy's, as are fifty per cent of the guests. The entire party cannot get over the fact that Mummy isn't drinking. They're suspicious – a bit like the world was when Harvey Weinstein declared he was innocent. They respond to the news with raised eyebrows and comments such as 'Have you hit your head or something?' or 'That's something I never thought I'd live to see.'

They remember a time not that long ago when we were all at Sean and Rebecca's wedding. By 11.00 a.m. on the day *after* the wedding Mummy was tucking into her fifth pint of cider for breakfast. She was most disappointed when the chap in charge of the wakeboarding activity wouldn't allow her to join in. Your mother did promise him that she was as sober as a rock, but she said this while staggering towards him with pint number five in her hand – ergo, he didn't believe her.

How are we getting away with it today? To be honest with you, Dory, I'm not sure we are getting away with it, but they've either accepted, or are pretending to accept, that Mummy has given up alcohol for Lent. She reinforces the idea that she's descended from an Irish Catholic family – you know, to make it a more plausible excuse …

Sunday, 31 March 2019 – Mother's Day

Today we tell the parents. First port of call – Granny Smurf. I've already sent her a card in preparation. Remember she was told not to open it. Let's hope she listened. I faff around for ten minutes trying to solve the enigma of recording a video call (I figured this would be a moment worth saving) and then I make the call.

She answers and promises that my instructions have been followed.

'Right, Mum, open your card.'
Here's what you wrote:

To my Nan, Nanny, Gran, Granny, Grandma or something else???

I'm not sure what you want to be known as. Can you let me know when I arrive in November?

I don't want to come across as a spoilt little embryo, but I require the following items created from wool (suitable alternatives acceptable): a unicorn, something offensive, a blanket, some little shoe thingies – and maybe matching jumpers for when I get a bit bigger?

I'm looking forward to catching up over a cuppa/bottle around mid-November. See you soon.

P.S. Happy Mother's Day :)

xxx

Her response is shock and then joy. She follows up with her title preference. She's opted for 'Granny'. An excellent choice (especially as I've been referring to her as that).

Granny Smurf also knew we were having difficulty creating life, so this has come as a wonderful surprise for her too. You will be spoilt – mostly with knitted unicorns.

The plan is to hold off from telling Granny Feeder and Grandad Tools until later on today. We're all going out for lunch together and then we're going to take them back to our house and show them how our renovation project is going. When they get to your room, there will be a sign that says 'Baby Dory's Room – reserved from November 2019'.

We're all in the kitchen making a cup of tea, and I hand Granny Feeder a Mother's Day card from me. She opens the card and I immediately realise that your Daddy, the silly sausage that he is, has made a critical error in our baby-reveal plans. I've only gone and addressed the card to 'The grandmother of my unborn child'.

Shit – I forgot I wrote that; I obviously meant to give her the card after the reveal.

Now Mummy, Granny Feeder and I are standing in the kitchen and Granny Feeder's face is an absolute picture. She asks if it's true. We smile and nod, and at that point she loses her shit and emits a scream that sounds like a pterodactyl raping a banshee. Seriously, this moment is to blame if you're born with brain damage.

Grandad Tools is in the other room and hears the screams (along with half the inhabitants of continental Europe), so Mummy and I shrug and tell him the good news as well. Not the way we planned, but still another long-lasting memory to add to the collection.

You're six weeks into your development and you've already brought untold amounts of joy to five people. For someone who doesn't even know what gender they're going to be, you're knocking it out the park.

———

The atmosphere this evening is identical to that of the morning – plus the eighteen bottles of Prosecco that have been eliminated.

I can hear Auntie Lisa (who now knows as well) and Grandad Tools conducting an alcohol-fuelled heart-to-heart. They're expressing joy at having another grandchild in the family. It's a drunkenly sweet moment, and now she's asking him how it feels to have you conceived under his roof—

Fuck!

I enact an emergency escape plan: I bypass Grandad Tools entirely without him seeing me and I make it upstairs to my temporary bedroom to watch a Marvel film.

Mummy arrives shortly after, in time for her to receive her first-ever Mother's Day card. This is what you wrote:

To my Mummy,

We don't know each other very well yet, but I already think you're wonderful. I know that growing me inside you isn't easy, and I am very appreciative of your efforts. So is my Daddy. He thinks you are doing a great job, even if you do feel tired and crappy all the time, and you can't remember what colour you decided to paint the downstairs toilet.

I'm still very small, but every day I get the tiniest bit bigger, the smallest bit stronger. This is all down to you. Every day you give me enough energy to keep growing, and I know that won't stop – even when you serve me a Section 21 eviction notice, and I have to relocate from your tummy at some point in November. You have committed a lifetime of love and energy to me.

This is why you absolutely deserve a Mother's Day card.

Happy Mother's Day, Mummy. See you in November :)

Lots of love,

Dory xxx

April

Monday, 1 April 2019 – You Had One Fucking Job

Yesterday I gave strict instructions to your Granny Smurf: 'Do not tell anyone about the baby.'

That was it. Nothing more, nothing less. You don't need a Turing machine to translate and decode that one, do you?

Imagine my surprise when I receive a message from Granny Smurf saying that she's told her friend. Apparently, she couldn't possibly keep it to herself.

This news is disconcerting, Dory. If I can't trust my own mother, with over fifty years of wisdom and life experience, to carry out my instructions, then what hope is there for you doing as you're told?

This is 'a thing', isn't it? Grandparents develop a defunct moral compass when it comes to following instructions from Mummy and Daddy. They say things like: 'I promise I won't give the grandchildren any sweets' and 'I promise I won't let them stay up late and swallow my last bottle of antihistamines.' But they lie, Dory, they all lie. I've heard this from many of the Mummies I work with. They describe it as grandparents taking revenge on them for being little shits when they were kids. And they know that they never have to deal with the sugar crash or the overtiredness fallout (and possibly an overdose), because they can return you home.

Tuesday, 2 April 2019 – Cheers, Mum

Your Granny Smurf continues to impress. I wake up to this message:

> I don't want you to be jealous, but if you have a son, there is a chance that you won't be my number one boy any more!

Cheers, Mum. Let's hope your number one boy comes to visit you in the care home, you back-stabbing heathen. I feel like a supermodel who's turned 26.

Wednesday, 3 April 2019 – Roll Out The Red Carpet

I'm walking to work with Mummy this morning and it's lovely. But – her scowls indicate she does not appreciate me treating her like a VIP. I've been holding up traffic like a warden with authority to allow her safe passage across the road. Further scowling suggests she also doesn't like me treating everyone in sight as a potential red flag and loudly vocalising my concerns through a set list of responses: 'a threat', 'definitely a threat' and 'that's a fucking threat right there if I ever saw one.'

After all, she is a VIP carrying a VIP. As far as I'm concerned, you can't get much more VIP than that. Mummy's issue was that she didn't recognise my actions as a hundred per cent altruistic, which is bloody bonkers, because they were. She somehow thought this was yet another example of Daddy indulging his own childish desires to 'act up'.

I think she's pissed off because she now needs a parachute to hold her tits in place. Looking out for you and Mummy is a thankless job, Dory.

Thursday, 4 April 2019 – There Be Storms Up Ahead

There's a wedding tomorrow, and Mummy and Daddy have the day off work to attend. It's been a while since we've spent time together other than during our house-renovation project. There's just one teensy-weensy obstacle I need to traverse first, and then I can relax and look forward to the weekend ahead.

The obstacle is that Mummy has nothing to wear. She's made a last-minute dash to your Auntie Lisa's house to borrow dresses, and she's about to start modelling them for me. She's asked me to provide 'honest feedback' on my preference. Anything less than honest would be a disservice to our relationship.

Normally, this would be a piece of cake. I pick the favourite and we're done. But as you know, Mummy is exhibiting unprecedented levels of emotional instability, and my Spidey-sense is telling me that I'm dancing on an insecure tightrope being part of this conversation, especially one where I have voter's rights! I must fashion my responses with absolute precision, Dory. There is a strong chance that the wrong answer might result in you not meeting your father.

Here comes Mummy with the first dress.

Mummy looks hot. I may have been a bit premature with my scepticism. 'You look great; I think you should go with that dress,' I say.

Mummy can tell when I'm being genuine and when I'm not, so I know she believes me. Job done. We can all go home – balls intact.

But now she's not sure. Uh-oh. She wants to try another one on.

Danger levels remain high, after all.

But my run of good fortune continues because dress number two is another big yes from Daddy. Once again, she looks great, plus she seems happier with this selection. The *HMS Mummy's Made A Decision* has entered the harbour; the crew are stationed above deck with guide ropes and are preparing to dock. Even the ship's rats look on with optimism.

Come on, Mummy, say yes to the dress, say yes to—

She doesn't, Dory. The crew have been told to stand down and the *HMS Mummy's Made A Decision* turns around and about and heads back out into the open sea. *We were so close.*

Consider the seven colours of the rainbow and the billions of permutations you can create from mixing and varying those colours. The possibilities are endless. Now, if you consider all those billions of colours, there is one – just one – that Daddy doesn't like, as far as fashion is concerned. That colour is teal*.

This shouldn't be an issue, as Mummy knows this.

So why, armed with this information, is your mother standing there in a teal-coloured dress and asking for my opinion? Is this a test? I don't understand.

I should lie for all our sakes, right? But I can't, because Mummy will know. Fuck – what do I say?

I take a deep breath in. 'I think the dress looks great, even though it's not my favourite colour, and if there was a gun to my head and I had to pick one, as difficult as it is, I would pick one of the first two, even though you still look great in everything you wear.'

I breathe out.

I've been honest, delicate and considerate. Have I avoided the noose, Dory?

No. Mummy says nothing; she's staring at me like the piece of shit that I am. I dare not speak. Another word could see me checking in at the morgue. Finally, she responds. 'You think I should go with one of the first two?'

'I absolutely do.'

I'm halfway through writing my acceptance speech for the award I'm about to collect when Mummy drops the mic. 'I think I'll try on the last one.'

NOOOOOO!

I'm sweating. Mummy is back on the catwalk in dress number four. Except it's not a dress, it's a full-length playsuit. Dory, I fucking hate full-length playsuits. They're good for handstand competitions, ball pits and not a lot else. I can't help it. And it's not like Mummy doesn't know this. She even comes into the room saying, 'I know you don't like these, but ...'

But what? Why is there a 'but'? Why is she torturing me like this? Did I

---

* Yes, I know the book cover is teal. I had several different colour options mocked up that I then sent out to friends, asking them to vote on their favourite. Unfortunately, teal was the clear winner. My choice would have been navy and red, but apparently the author of this book knows fuck all about how to present it.

burn down a school full of children in a previous life? This is the opposite of logical. I've travelled far and wide, emotionally speaking, during these last ten minutes. And now, the finishing line is within touching distance, but I'm being sabotaged by the very person I signed up to help.

I attempt to deflect. 'Wear whatever you will feel most comfortable in.'

No dice; she's pushing me for an answer, Dory. I can't take this any more. I say, 'I don't like that as much, but I love the first two.'

And like that, I've blown my mission. Mummy storms off, no doubt for another full-blown pregnancy breakdown.

Friday, 5 April 2019 – Wedding Day

It's a beautiful day. Mummy looks great (obviously, she went with the first dress she tried on last night), and your old man doesn't look too bad either. A lot of our friends are asking about transport arrangements. Mummy casually announces that a) we're broke from doing our house up, and b) she's still recovering from a Crohn's flare-up, meaning she'll be doing the driving. The bride is the friend whose hen weekend Mummy bailed out on two weeks ago.

Everyone seems to have bought our bullshit, but to extinguish any lingering doubt we switch glasses at key moments so that it appears Mummy has at least had a couple of drinks; she also announces to anyone who will listen that she's drinking vodka and cokes when she's only drinking cokes – despite also proclaiming that she's driving!

I look around at all my mates who have children. I wonder what arrangements they had to make to come here. Do they have to leave early to pick their children up? Can only one parent drink or can both? And did any parents not make it here today because they couldn't find a babysitter? Maybe others were invited but they didn't want to come, and so they used their children as an excuse. I can see me using you as an excuse to forego attending social engagements.

The rest of the day proceeds more than smoothly. I'm desperate to tell everyone about you, but I manage to keep my mouth shut.

I'm met with suspicious eyebrows when I announce it's time we were leaving. 'Why? You don't even have kids,' says one friend. But I remind them that we've got 'stuff' to do on the house and then I say a sentence that has the word 'Crohn's' in it eight times. No one says anything (at least, not to our faces).

———

We're back home, and Mummy is in bed fast asleep. She looks beautiful. I'm trying to process the fact that life is being created and shaped inside her body in this instant. I know that happens every day for the millions of species that inhabit the planet, and I know it has done so for millions of years – and will do so, hopefully, for millions of years to come, but it's the first time it's hit me in such a poignant and direct way. I've helped create life.

It's a cliché for parents to say that their greatest achievement is their children, but it's a beautiful cliché, and it's one scout's badge that I can't wait to sew onto my sleeve.

Monday, 8 April 2019 – Our First Midwife Appointment

We're holed up in the doctor's surgery, waiting for our first midwife appointment. While we wait, we're treated to a little pre-birth parenting education by a young Mom and her toddler, Jack. I'm not sure what the Mom's name is, but I've taken to spelling her title with an 'o' instead of a 'u', as 'Mom' in this case stands for 'Mother of Magnificence'.

Mom has levelled up in several key areas of parenting. First, she has mastered the ability to ignore her son and instead focus on her phone: an admirable accomplishment. Using only his vocals, young Jack is giving it everything to capture her attention, but despite his best efforts he's failing. He will need to do better.

Jack reaches out and taps Mom on the knee. At first glance, I can't see his results improving; a tap on the knee is undoubtedly no match for a smartphone and a Mother of Magnificence. But I've misjudged him; a closer look reveals he's using a half-eaten sandwich as his 'poking stick' of choice and, from where I'm sitting (four metres away), it looks like it contains mayo. Good choice, bud; I love mayo.

Mom does not like mayo. Actually, I think Mom has mayophobia, because the look she is wearing on her face is one of disgust and contempt. The smartphone no longer holds Mom's attention.

Objective complete, little guy. Take a bow.

Mom moves straight into the debriefing stage. I know how this works, Dory, I've read enough James Bond novels. The agent's superiors question the spy about why he or she took certain actions in the field. They evaluate the agent's choices and provide constructive feedback – for developmental purposes. It makes perfect sense that parents borrow from the world of espionage.

Mom opens with a classic: 'Why did you do that?'

The little agent struggles to respond; maybe he finds the debriefing stage intimidating, or maybe it's because he's not yet learnt to speak. Mom repeats the question, but this time she injects a little more urgency into her voice.

Once again, nothing from Jack. Mom glances around the waiting area, weighing up her next move, before enlisting the support of a friend sitting nearby. 'Is he some sort of an idiot or something?'

Jack decodes this as a joke and starts to laugh.

'That's not funny, you've wiped your sandwich on my knee and now I'll have to wash my trousers,' says Mom.

Jack starts to cry, so Mom throws her phone at him. 'You'd better not break it or you'll be in big trouble.'

The midwife appears and calls us in, thus bringing the lesson to an end. Good luck, Jack. I wish you the best in your future endeavours.

——————

We meet Kat, who was also Auntie Lisa's midwife. A glance behind Kat reveals a wall featuring hundreds of baby photos and thank you cards from parents. This is all positive stuff, Dory.

Kat tells us Mummy is eight weeks into the pregnancy but only six weeks post-fertilisation. That's confusing. Kat explains that you calculate a baby's due date from the first day of the woman's last menstrual period, but the actual date of conception will be roughly two weeks later when the woman releases an egg and the man's sperm fertilises it. I'm still confused, but it's fine.

We tell Kat that Mummy is eating well, she's reduced her caffeine intake, she's not smoking, she's taking vitamins, blah, blah, blah.

Mummy reports that while she's doing everything to ensure you're getting your five a day, her Crohn's means she isn't certain she's absorbing what she's putting into her body. Therefore, we cannot be sure you're getting what you need, especially iron. Kat suggests taking iron tablets but Mummy explains that her Crohn's will fuck her body up if she takes them (last time this happened, she extended a hospital stay by three days). Kat weighs up this information and decides that Mummy needs to be considered high-risk.

We're not worried (for the first time during the pregnancy): Mummy will be assigned a consultant, and she may have to undergo further tests and observations, which is fine by us. If there is anything wrong, the right people will know about it sooner, and the experts can help make the wrong things right again.

We end the appointment feeling excited – another milestone crossed off the list, Dory.

Wednesday, 10 April 2019 – My Biggest Fear

I woke up exhausted today, Dory. I wouldn't normally bore you with such a mundane update; after all, people get tired, and parents of babies operate on less sleep than they need on a full-time basis. But here's the kicker: when I don't have enough sleep, my productivity doesn't just drop, it sinks to the ocean floor and evaporates. (Shut up, physics; that can happen.)

I'm writing to you today to confess my fears. Short of anything happening to you or Mummy, a lack of sleep is my biggest concern going into parenthood. I want to be more than an able parent (a lifelong challenge in itself, no doubt).

When I'm tired, I experience cognitive shutdown. The routines that I have in place for my regular operating system start glitching and become unstable. The system then collapses and I find moving my little finger akin to facing a final-level boss battle on the hardest setting. I'm ashamed to admit it, but I become hopelessly pathetic.

If I fail at the basics, what will I be like when it comes to sterilising bottles, changing nappies, soothing a distressed Dory and getting you off to sleep again at 3.00 a.m. (potentially all at once)? Other parents tell me, difficult as it is to imagine, that you find a way to cope because you don't have any other choice. Granted, coping might be enough to maintain your survival, but we can do better than that. Right?

I'm worried I'll be less of an asset to Mummy. This means she'll be forced to use up more of her energy, which will, in turn, deplete her resources quicker and cause us to fall back into that bracket of parents who 'cope' – all because Daddy's a wet paper bag without his eight hours of uninterrupted sleep (only broken by the odd occasions when I wake in the night for a sit-down wee).

I do not accept this – and I've given it a lot of thought.

Granny Smurf is moving up to stay with us soon. She'll be living in our house temporarily, but she'll almost certainly be around when you're born. Call it good timing on your part, but having that bolstering support network close by can only be a good thing. Additionally, it affords Granny a more hands-on experience; something she recently admitted to never thinking would happen – which shows the confidence she had in her only son holding down a relationship long enough to settle down and start a family.

Another area ripe for exploration is our maternity and paternity options. Although the role of the patriarch has changed from past generations, for the majority it still follows a particular pattern: Daddies take two weeks off (plus any holiday leave they might have access to), and then they go back to work full-time.

This, to me at least, is about as appealing as shitting in a sleeping bag and riding it down the log flume at Butlins. I won't have a lot of time to watch you grow and develop in the early stages of your life, which is counter-intuitive to wanting children in the first place. As wonderful as technology is, I don't want a video file of my child smiling for the first time; I want to be there witnessing it with my own eyes.

Fortunately, the UK has a scheme that allows parental leave to be shared.

Instead of Mummy taking the whole year off, we can split it so Daddy takes more than the standard two weeks.

I shall need to give this further thought. In the meantime, I'd be grateful if you can ensure you're sleeping through the night by week three.

Thursday, 11 April 2019 – Mummy's Social Gene

The more I consider the social gene on Mummy's side of the family, the more I worry about how contagious it is. I think every one of her cousins carries it, and her parents carry it too, along with her aunties and uncles. Realising this evokes a terrifying thought: what if you're a girl and you inherit Mummy's social skills? Fuck, Dory. It's hard enough for a father to watch his daughter reach an age when partying and sex become objectives, let alone fathering a social overachiever.

I should also add that, at 34 years of age, I've undergone a huge transition from my twenties. I'm a lot more … Mummy says 'boring'. I recall one family wedding where Mummy was most disappointed in my partying stamina, when I announced at 5.00 a.m. that I was about ready to knock things on the head and go to bed. You should have seen the look of disgust and disappointment she threw me. These days, I choose the comfort of books and sleep over tequila shots and kebabs. It never used to be this way. I have my own vault fully stocked with drunken stories and episodes of behaviour that I'm less proud of now than I once was.

One of the reasons we're not finding out your gender is because we don't care, but, as sexist as my remarks are, I don't look forward to having a teenage daughter going out drinking (not that I would stop you) and going on dates. It's every father's worst nightmare. Maybe you will be a girl who isn't into boys. I'd still worry about you going out, but at least the boy threat would be eliminated. But to say girls aren't capable of taking emotional advantage of other people is ludicrous and untrue. What about if you're a boy who likes boys? I couldn't care less if you were gay. If it's legal, you can do whatever you want and be into anyone you want, and I can guarantee Mummy and Daddy will support your decision. But I hate the idea of anyone taking emotional or physical advantage of you –

regardless of what gender you turn out to be and who you like to sleep with.

It makes me feel sick, and you've not even graduated to the foetus stage yet – is this mental?

Friday, 12 April 2019 – My Not-So-Bright Idea

Mummy is struggling with exhaustion. She thinks it's down to a lack of iron and being pregnant with you. To help solve this puzzle, I've had the inspired idea that Mummy should consume a water-based iron supplement (gentle on the stomach so it should work with Crohn's), along with a stomach-friendly laxative.

The rationale for my hypothesis is simple maths: Mummy took the iron supplement the other day; she struggled with digestion, but she wasn't in pain. So, if Mummy takes it again, along with a little something to help ease it on its way, then we should have a workable solution that solves all our problems. You get your iron, Mummy isn't as tired, and Daddy gets to collect his doctorate in medicine.

═══════

The mission isn't proceeding as intended; we have an operative down in the field. Agent Mummy has a digestive flare-up and is in considerable pain. This is almost certainly owing to poorly calculated maths on my part. There is nothing Daddy can do except rub Mummy's back, and there is nothing Mummy can do but wait for it to pass.

Usually when this happens to Mummy, it's without an embryo in her uterus, so it goes without saying that I hope you're OK. This mission will be recorded as a complete fuck up, with no appetite – pun intended – for a second attempt.

Damn it, Dory. Back to the drawing board.

I feel awful. I'm concerned that a lack of nutrients could mean developmental complications, but my actions could potentially orchestrate the exact thing I want to avoid – I'm sure there is a life lesson in this.

After ninety minutes of discomfort, the worst of it seems to pass and Mummy falls asleep. Thank fuck.

Saturday, 13 April 2019 – Who Are You Calling A Parasite?

Yesterday was a disaster. I don't know what to do going forward – that's if we even need to do anything. I will admit my paranoia is fed by a lack of knowledge about the impact that Crohn's disease has on the development of a foetus. I do know that iron is important for your development, that Mummy doesn't get enough of it, and that Daddy, with the best of intentions, put her in a lot of pain last night messing with stuff he's not qualified to mess with.

Mummy has a blood test scheduled, but it's not until 25 April – the ten-week mark (or eight weeks since fertilisation). That's near the end of the first trimester, and that strikes me as a bit late to start fussing with blood tests.

Let's rationalise this. Positives first.

All new parents must experience this stuff, with the vast majority having their concerns amount to nothing except the birth of a perfectly healthy baby boy or girl. If it's not Crohn's, there are a million other things to keep a soon-to-be first-time parent awake at night.

Mummy is not the first person in the world to suffer from Crohn's and get pregnant. If the risks were that great, Kat would have told us during our first midwife appointment. This suggests to me that having a blood test at the ten-week mark is not a red flag.

Our species has been around for approximately two hundred thousand years; we were here before Google, the NHS, blood-analysis technology, water-based iron supplements and factor 50 sun protection.

Finally, the new *Avengers* film is out the week after next.

Over to the 'Worry' column: no one cares about you more than we do; therefore, no one has as much to lose.

The NHS is woefully underfunded. I worry that they simply do not have the infrastructure to give patients full care and attention – something could get missed or not be fixed in time. I'm torn between telling myself to chill the fuck out and not letting ignorance drive my actions. As far as I'm concerned, I'm already a Daddy and I have a job to do. Mummy feels the same way.

But as soon as either of us tries in ignorance to take control of the steering wheel, we realise a few things: we've never driven in this location before and we don't know where we're going. We have plenty of satellite-navigation options to assist us, but none of them are perfect – and they all contradict each other.

One thing I do know is that your mother is prone to drama-filled episodes concerning her health. We're talking about the same woman who once broke her nose while opening a car door, who's trodden on a scorpion, and who lasted twelve minutes on her first ski holiday before rupturing her knee.

Mummy has no idea that I'm battling with any of this (at least, not to this extent), and I don't want her to know this stuff worries me as much as it does, in case it worries her.

———

I have a glaringly obvious solution to our problems, and it's one I should have sought out three seconds after learning of your existence. Do you recall we recently visited our friends Rebecca and Sean for their daughter's first birthday? Well, Rebecca happens to be a midwife (I know, I know – silly Daddy). We've been meaning to visit them and give them the good news as friends, but now our visit carries a dual purpose: to share our news and to mine Rebecca for information that might help to assuage our concerns.

We arrive at their house and knock on the door. Sean greets us – but he's wifeless. Damn.

'Where's Rebecca?' Mummy casually enquires, in a tone that says, 'I don't care that much.'

'She's back at half past seven.'

I have a small issue with the way he said that. Did he mean p.m. or a.m.? Midwives don't exactly get the privilege of a nine-to-five job, do they?

God damn it, Sean.

Thankfully, the Matriarch is ready with a piece of dialogue that will solve the a.m.-or-p.m. mystery. I forget the exact wording she used, but it was something like this: 'Not that we give three shiny fucks about the answer to the question I'm about to ask, but I'm compelled to offhandedly enquire if that's 7.30 a.m. or 7.30 p.m. If you don't want to answer, that's fine. I'm not too bothered; I'm only asking for a friend – one who's dead.'

'7.30 p.m.,' says Sean.

In that case, we'll stay for a cuppa.

Rebecca returns home right on schedule – we are a *go,* Dory. I repeat, the mission is a *go.*

The first step is to tell them the news – we're going to have a baby.

After the display of emotion subsides, we finally get to it. I dump all our worries and fears onto Rebecca like a piano dropping from a forty-storey building.

Rebecca's first response is to smile. I would have signed over our house alone for that smile.

Rebecca answers all of our questions. In short, we're doing what ninety-nine per cent of new parents do, which is to worry – probably over nothing. Rebecca explains that, at this stage, embryos are like parasites; you're more than qualified at taking what you need from Mummy's body. Phew.

Hang on a minute. Parasite?

Sunday, 14 April 2019 – Santa-Isn't-Real Moments

I've been thinking about my childhood experiences – everything positive, everything negative, and everything poignant – and about how those experiences influenced my journey to adulthood through the many rites of passage along the way. But I'm finding difficulty in attaining any worthwhile parental insights from this reflection exercise. Certainly, some of my negative childhood experiences taught me valuable lessons. For example, Granny Smurf hasn't exactly been one of the lucky ones when it comes to relationships and men. I've watched her experience, and have experienced myself, treatment from men that I don't wish on anyone, particularly those I hold dear. Especially you.

That said, Granny Smurf never allowed herself to be a victim. Instead, she's emerged from every negative experience stronger and wiser. She's learnt from all of them.

In turn, as an observer and a passenger, I too have learnt from her experiences. They helped shape the way I treat people. They taught me humility and empathy, and I learnt that value could be obtained through suffering. It's from failure and things going wrong that we gain our most valuable insights into life.

However, ask any parent, including both of yours, if they want their children to suffer and their response is unlikely to be anything other than a resounding no.

That's why I'm struggling to translate my thoughts and experiences into actionable parental values. I don't want to place you in a situation that would harm you or cause you pain. I want to protect you. At the same time, I need you to know the truth about the world and about people, so that you're not ill-equipped when you go out there. I want you to see not only the good but also the bad (both of which rarely, if ever, exist in isolation) and everything in between. I want those insights to inform how you see the world and where you fit into it – how you treat others and how you allow others to treat you.

There have been many of these key moments in my life. I have a term for them. I call them 'Santa isn't real' moments. They're moments when I've discovered the truth about something – moments which turned a pleasant belief into an unpleasant reality. Examples include 'Not everyone is nice', 'Grown-ups fuck up too' and 'Santa isn't real'.

How do I turn this self-reflection exercise into parental actions? I honestly don't know the answer, Dory – but thankfully, I've got time. I certainly don't want you learning these lessons too early on in your life.

Childhood innocence is a joy to behold. I can't wait to see you running around playing with your toys – watching your imagination conjure up all kinds of wonders. I think being armed, as soon-to-be parents, with the knowledge that childhood is fleeting will help us ensure we treasure those moments. Because one day, your Mummy and I will have to sit you down and explain to you that Santa isn't real. It's a hard lesson to learn. I wonder if it will be harder to teach.

Monday, 15 April 2019 – My Greatest Passion

I wouldn't class myself as a materialistic person, but books prove an exception to the rule. One of my favourite things to do is read. I read every day, and I read both made-up and non-made-up stories – made-up stories are one of the few tools I possess for truly disconnecting from the noise inside my head that accompanies me almost everywhere I go.

I cannot wait to read to you, Dory. I learnt the other day that you'll still be in Mummy's tummy when you can start recognising voices. When that day comes, I'll start reading to you. Mummy's favourite children's books are the Dr Seuss series, and you can bet ten tins of baby formula that you'll have the full set sitting on a shelf in your nursery before your first birthday. I was more of a Roald Dahl kid growing up. *The Enormous Crocodile* and *Charlie and the Chocolate Factory* were two of my favourites, and I think I was about seven or eight the first time I read *The Hobbit*.

Non-made-up storybooks are responsible for the majority of my learning these days. To me, buying and reading a book and then learning something from it represents the greatest possible value for money. It still blows my mind that you can spend a few quid and gain access to so much knowledge and information, and then use that to make improvements in your own life.

When you begin to expose yourself to different subjects and areas of life, you may at first be overwhelmed; life can be viewed through a seemingly infinite number of lenses. But if you continue to pursue knowledge and experiences, you build connections – connections that soon begin to reveal themselves more frequently. They become deeper and richer, and that feeling of being overwhelmed is replaced by something less scary – something that hopefully makes you say, 'Aha!'

A commitment to learning can help you to find your place in the world – at least, that's the excuse I give Mummy when I want to get out of doing the dishes and go and 'work'.

To recap: reading made-up stories can help you escape from reality (something everyone needs occasionally), while reading non-made-up stories helps build truth and clarity within your own reality (although that isn't to say you can't find truth in made-up stories – quite the opposite; but

I hope you take my point).

Find the value in the books and stories that you read. Always seek out knowledge. And share what you learn. Do these things and you will make the world a better place and its inhabitants will benefit from it.

Wednesday, 17 April 2019 – Minus Eighteen And Dropping

We're driving back from some friends of ours, and Mummy decides to work on her personal development plan. She asks me for some feedback about her driving: 'Do you think I'm an aggressive driver?'

My first thoughts make a beeline towards déjà vu, owing to the other night's dress-modelling drama, when I was ambushed by spiralling hormone levels. I refuse to repeat the mistake of walking carelessly into a self-immolation party.

But how can I not? We're in the car; I can't escape. I need to tread lightly, but I'm fucked if I know what direction to head in.

First, the answer to Mummy's question is a resounding and firm yes. Yes, yes and yes. Capitalise the yes, bold and underline it, and then code in some flashy lighting effects. Mummy is an aggressive driver; you and I have already worked this out, Dory.

But I daren't say that, for reasons that should by now be bloody obvious.

Also, I feel confused. Over the four and a half years that we've been together, I have, on occasion, told Mummy she's an aggressive driver. Come to think about it – I tell her every time she exhibits road rage, which happens to be every time we're in the car!

Can you see my quandary here? Why is Mummy asking me a question to something she gets the answer to regularly? I sense a trap – a big fucking trap, Dory.

If I answer honestly, I'll upset Mummy, and if I lie, she'll call me out as a liar and a villain.

Rightly or wrongly, I select option one to maintain my integrity.

'Yes, I can confirm you are an aggressive driver. I tell you this all the time, so I'm a little in the dark about your motives here.'

Mummy looks like I've just confessed to a three-year affair with her best friend. She genuinely appears to be learning this information for the first time. How, Dory? How the fuckety, fuck, fuck am I in this position again? Unsurprisingly, the rest of the journey is frosty – minus eighteen and dropping.

Thursday, 18 April 2019 – 'Shells'

It's date night, and I've taken Mummy to see a live orchestra performing music from the films of Pixar Studios. You won't believe who we're looking at right this second. It's you, Dory, on-screen – or, at least, the Dory your pre-birth name is based on. They're playing music from *Finding Dory* and a background display is showing Dory as a baby (more of a toddler, actually), and it's beautiful. I quickly Shazam the music; the song is called 'Shells'.

Next film on the set list is *Up*, one of Daddy's favourites. Scenes from the film are on display; Carl and Ellie are getting married. Nothing but positive feels engulf the theatre. And now they're showing … oh shit, I forgot about that scene. Wait, why isn't anyone turning it off? Someone cut the cables now! KILL IT WITH FIRE!

It is the scene where Ellie miscarries. It's always been sad, but now it's terrifying. Thankfully, we move on to *The Incredibles* – a family with three perfectly healthy children. I welcome the distraction with open arms.

Friday, 19 April 2019 – The Tail End

Today we're off to pick Granny Smurf up from her home in Kent and bring her back to Northampton to start a new life – as a resident and soon-to-be grandmother. Mummy is accompanying me, but she's been given strict instructions not to lift anything – especially as she has been complaining of a pain in her tummy today. Full disclaimer, Dory; you're getting the blame for it. Don't take it personally.

Granny Smurf's relocation to Northampton is something that we've been discussing for the last few years, and now it's finally happening.

There's a blog article by Tim Urban called *The Tail End*. In it, he uses charts to illustrate a person's life in days. His metric leans heavily towards optimism and assumes you live to be 90. A quick calculation tells me that 90 (years) x 365 (days in each year, not including leap years – I can't be bothered to work that out) gives you 32,850 days alive.

Tim then calculates how often he sees his parents (with built-in assumptions) and then cross-references the data with his parent-days metric to reveal how much of his total time he's already used up seeing them and how much time he's got left.

Applying his maths to my own circumstances makes for some shattering realisations.

As I write this, Granny Smurf is 53 years old. Let's be optimistic like Tim, and assume Granny lives to 90 and that she retains all of her faculties. That means she has thirty-seven years remaining.

First, using some built-in assumptions myself (again, fuck faffing with leap years), I'll calculate roughly how many days I've spent with Granny Smurf.

The numbers below have been captured by reviewing my circumstances at that particular age. So, from age 14 and upwards, you can see I started to spend less and less time at home.

14 x 365 (0-14 years old; every day at home) = 5,110 days

2 x 312 (15-16 years old; more time socialising) = 624 days

2 x 208 (17-18 years old; when I started working) = 416 days

3 x 36 (19-21 years old; when I was at uni) = 108 days

11 x 3 (22-33 years old; twice-yearly visits, each of 1.5 days) = 33 days

Total = 6,291 days

Next, I calculate how many days I have left to spend time with Granny Smurf, assuming I continue the current pattern of twice-yearly visits. Let me remind you that this exercise assumes that Granny Smurf lives to 90, with good enough mental health to recognise who I am and to know that drinking lead paint isn't that nutritious.

If I add the total days spent to the total days remaining, I get 6,365 days. Ready for the results?

I've used up 98.838% of my time already and I have 1.162% remaining – or seventy-four days.

Let that sink in.

This is the tail end, Dory. As someone who is about to become a father, I think this is tragic.

Until today.

The time I have remaining with your grandmother isn't the tail end at all, it's the middle section. The trajectory has changed and the projections have altered. Not everyone is this lucky; life has a way of cementing people's routes all over the world, more so today than ever before because of how accessible the globe is.

Your Mummy sees her Mummy and Daddy and your Auntie Lisa most days – and has done since she was a child (other than during periods of travel). She's yet to enter the tail end with them.

You will grow up with your grandparents almost as much as you will with your parents.

I don't want you to think this is a roundabout way of manipulating you never to leave your parents; it's not (unless you can't afford the rent). We want you to forge your own path: forge it far, forge it wide and forge it deep. But it's something to think about.

This exercise isn't restricted to immediate family – its focus is on relationships in general. The article ends with Tim's deductions from the exercise, with which I fully agree: living in the same place as the people you love matters, priorities matter and quality time matters.

Saturday, 20 April 2019 – As Things Stand

Granny Smurf now lives in Northampton, but we're not hoisting the bunting up yet. Ideally, we could have done with another eight weeks before welcoming Granny, as we haven't quite finished our renovation project – we're close, though.

We began it last July, and we hilariously thought it would be ready in time for Christmas. However, development is something your parents didn't have any experience in at the time (Daddy didn't know how to spell 'screwdriver', let alone use one – I still don't, to be honest; I had to spellcheck it just now), and we made every rookie mistake going. This resulted in the completion date moving forward again and again, with the cost mounting up more and more.

But we'd pencilled in 19 April to collect Granny Smurf and, once that date was locked in, it was locked in. She handed in her notice for her old job and told her landlord she was moving out.

The situation today looks like this: Granny Smurf is living in our house despite it having hardly any furniture – it has an old sofa, and she has a bed, but there's not much more. Mummy and I are still living at Grandad Tools and Granny Feeder's house. We haven't begun to think about packing up yet – there's still too much to do. Hopefully, we'll be able to move back in a few weeks. Granny Smurf will live with us for the foreseeable future – so she can settle, get a new job, and so forth – before thinking of her long-term housing arrangements.

Enough about future planning. Mummy says her side is still hurting – everything OK, kiddo?

Sunday, 21 April 2019 – Easter Sunday

Happy Easter, Dory. I've opened the unicorn egg that I bought you on my day of discovery and I may have eaten all the chocolate, but Ruby the unicorn is still hanging about waiting for you.

Despite Ruby's best efforts at reminding us that we have a Dory in Mummy's tummy and that we should be excited, your parents aren't doing that great today. The pain in Mummy's side has increased – a lot.

We've dialled the NHS 111 advice line and we have the phone on loudspeaker while we talk to an advisor. They ask Mummy if she has pain in her neck and in her shoulder. The question sends chills up my spine – I know exactly why they're asking that: they're determining whether you might be an ectopic pregnancy.

I know this is routine procedure – you find out what something is by finding out what it isn't. However, Mummy does have a sore neck, and the side cramps have been severe. *Fuck, Dory*, you'd better be at home in Mummy's uterus and not anywhere else!

The other thing that's beginning to shit me up is seeing Mummy in pain. I've seen her experience pain many times before and she handles it remarkably well. Over the years, I've learnt that if Mummy says something hurts, she's not fucking around – it hurts.

Please be OK.

The NHS advisor tells us to come to the hospital.

6.20 p.m. The hospital is crazy-busy – as in the front row of a headliner act at Glastonbury. There's nothing we can do but wait.

Nearby, a young family occupies our attention while we wait: a Mummy, a Daddy, their son (about 7) and their daughter (about 4). We've just witnessed the girl spit in her Mummy's face because she couldn't have money for sweets.

Please don't ever spit at Mummy, Dory.

Now the little girl is singing 'Twinkle, Twinkle, Little Star', which would be cute if I hadn't watched her catapult phlegm over the woman who gave birth to her.

Her older brother has now decided to try his own voice at singing 'Twinkle', but he's amended the lyrics: 'Twinkle, twinkle, little star, I will hit you with my car.'

His wordplay has caught me off guard, causing me to laugh. I tried to do this discreetly but, like I said, I was caught off guard, and now the kid has zeroed in on the fact he's had a positive response from an audience member.

He's now begun his version of 'Twinkle, Twinkle' from the top – his eyes fixed on mine. The problem with children and comedy is that they have no concept of the law of diminishing returns. If an action, particularly one of misbehaviour, causes someone to laugh, they assume that to repeat said action again and again will elicit a similar response.

This is not true, Dory. It gets soul-crushingly boring in no time at all. The kid is only 7, bless him, but in my head, I repeat the mantra: 'Shut up, bellend.'

Thankfully, we've been called in to see the doctor.

6.40 p.m. The doctor is concerned about the pain in Mummy's side and she has referred her over to the gynaecology department. Unsurprisingly, they too are busy, so it's back to another waiting room to sit it out.

I text Rebecca on the off-chance that she can do something, but she's on holiday in the Lake District, so we're on our own.

9.36 p.m. We see … someone: another doctor, I think. She asks similar questions to the last one and agrees that Mummy needs to go to the gynaecology department (if they can fit her in). She takes a blood sample from Mummy and tells her not to eat or drink anything – in case she needs to go to theatre for surgery. *Theatre? Surgery?* Why would she need to do that? But by the time I've stopped throwing up in my mouth, she's already left.

11.36 p.m. More blood tests, this time to establish Mummy's blood type – in case she needs a transfusion. The nurse taking the blood also confirms that the scan you and Mummy need won't be carried out until morning. *Why not? Is it because they think she will need surgery but they can't perform it tonight? What the fuck is going on? It's a quick scan – it will only take a few seconds.*

At this point, I am more scared than I have ever been before in my life. Mummy is the same – I can read it in her eyes.

The doctor gives her something for the pain.

Monday, 22 April 2019 – The Second-Longest Night Of My Life

??.?? a.m. Despite someone telling us that Mummy won't be scanned until morning, we learn that staff in the gynaecology department now want her scanned urgently. We're instructed to wait until a porter becomes available to collect us.

??.?? a.m. Mummy has checked into the new ward in the gynaecology department and we've been told to wait for someone to come and perform the scan. We try everything we can think of to keep ourselves distracted. We plan our trip to Amsterdam next weekend, but we don't bother booking airport parking.

Not yet.

I don't say it to your Mummy and she doesn't say it to me, but we each wonder if you're still alive.

Next, we order new blinds for the house. Fucking absurd, right?

5.00 a.m. A nurse arrives and explains that they don't have anyone available who can scan Mummy until 9.00 a.m., so I might as well go home and try to sleep for a few hours. I'm pissed off, Dory; we've been up all night, told one thing and then another. We could have stayed at home and arrived ten minutes before the scan.

I feel tired. I feel sick. I feel scared.

I kiss Mummy goodnight and tell her everything will be fine. I kiss her belly and hope to anyone who's listening that you're still swimming and that I'm not lying to Mummy when I tell her everything will be fine.

Since my day of discovery, I've been writing to you every day. I even gave you a temporary pre-birth name, Dory. Was that a mistake? Has this exercise strengthened my emotional attachment to you, something I should not have done until later on in the pregnancy … just in case the worst should happen …

5.30 a.m. I crawl into bed and take Ruby the unicorn with me – I hold the inanimate soft toy in my grasp until sleep eventually takes me.

———————

8.45 a.m. I stumble downstairs to make a plan with Granny Feeder. We agree to take two cars to the hospital because we don't know how today will play out and who will need to run what errands. Next, I drive to our house to see Granny Smurf and tell her today is going to either be a good day or a bad day – there will be no in-between.

Mummy texts me to say that she's still in pain, she hasn't slept and she's terrified.

9.20 a.m. I arrive at the hospital ahead of the scan. Granny Feeder is here with me, but she waits outside.

9.25 a.m. We've been moved into yet another room, and a nurse named Julie arrives with the ultrasound machine. Both your parents are stone. We grip each other's hands and wait.

9.26 a.m. Julie rubs jelly on Mummy's tummy and prepares the probe. At this moment, I would trade anything I own for the news that you're OK. An image appears on-screen. It's you … I feel as if I've been shot in the chest. There's more – you're moving. I can see your arms flailing around. I allow a sliver of hope to creep in, but I daren't breathe. I need more information.

'Your baby is where it needs to be,' says Julie.

You're not grounded, Dory.

'And there's the heartbeat. Your baby is fine.'

The stone melts away and is replaced with unmeasurable relief.

In that moment, I realise that you are the most precious thing in the world to me.

Julie lets us keep the scan photos. I take them straight out to Granny Feeder and show her. Now she can breathe. Next, I take pictures of the scan pictures and send them to Granny Smurf.

So, what is up with Mummy, Dory? We don't know. No one knows. All they know is that it's not anything to be worried about. Apparently, pregnancy can cause a multitude of cramps and pains, and that's normal. Even severe ones can occur this early in the pregnancy. While I'd take this scenario a million times over, I cannot believe the journey we've been on over the last eighteen hours, only to get '… it could even be trapped wind.'

Wow!

Wednesday, 24 April 2019 – Whatever Doesn't Kill Me

Today I'm the one in pain. It's my back. My fault – I did a few unaided tip runs yesterday. Usually, I would suck it up and wait for it to subside, but not any more. I often suffer from back pain due to an ongoing injury involving two bulging discs in my spine that resulted from some not-so-clever gym work a few years ago. Renovating my house does little (nothing) to aid my recovery – an office day job doesn't help either.

This concerns me as it puts at risk our future lightsaber duels, not to mention den-building, handstand competitions, pretending Daddy is a horse, and missions to the soft-play adventure park.

I've heard of parents wanting to have kids early on in life so that they're still fit and healthy enough to play with their children. This is sound logic. While I'm closer to Granny Smurf's age than I am to yours, I don't consider myself in the same age bracket as Gandalf the Grey – I feel short-changed at the prospect of having to say no to you when you need a sidekick to take on the world, because of my twatty back issues.

Now that our renovation project is almost complete and Granny Smurf has moved in, Operation Get a Better Back needs to be the next item on my to-do list. All available resources will be called upon to serve the objective.

I'll report back on my progress in a few months.

Game on.

Thursday, 25 April 2019 – How I Know I'm Still 5 Years Old

I had two important dates marked out on my calendar for 2019, both of them film releases: *Avengers: Endgame* and *Star Wars: The Rise of Skywalker*. I say 'had' because you now make up the third important date. Congratulations on making the cut.

It should be abundantly clear by now, but in case it's not, you do realise your father is a big film geek, right? Good.

Avengers: Endgame is out today and I'm excited. Embedded in my excitement is an important lesson that I think we forget as we grow older. And that's to have fun as adults. Every one of us is a child at heart, but (and I'm ashamed to say I include myself in this) we forget that as we grow up. Or rather, we don't forget it, but we don't make a strong enough priority of having fun and playing.

Adults might grow out of Barbie and Action Man, but if we look hard enough, we can find something to replace them that serves that same purpose of letting go of everything plaguing our minds for a small amount of time to have fun: reading books, going hiking, hanging out with our mates, playing video games – or going to see *Avengers: Endgame*.

I hope you learn this, and I hope you'll remind me of it as well.

7.20 p.m. The film is about to start and I have an erection the size of four flights of stairs – I act cool but inside I'm my 5-year-old self again.

11.00 p.m. Jesus fucking Christ, that was an epic three hours well spent.

Friday, 26 April 2019 – Our First Family Holiday

Today we're off on our holidays, Dory. It's our first family holiday of many. We're off to Amsterdam to not get drunk and not get stoned.

Your parents love to travel. Since we've been together (four and a half years at the time of writing), we've spent twenty per cent of our entire relationship travelling. It's such a rich and rewarding experience, and we're addicted. For us, travelling is like filling the car up at the petrol station so it can continue moving forward a few more miles. Except in this analogy, we're the cars and the fuel isn't diesel, it's passport stamps.

Your old man has dived with bull sharks in the ocean, seen the African Big Five up close in the wild, jumped out of an aeroplane nineteen thousand feet over glaciers in New Zealand, enjoyed local hospitality in several rural Asian villages and done much more besides. I've been incredibly lucky.

I want you to have this. Mummy and I have already promised each other that you will be spoilt; not with inanimate, materialistic 'things'* but with enriching experiences. Hopefully, these experiences will teach you to live in the moment, cherish all corners of the planet and transcend cultural barriers.

Living life to the full is the ultimate fuel source for the mind, body and spirit.

Sunday, 28 April 2019 – The Happiness Project

Today we're off to take a look at *The Happiness Project*, an exhibition at Body Worlds. This display features anatomical real-life human bodies

---

* Lego is not included in my list of things that are materialistic; you must have lots of this or what is the fucking point of childhood, right? We might as well take you straight to the clinic and get you aborted – it would be kinder!

preserved through a process called plastination. You could say I have – incoming Daddy joke – a morbid curiosity. The display promises to take us on a journey that examines the effects of lifestyle and mental health on our bodies and in turn our happiness.

Seeing our species in the way that it's presented is fascinating. There are people of different shapes and sizes running, vaulting, playing instruments and having sex. The main message from the expo is this: if you feed your body and your mind all the good stuff, you'll convert it and output it as great stuff; but if you feed it junk food, negative thoughts and long periods of inactivity, then you'll output something else entirely, toxic stuff – not something you want, Dory. This is another lesson I hope to impart to you one day.

We've arrived at the next floor of the expo and I'm looking at an eleven-week-old foetus. It died at the same age as you are now. It brings back memories of last week. I don't find it upsetting; it's strangely cathartic. At this age, the foetus is translucent; you can make out the bones and early signs of organ development – captured, preserved and then presented in the most beautiful way.

Travel never fails to reward and impress.

Tuesday, 30 April 2019 – Maybe

We're back from our trip but I feel like I need another holiday already. Today is not going well. I've colossally overestimated how much money I can take back out of our house through a remortgage now that we've completed our renovation project and the property is worth an extra few quid – the bank will only lend me so much and it's not as much as I wanted.

This has two financial implications. It means we can't reinvest the money which I had planned to use to help Granny Smurf buy a house. It also puts financial pressure on Mummy and me when you arrive, because we can't quite pay off all the loans that we took out to carry out the house renovations in the first place.

I still haven't figured out what my working situation will be like when you're here, but I want to take more than the standard two weeks' paternity leave. Unfortunately, doing that would potentially mean taking unpaid leave – something I now might not be able to do.

Mummy and Daddy have done the most productive thing a couple can do when faced with a problem (particularly a financial one), which is to have a row and blame each other. We're not winning any prizes for problem solving today.

I get annoyed when I allow this sort of stuff to beat me up. It's embarrassing. I'm lucky; I have more to be grateful for than most people I know and that was before I learnt about you. Remember, it was only a week and a half ago that we thought our parenting journey was over before it had begun! Humans are ruthlessly efficient at redefining their baselines!

I've listened to 'Shells' on repeat. I figured it might help me refocus, because the music reminds me of you.

It's working … very effectively.

I'm looking at this through a different lens, and from another angle it's not a money problem we have; it's a plan that's hit a roadblock. That's all. We're lucky to own our own house and make it the way we want, as well as having our family living close by. What's important is you and Mummy. You're both healthy – I have nothing to complain about. I've sent an apology to Mummy.

I cannot overstate how effective listening to 'Shells' has been for my mood today. Music has been a powerful ally of mine for many years; it helps me with focus levels by removing distractions, and it sometimes helps me pause long enough to look out of the window. But having a track that triggers thoughts of you has multiplied the effect tenfold.

Imagine if every parent had a song that they associated with their child. If parents fought or had a bad day, then playing that song might help them to reframe and settle their emotions. It's like a psychological trigger.

It's remarkable how listening to one song on repeat has turned a shitty day into an insightful one.

There is a Taoist parable about a farmer. One day, the farmer's only horse runs away, and the farmer can't work his farm. The neighbours offer their sympathies to the farmer. 'Such bad fortune,' they say.

'Maybe,' replies the farmer.

The next day, the horse returns with three other wild horses – the farmer now has four horses. The neighbours return. 'Such good fortune,' they say.

'Maybe,' replies the farmer.

The next day, the farmer's son tries to ride one of the wild horses. He falls off and breaks his leg. The neighbours appear again. 'Such bad fortune,' they say.

'Maybe,' replies the farmer.

The next day, military officials arrive at the farmer's village and conscript young men into the army. They don't bother with the farmer's son as his leg is broken. Once again, the neighbours visit the farmer. 'Such good fortune,' they say.

'Maybe,' says the farmer.

Powerful stuff, Dory.

May

Wednesday, 1 May 2019 – Financial Planning

The first day of a new month reminds me of how long we have left until we meet each other: roughly twenty-eight weeks. We have your first official scan in a couple of weeks. I'd appreciate it if you could keep the life-threatening scares down to somewhere between zero and none.

I've spent the day trying to figure out a new financial plan based on yesterday's not-so-good news. I think I've found a solution. It's by no means bulletproof, but it's a start.

I've discussed alternative mortgage products with my mortgage broker. He's found another product through another lender who will let me borrow more money. This reintroduces the option of me taking additional time off work when you arrive. Bingo.

You see? *Maybe.*

But I first need to understand what our total expenditure and combined income is. I've not had to think about that in years. Fun fact – did you know that Mummy and I have only ever spent four weeks living alone together under the same roof? For the rest of the time we've been living with family or friends, or we've been travelling. We've never sat down to look at finances, just the two of us. We've never had to.

Before I calculate income and expenditure, it's worth baking in a few assumptions. Right now, Mummy works, but soon she won't. She'll have statutory maternity pay, but at some point that will run out. Between you and me, I don't think Mummy will want to go back to work if she doesn't have to. I therefore need to factor in the possibility of us becoming a one-income household.

To calculate our household outgoings, I need to work out what the minimum cost of our household would be, with overestimations factored in and allowances for you when you arrive. I don't know if you will be breastfed or formula-fed, so I've budgeted for formula as I presume that's the more expensive option.

Finally, I've budgeted a small personal allowance for Mummy and me. We don't need a lot. It's not that your parents are naturally frugal, we just don't buy a lot of stuff for ourselves. The bulk of my expenses go on second-hand books and travelling. Luckily for me, second-hand books are cheap (not that I envision much reading time when you're here) and, while travelling isn't as cheap, we won't exactly be heading straight from the hospital to Heathrow airport when you're born, will we?

With the above in mind, I've arrived at a figure. It's 2.5k. Remember, that's an overestimation, and it doesn't allow for savings, but that's the minimum we need coming in each month to get by. So, if I want to take additional time off, and if Mummy wants to take some time off from jobbing to do some full-time mumming, I need to ensure there's enough in the bank to cover our expenses each month. 2.5k is the target, Dory.

I suggested a couple of money-saving ideas to Mummy, but was shot down quicker than an Iranian fighter jet in US airspace. Apparently, my old slippers aren't suitable teddy-bear alternatives, and we can't substitute Early Learning Centre toys for Granny Smurf's dentures.

Thursday, 2 May 2019 – Needs More Nerf Guns

I've read a fantastic example of parenting done right: *The Magic of Thinking Big* by David Schwartz. In it he references a case study. A child, Billy, cries out one night. Billy can't get to sleep because he's been watching a film featuring aliens. He is scared. Now, the default action of a parent (it would certainly have been mine until now) would be to reassure the child, tell them aliens don't exist and hope they settle. Not this Daddy, Dory. He proceeds to carry out a thorough inspection of the room, ensuring the windows are locked. He then gets hold of Billy's plastic toy gun and places it on his bedside table with the instruction 'Just in case'. Billy is flat out asleep four minutes later. How cool is that? I've underlined the shit out of that paragraph. I've begun the habit of underlining anything that I think serves as a parental lesson; anything that I think will be useful for us in the future.

What would I do in that situation – maybe tell you that aliens don't exist, but give you some weapons as backup and reassurance? Actually, scrap that, who doesn't want to believe aliens exist? I'd better stock up on Nerf gun bullets!

Reading about Billy has led me to recollect a few fond childhood memories of my own. I've already told you about my black-cat soft toy, Charlie, right? He was my best bud and he was more than my cat. He used to accompany me through every one of my night-time adventures from bed. Every night, we would go on a space mission. I'm not sure why it was space; maybe it's because I grew up on *Star Wars* movies or maybe it's because it was dark, and space is dark.

I remember feeling comforted by having Charlie by my side whenever things got a bit hairy, and there were plenty of those moments. Whether it was manning one of the side cannons, hiding with me while we waited for trouble to pass, consoling me when I was upset, or just plain old hanging out, Charlie was always around. Dory, you need a Charlie.

Ultimately, I think it needs to be you who decides who your Charlie is – I'm sure by the time you're old enough to make that decision you'll have plenty of soft-toy options to select from.

Sunday, 5 May 2019 – News Just In

Breaking news: Mummy's boobies have swelled to a size of planetary proportions. Dory, I'm in awe – they can't continue growing at this pace. It's unsustainable. My sympathies, you probably don't want to hear about this, but in case it isn't clear: your Mamma currently got dem big-ass titties on the go.

Sticking with female body transformations, we've noticed a baby bump!

It's you, Dory! You've grown lots in the last couple of weeks. According to our pregnancy development app, you're about the size of a plum. Another pregnancy-proud Daddy moment. I take a photo of me kissing the roof of your rental home and then I kiss the owner of the property. Both tenant and landlord are doing a fine job. A fine job, Dory.

News update: Mummy has signed a contract with Ben & Jerry's to be their main milk supplier.

Monday, 6 May 2019 – The Orwell Protocol

We're out for breakfast with the family this morning, and Granny Smurf is recounting how she used to manipulate me.

She says, 'I used to pretend that I'd had an injection that instantly alerted me to any wrongdoing.' Apparently, this inspired little narrative came about after a recurring period of me asking how my Mummy always knew I was up to no good.

At first, I'm horrified. How fucking dare she lie to her only child? However, I'm no longer a child (allegedly); I'm about to become a father. Things are falling into place, Dory; I'm now appreciating the coin from both sides. These manipulative techniques will come in useful. I must develop and grow as a person, be open to new ideas and accept an ever-evolving belief system. Telling you whatever fiction I can conjure up (an inexhaustible resource, I'm afraid), in order for you to obey me without question, needs to be part of my parental framework.

However, 'special injections' are a little old-fashioned. They served Granny Smurf well, but I need something more in line with the times. I need to update the narrative.

How's this for a starter for ten:

There are cameras everywhere. In every room in every house, in every shop in every street, in every garden in every town, in every space that you can seek. These cameras are always on – every second of every hour, every hour of every day and every day of every year of your childhood. These cameras need zero downtime for maintenance or system upgrades. They don't need sleep. They work over Christmas (pause for dramatic gasp).

These cameras record everything you do.

Storage capacity is a non-issue; all data files are instantly uploaded to the 'child behaviour cloud'. It utilises over ten octillion satellites, so no amount of bad weather will incapacitate the file-upload process.

And if that weren't impressive enough, these cameras have a complex binary camouflage system. This means that children cannot see these cameras – only grown-ups can.

This network is affectionately called the 'Orwell Protocol'.

When a child is born, its DNA is uploaded to the Orwell Protocol mainframe. Parents can access their children's profiles from an app on their smart device. I'm afraid the app is devastatingly intuitive. You so much as think about thinking about helping yourself to a chocolate biccy and the app will alert us to your intentions. The punishment will be swift. It's not worth it, Dory. Luckily for you, if you do everything your parents tell you to do, you will never have to worry about getting into trouble.

Long live the Orwell Protocol.

Tuesday, 7 May 2019 – Just In Case

I've spent the day thinking about, and planning for, death. Your existence has served as a welcome jolt to the ribs for me to sort out our family affairs, just in case something awful should befall one of your parents. I have instructed an estate planner to take care of the legal necessities. With his help, our assets and wishes in the event of our deaths are soon to be protected by law.

Talking about death is never a serotonin booster, but not talking about it is worse, and not preparing for it worse still, particularly for those left behind – you. The red tape involved in probate is said to be painfully difficult to cut through.

Don't despair at all this talk of death – it's just a precaution. You will be born into the world at a time when things have never been so good (depending on your perspective). With today's media capitalising on dreaded events and manipulating us into believing the apocalypse will be along at any moment to erase our species from existence, it's difficult to reframe our world view into something a tad more cheerful.

But cheerful it should be; history shows us how far we've come and the projections for the future are brighter than a star living in its prime. Yes, we have problems to solve (that will never change), but if you look at the global collective well-being we've never had it better!

Try and remember this as you grow up, and if you find yourself struggling, think about, and then empathise with, your poor parents, who somehow trudged through their childhoods without smartphones, the internet and Netflix.

Wednesday, 8 May 2019 – No Killer Whales For You, Dory

The other day I sent an email to a tour operator asking about the age restrictions on a killer-whale trip that I've been wanting to take for years. It's bad news. You can't go until you're sixteen. I expected this. But I was curious, so I asked.

It's not all doom and gloom, though – Mummy and Daddy can still go. I say this as a joke, but it's got me thinking. What are the parenthood rules for going away or doing stuff without your kids? Is a trip to the cinema OK, but a biannual three-week Mediterranean cruise a piss-take?

It's not something I've considered before, but I do know one thing: I want to go swimming with killer whales in the wild, and I want to do it within the next sixteen years. Also, I don't envisage a scenario where your mother won't want to come, which means you'll probably have to stay behind with your grandparents. Don't worry, Daddy will bring you back a fridge magnet.

I hope you don't think I'm a terrible father who regrets having children even before he has any. That's not the case at all; it's just that I know of parents who put their kids' 'needs' before themselves in everything they do and deny themselves their own lives. I don't understand this. They might identify as parents first, but every one of us on the planet is an individual, and we keep many different identity hats in the wardrobe: husband, wife, surgeon, chef, traveller, film geek – these are all identity hats, some of choice and some not. But nonetheless, all these hats are fidgety, and they all need wearing. Date night is needed, time alone in front of the TV with an Xbox controller is needed, and time away from the kids has to be something that's needed as well, right?

I realise this is all conjecture – much like all the thinking I do about parenthood, as I've yet to begin my tenure. That said, I believe that parents who claim to put their children's needs first and never leave them on their own don't achieve putting their children's needs first at all. How can we be the best example for our children if we choose to wear the same hat every day?

I take the point that our children are our top priority – but they're not the only priority. I think the denial of this fact comes from self-manufactured parental guilt. It's something I've been told about many times even if I can't fully relate to it myself yet.

What does going away without your kids look like, anyway? Let's work through this right now. We'll use the killer-whale trip as an example.

The trip is eight days long; let's say ten to include travel to and from Norway. Ten days feels like a long time to be away from you (despite what I've said above). Whenever I leave Mummy and go away, I miss her. Even if the trip is epic and I don't have a second to be bored. I can't imagine things being any different with you. If anything, it's likely to be worse. But when I look back at some of the experiences I've had without your mother, it's those experiences that register in my mind first, not the periods where I missed her. There is a lesson in that.

What about your perspective? Ten days feels like a long time to be away from my family as an adult; to a child it must feel like forever. I remember being away from Granny Smurf for two weeks one summer when I was about 7 or 8. The first week was great, but during the second week, I was homesick. The fact that it's such a strong memory suggests it was a real issue for me psychologically. I also remember being bored in the second week. I had no one to play with, and I'd spent all my pocket money – so maybe we need to ensure you have some epic adventures lined up for when we're away. Failing that, Wi-Fi.

Would Mummy and I have to go at the same time? If I had a choice, I would prefer to go with your mother. However, this trip will be one of the most unique experiences we've ever had, and it will still be memorable if we're on it together or separately. This is a valid option. You have at least one of your parents with you at all times, and we each get to go on the trip. Might this be a good compromise?

I think part of this picture will be defined by your personality and by how strong your relationship is with the rest of the family.

Will we be lucky enough to get a single trip to the cinema in the first two years of your life, the odd city break between years two and five and then our trip with the whales when you're 6 or older? Who knows? Like I said, it's all guesswork and this thinking is premature, but it's something I'm mindful of going into my dadship programme.

By the way, you do realise that you'd get a fridge magnet every time we left you, don't you?

Just saying.

Thursday, 9 May 2019 – A Promise

You are twelve weeks into your development, Dory, and you are about to graduate from the first trimester. I want to congratulate you and Mummy on a job well done so far. We only thought you had died once, so that's a figure that could have been worse, right?

What would you like as a reward for your hard work? I'll tell you what – here's a promise, kiddo. One day, when you're older, you can ask me for something. In fact, seeing as I like to advocate travelling to anyone who will listen, you can have an all-expenses-paid trip – provided you stay in hostels, eat street food and use local tour operators.

It can be anywhere in the world. It doesn't count towards any birthday or Christmas presents. Family holidays are also exempt. I strongly recommend you save this up until you're in your late twenties, but I'll leave it to you to make that decision for yourself. You just have to remind me of this promise, and I'll find a way to ensure you go. I'm so grateful to be a soon-to-be Daddy and the commitment will remind me of this moment.

Friday, 10 May 2019 – Anyone Seen My Erection? No, Me Neither

Are you OK, Dory? Can you breathe? I hope you're not claustrophobic. The reason for my concerns is that Mummy is trying to get into her jeans and, oh boy, are they snug. But she's choosing not to recognise the magnitude of the situation; she's decided they fit her fine. This is an incorrect assessment, Dory. They do not fit fine.

However, never one to be outdone by logic and sound reasoning, your Mummy has decided she's squeezing you in one way or another. It reminds me of when I go camping and I'm endeavouring to somehow fit my oversized sleeping bag into a sack the size of a crisp packet.

Arousal levels are minimal.

It is quite funny, though.

Sunday, 12 May 2019 – Be More Like Haylee

In the past, I've instructed you to be your own person (the Orwell Protocol notwithstanding). I'm reconsidering that directive and editing it to read: 'Be more like your cousin Haylee.' You see, Haylee came to stay with us last night and the wonderful little darling slept in her travel cot from 8.00 p.m. until 7.30 a.m. She didn't wake up for a feed, a nappy change or anything else. Mummy and Daddy even woke up before her. And when she did finally open her eyes, she was all smiles and cuddles for her auntie and uncle. Do you see what I'm driving at here, Dory? Has the penny dropped (safely away from your head)? Haylee is a well-behaved baby; by well behaved, I mean someone who makes the adults' lives easier. Don't misunderstand me, I'm still an ardent advocate of individuality. I promise. However, when it comes to sleeping, let's aim to be more like Haylee, Dory.

Monday, 13 May 2019 – Progress Versus Impact

Progress versus impact. Victor Vescovo becomes the third person to descend to the furthest depths of the planet, the Mariana Trench. This milestone dive resulted in the discovery of new species. That is progress.

He also discovered a plastic bag and sweet wrappers. That is impact.

Plastic is having devastating consequences on the environment – both on land and in the seas. This prods at my conscience, Dory. What can I do as an individual to help mitigate the problem, and how does a newborn baby come into my thinking?

When it comes to babies, westernised culture is dependent on plastics: nappies, nappy sacks, bottles, wet wipes, tubes and pots of baby creams. I'm sure that shortlist covers but a tiny fraction of frequently consumed single-use-plastic products for babies.

I am looking at ways I can trade plastics for something a little friendlier to the environment. On paper that's fine, but how can I plan for something I have no experience in, and how do I get other people on board with me?

It's easy for me to write to you right now from my height-adjustable desk, without any distractions, having had a full eight hours of sleep and with a structured routine in place, telling you how Mummy and I have enlisted in the enviro-army. But what happens when you wake up for the fifth time in one night or when you shit triple your body weight and scream the house down? Am I going to be running for the cotton wool and ceramic bowls of warm water?

Progress has meant that life is more convenient than ever before, and you will learn that we as a species are unfailingly effective at normalising our standards and expectations every time our lives improve – so the prospect of returning to a time where reusable nappies are the new norm in the eyes of many becomes an uphill climb.

That is impact.

Tuesday, 14 May 2019 – Beware Miss Heidi

Mummy is not Mummy today. She's that other thing that suddenly appears without warning and steals Mummy's smiley, happy self and replaces it with something more unpleasant. You and I both know this thing, don't we, Dory? We should, we helped create it – and we've seen it in action terrorising little old men in their Fiats.

Research tells me that it's a known condition that women suffer from when pregnant. In scientific terms, it's called something that's long and unpronounceable, but more commonly it's known as the Miss Heidi effect. Symptoms of the Miss Heidi effect are as follows:

- Hating the Daddy for no rhyme or reason, and believing that he is a vile-looking degenerate of a man and a waste of grey matter.
- Taking deep offence at people carrying out mundane activities like eating.
- An allergy to the phrase 'Are you OK?'

Seriously afflicted sufferers also report feelings of a deep sense of curiosity as to why they even agreed to make a baby with the Daddy in the first place.

I daren't ask how many of those symptoms your mother has, but something tells me she needs to yell, 'Bingo!'

Beware Miss Heidi, Dory. In fact, every man, woman, child, animal and living or non-living thing should beware Miss Heidi, as she has the wrath and destructive capability of a family of hangry Godzillas.

Beware Miss Heidi …

Wednesday, 15 May 2019 – Scan Day (Official One This Time)

Today we have our first official Dory scan. Because of the little scare we had the other week, I don't feel nervous. It's a wonderful feeling and I'm excited. My excitement manifests itself in the following ways: skipping down the road on our way to the hospital, cheering loudly in the hospital waiting room when we're called in for our appointment, and high-fiving myself for a job well done. I'm told off by your mother for all of it.

10.25 a.m. Jill, the sonographer, rubs jelly on Mummy's tummy. Can you feel that, kiddo? Is it cold?

10.26 a.m. And there you are – my absolute world. You've grown a lot in the last few weeks. I can see your limbs, and I can see your heart beating. It's tiny but powerful. Now you're moving.

Once again, I'm thankful for the technological advances we've made in medicine. I'm looking at my child on a display monitor. I can see my child moving, and I can see my child's heart beating. I can see all of this, even though you aren't even fourteen weeks into your development and you're residing under multiple layers of organic tissue. And yet, thanks to technology, I can see you.

You did it, kiddo; you got us through to the first scan. Daddy is super proud of you. And he's proud of Mummy too. She's coped with the pregnancy wonderfully well so far, and she deserves the feelings of love and joy that she's experiencing right now.

For the first time, I believe we'll be all right – all of us.

According to Jill, you're not in the right position for her to accurately measure your height, which she needs in order to forecast your delivery date. The scan results from last time are apparently void. I'm not in the least bit concerned about any of this right now – your position on the scan makes you appear to be sitting upright. My mind can't take much more of this – incredible stuff.

But Jill does need to measure you, so she dispatches Mummy to the canteen for tea and cake. Movement and a full bladder on Mummy's part should hopefully push you up into a better position to be measured.

11.15 a.m. We're back, and Jill is using the ultrasound probe to encourage movement. By 'encourage', I mean she's prodding at you with the probe far too enthusiastically for my liking – this isn't a spearfishing competition, Jill! Eventually, she gets what we need – a measurement reading. You're 9.6 centimetres long and thirteen weeks and one day into your development. Your due date is 14 November 2019.

Roll on November, kiddo!

3.15 p.m. I'm supposed to be working, but I can't concentrate. I'm too excited.

Thursday, 16 May 2019 – Embargo Lifted

Now that the twelve-week scan has passed, the announcement embargo can be lifted – to a degree. Mummy doesn't want anything on social media yet because we have a couple of family-gathering events, which are the ideal opportunity to break the news face to face.

However, anything other than that is fair game, so I've wasted no time in sharing the most important news of my life with everyone and their dog. All of Daddy's friends now know, as does the random high-street banking employee who watched me kiss Mummy's tummy in public this morning.

Telling people is a relief for many reasons. First, announcing to the world that you're expecting a child typically means you've got through the first stage of pregnancy (which we have): the one that happens to be the stage with the highest risk. It doesn't mean we can slow up on the 'just keep swimming' motto, but it does mean we can come up for a rare breath of air.

Second, our baby-support network has exploded, owing to how many people we know with children, so telling people has practical benefits.

Finally, I want everybody on the planet to know (even if they don't give a shit). I'm thrilled about what's happening to me and what's going to happen. Life is such a miracle on its own, but add to that new life – new life produced by Mummy and me – and you have something that, in my eyes, is majestic.

Friday, 17 May 2019 – Chicken, Cooked Or Uncooked?

There has been a communication breakdown that has led to a live incident. It started when kitchen rock star and first-class family provider Granny Feeder cooked for the household. Daddy and Grandad Tools got the usual Irish delicacy of meat, veg and potatoes. Nothing out of the ordinary so far. For Mummy, because of her Crohn's, she prepared something a little lighter. Chicken. Now, Granny Feeder purposely didn't cook the chicken all the way through; she sealed the edges only. She did this because she didn't know what time Mummy would want dinner and Granny was going out dancing with the girls. Granny's intention was for Mummy to finish off the cooking when she was ready to eat. A solid plan, but she forgot one vital part – to tell Mummy that the chicken wasn't cooked!

Fast-forward an hour or so and Mummy took one look at what she thought was perfectly cooked chicken, plated it up and began eating. But it wasn't cooked, and Mummy didn't realise until she was a few mouthfuls down. Dory, some meats you can get away with eating undercooked, but chicken is not one of those meats. Chicken is very much not one of those meats. So now we're standing in the kitchen, unsure how to proceed.

A quick Google search tells us that food poisoning won't harm you, Dory. Everything you read online is a hundred per cent accurate, right? Right?

But Mummy doesn't want to take any chances, so she's now in the bathroom making herself throw up. You've got to hand it to Mummy; she always has your safety in mind.

A few hours later and Mummy appears fine. Whether the self-induced vom-sesh was needed or not, it looks like food poisoning has been averted.

Saturday, 18 May 2019 – Oh Dear, Emma

Last night I went to bed with Mummy, but I've woken up this morning with Miss Heidi – and she is pissed off. Fortunately, the actions of Emma from an online furniture retailer have spared me from a full-frontal assault. You see, Emma has made an ill-timed email response to Mummy, explaining that the spare parts for the vanity unit we were expecting to receive would no longer be arriving, despite her previously agreeing to send them out.

Oh dear, Emma.

Here are some examples of what Miss Heidi said about Emma: 'Emma's a fucking dick and she can go fuck herself, the stupid twat.' 'Can't she fucking read? She's not even on about the right part!' 'She can't say she'll do something and then change her mind; is she some sort of fucking idiot, or what?'

Beware Miss Heidi, Dory.

I'm now lying in what is probably an identical position to yours. I'm scared, and I don't know what to do. And if that isn't bad enough, Dory, your mother – sorry, I mean Miss Heidi – has expelled every element from the periodic table out of her bottom and now the room smells like Chernobyl.

But then, suddenly, Miss Heidi vanishes without a trace (*if only the smell would follow suit*). I can't explain it. One second she was there: nostrils flaring, eyes bulging and steam pouring out of every orifice above the neck. But in the next instant, Mummy returns with big smiles and affectionate cuddles.

What the actual fuck, Dory? Now she's telling me she has a surprise for me.

I know I've said it before, but this pregnancy stuff is fucking nuts.

Mummy's 'surprise' is a bag containing our first lot of baby clothes. They've been donated by a friend. They're gender-neutral, cute and rather adorable. A standout favourite is a panda outfit complete with a panda hat with little panda ears. I never imagined myself getting excited over panda hats, but there you go.

———

My day continues to improve. We're out for dinner with Mummy's cousins and their partners – whom Mummy is incredibly close to. We had planned for this evening to be our moment to share our news. Mummy has asked me to make the announcement, and I didn't know how to make it until a couple of seconds ago.

Here goes.

I ask Cousin John to take a photo of Mummy and me, but I deliberately make a song and dance about my request, so that all surrounding conversation is interrupted. Now, all attention is focused on us. We stand and pose for the photo.

'Ready; one, two, three,' says John. But before he can take the picture, I drop down and give Mummy's tummy a big kiss.

69

We've nailed it. The response is right on the money. Lots of cheering, lots of hugs and lots of smiles – another happy memory to add to the collection.

Sunday, 19 May 2019 – Hormone Lockers?

We're off to the Baby Show Expo in Birmingham. Our primary objective is to test drive a buggy that Mummy has already selected as her number one contender for you (I wasn't part of the selection process). We've brought Auntie Lisa and your cousin Haylee along for the ride.

If I'm honest, I'm not looking forward to it. I believe it will be a demonstration of marketing psychology at its finest. I can already hear the sales pitch in my head: 'I'm sure you want the best for your child, and that's something that you can't put a price on, don't you agree?' We'll be small fish in a sea of sharks. I must be on my guard.

We arrive at the entrance, and I ask the gentleman checking the tickets if they have a locker for Mummy to store her hormones in for the day. He looks at me as if I'm a suicidal religious fanatic, before encouraging me to look around and see how many pregnant women are in attendance today. His point is well made.

Breast-milk cereal bars are tasty. I've just smashed back my third, after discovering a box of them in Mummy's mum-to-be care package that she was given on arrival. It's not like she needs them yet, anyway, and I didn't get a chance to eat breakfast.

Dory, this place is gigantic. They have everything you could imagine that's linked to babies. There's a pram test-driving track (it's actually called that) where you can push prams over different terrains and surfaces, baby-furniture stands, carry-case products, travel cots, car seats, baby clothes, photoshoot companies, bottles, sterilisers and a ton more. It's a little overwhelming – I'm out of my depth.

Mummy has spotted a maternity-clothes stand and she beelines for it. However, she suddenly pivots and performs a 180-degree turn, and then she storms off in a sulk. I'm not sure why she did that, but it might have something to do with me and Auntie Lisa humming 'Pink Elephants On

Parade' from *Dumbo*. However, that's not confirmed, so this mystery will have to remain unsolved.

It's buggy-testing time. I have to hand it to Mummy; she's done all the legwork, and she's selected something she believes will appeal to both our personalities. Said buggy is designed for off-roading, with an interchangeable car seat, bassinet, go-cart seat and however many more seats we'll need (I still have no idea); it has manoeuvrability akin to that of an X-wing starfighter; and finally, it collapses quicker than a stroke victim, which is excellent for logistics (particularly in the rain). And it's not horrendously priced. I'm sold.

That said, the statement 'not horrendously priced' is relative to my baby-product baseline, which has been set in the uber-expensive bracket. I now think anything baby-related that costs under ten grand or only three limbs is a bargain.

It's later on in the day and we've finished at the expo. Everyone is tired, and Haylee has decided it's meltdown time – hip, hip, hooray for the one-hour car journey home.

I enjoyed today but I can't help feeling saddened by the whole affair. The level of consumption was off the charts – even by westernised standards. The thing I can't wrap my head around is that all this baby stuff is needed for such a short amount of time. And none of it is cheap. One of the biggest-selling products today was something called a 'Sleepyhead', retailing for around a hundred and fifty quid (depending on what version you buy). It's essentially a blanket with built-in pillow protection around the sides, making it like a pod. To me, that's mental. Surely you can cobble something together at home from a few pillows or a towel? Don't misunderstand me – it's a beautiful-looking product, and I have heard parents rave about them, but it still doesn't detract from the fact that it's a hundred and fifty pounds for a pillow that will last, what, a matter of months?

Once again, I remind myself that I've not begun my tenure as a father, and I'm prepared to eat my words and go out and buy ten Sleepyheads if it helps. But until then, we'll continue to make do with hand-me-downs – don't judge us. Besides, any money we save can be spent on things that we actually need, like a surround sound system – at least that should last longer than three bloody months!

Monday, 20 May 2019 – With Every Heartbeat

Thud-thomp, thud-thomp, thud-thomp. That's your heartbeat, Dory. I can hear it beating louder than ritual drums at an ancient tribal sacrifice.

It's beautifully evocative.

I didn't expect to hear it so soon but Mummy and Daddy are at Rebecca and Sean's house for dinner, and the first thing Rebecca offered us as we walked through the door was to get out her Sonicaid so we could listen to your heartbeat.

Thud-thomp, thud-thomp – biological wizardry performing at the highest of standards.

You anticipate these moments, Dory. You wonder how you'll feel when they happen – if they'll meet your expectations or fall short of them. Or, if you're lucky, exceed them. No prizes for guessing where this one ranks; my head is above the clouds with only the stars and zero gravity for company.

Thud-thomp, thud-thomp.

Hearing the rhythm of your heartbeat tells me that you're OK, that you're growing stronger.

That you're real.

Tuesday, 21 May 2019 – And Breathe, Dory

I've met Mummy after work. We both get in the car, and the first thing she does is undo her trouser button and you explode out; it would seem you've had a growth spurt. Mummy's bump is developing nicely – I trust you obtained the appropriate planning permission from your local authority for your home extension.

While we're on the subject, when is Mummy going to admit to herself that her clothes don't fit any more?

You ask why I don't tell her. Probably because I like my ribs unbroken. But then …

'I need to think about getting some maternity clothes,' Mummy says.

Thursday, 23 May 2019 – The No-Holds-Barred Club

I've heard women give accounts of their labour experiences before; however, I now realise that those accounts never exceeded a PG-13 rating. Now that I'm to witness childbirth up close, I'm entitled to more detailed, richer and quite frankly graphic descriptions of the miracle of life, courtesy of some of the other Mummies I work with.

I've heard Sam describe her placenta as a giant tampon and the umbilical cord hanging between her legs as a giant tampon string. She capped the story off by telling me how she was diagnosed with a gristly vagina. I've heard the most remarkable descriptions of vaginal discharge and other bodily fluids that I confess I never knew existed. Angie tells me about the hilarious moment when her other half popped his head over the screen they use for C-section procedures, only to see his wife's insides lying on a tray next to her. Unsurprisingly, he nearly passed out.

It's not only spoken accounts either: my pal Gemma performed a live re-enactment of getting her lady garden stitched up after a nasty tear, following labour. She admits the pain level exceeded that of giving birth.

I was hungry a second ago …

Let's keep this between you and me, kiddo. Otherwise, Mummy will freak out and lose her shit – which, by all accounts, she stands a strong chance of doing in labour, anyway.

Friday, 24 May 2019 – Oopsie Daisies

Miss Heidi has appeared – it looks like she'll be driving us to work today. You know the drill, kiddo: keep quiet, do not move, do not breathe – do not think!

We leave the house at eight o'clock.

A few minutes later, the bus in front of us pulls over to collect passengers (as per its job description). We can't get around the bus because the gap is too narrow – we're on a single-lane road and it's busy with traffic. Miss Heidi has no choice but to hastily apply pressure to the brakes and bring the car to a stationary position. 'Why the fuck aren't we moving?'

My brain prepares the obvious riposte and readies it for vocal delivery, but then it becomes my turn to hastily apply the brakes as I consider the consequences.

Tension mounts.

———

It's been three seconds since my last report, Dory, and Miss Heidi is about to go nuclear because we're still not moving.

Another two seconds pass. Miss Heidi has now endured five complete seconds of remaining stationary in a vehicle, a new personal best. I wonder how long she can keep this up.

She lasts another two seconds and then makes her decision. 'Fuck this,' she proclaims.

Miss Heidi pulls out on the opposite lane – the one with oncoming traffic – as she thinks she's spotted a gap.

In case you're wondering what that smell is, Dory, it's burnt rubber. The tyres have come screeching to a burning halt three feet shy of the bumper belonging to a Vauxhall Astra. It seems the 'gap' wasn't gappy enough. The driver of the Astra is stunned as to what's happening. He's shaking his head in disbelief.

But rather than face up to the responsibility, Miss Heidi vanishes and sends back Mummy, who starts chuckling – *fucking chuckling*?

'Oopsie daisies,' says your mother.

Oopsie daisies? How are we operating at *oopsie daisies*?

Beware Miss Heidi, Dory.

———

We're parking up after the longest day ever, but at least the three of us are alive. While reflecting on this morning's little road incident, I notice that one of the back seats has dislodged itself and is now lying in the footwell.

'The back seat is broken,' I say.

'Oh well, you know that seat's been a bit dodgy ever since we've had this car.' Mummy's suspiciously dismissive, Dory.

'Yes, my sweet, but why is it on the floor?'

'Beats me.'

And then it dawns. 'Is it there because of how hard you had to squeeze the brakes this morning?'

Mummy doesn't respond.

Oopsie daisies, Dory.

Saturday, 25 May 2019 – Another Milestone Reached

My day job is similar to that of a project manager. At the start of a new project I create a project milestone plan. I record all the actions that need to happen, and I bold out the most important ones.

If this pregnancy were a project, then I would have just crossed off one of the bolded-out actions – getting the results back from your 'Combined Antenatal Screening For Foetal Anomalies' report.

The news is positive. You have a 1 in 543 chance of being born with Down's syndrome and a 1 in 100,000 chance of contracting Edwards' or Patau's syndrome. Good work, kiddo.

Why is this a relief? Well, for starters, if you have Edwards' syndrome you are all but guaranteed to die before birth or shortly afterwards. It's a similar story for Patau's syndrome. The chances are rare, but it happens, and it could happen to you. I guess it still might, but a 1 in 100,000 chance means I'm less concerned about your odds than I was yesterday.

Down's syndrome is a bit different. I don't know enough about it, to be honest. I know what it is and what causes it, but I can't fathom the impact it has on both the child and the parents. Mummy tells me our jobs would become a lot harder, but it doesn't mean you're likely to die before birth (or shortly after) and, by all accounts, you would have a decent quality of life.

I can't imagine what it's like for parents having to weigh up the arguments about allowing their unborn child to live or die because of a condition or severe disability that they will be born with. This was one of many fears that I've been carrying since my day of discovery, but thankfully this letter helps alleviate those fears (slightly).

Sunday, 26 May 2019 – Haylee's Christening

It's Haylee's christening today, and Mummy and Daddy have been asked to be godparents. It's a privilege to be able to say yes. We both adore your cousin. However, I am feeling a little apprehensive.

Today's proceedings are being observed through the lens of Catholic traditions, in a Catholic church. I do not subscribe to Catholicism or any other religion. I'm an atheist. Outside the context of historical and photographic interests, churches represent something I'm not comfortable with.

But Haylee's christening isn't the reason for my apprehension. I'm happy to make promises to God (which will probably all be broken), become her godfather and look forward to a few beers with the family afterwards. The reason for my apprehension is that I know Mummy will be thinking about your own christening. We've had a brief discussion on the subject and Mummy has said that she wants you christened. I've said that I'd prefer we spent the day watching repeat episodes of *Fawlty Towers*. I feel there will at some point be a more 'formal discussion' on the subject.

Mummy is wearing a yellow dress that looks like it was tailor-made for her. She looks gorgeous. It's just a shame I have to get in the same car as her again.

We arrive at the church in time to make small talk with the family while waiting for the ceremony to get under way. I've had to listen to several members of the family remind me how it won't be long until you'll be christened. *Awkward.*

Did I mention how attractive Mummy looks today?

The priest arrives and announces that the water and oils he will be using today have all been blessed by a bishop in another part of the country. That's a relief; can you imagine if they hadn't, Dory? I daren't consider the implications.

The ceremony begins. Haylee, her parents (Auntie Lisa and Uncle Matt) and your parents are all standing at the altar listening to the priest do his bit and baptise Harlee. Sorry, did I say Harlee? That's because the priest keeps saying Harlee instead of Haylee. He's got your cousin's name wrong three times now. Not the hat-trick-hero accolade he should be aiming for.

I'm confused. He can project-manage the logistics of getting holy water to and from the bishop to be blessed, but he can't read a name written on a bit of paper right in front of him – spelt out in capital letters and non-joined-up writing.

Mummy tactfully educates the priest, but he responds by first telling her off and then reminding her that he does in fact know the baby's name.

We must be coming to the end.

But the priest is overseeing yet another round of prayers (I think we're into double figures by now) and divine commitments. We're still standing at the altar, and your mother's impressive chest display is working well to distract me from getting bored.

I'm contemplating a sly nose pick when Mummy leans in and whispers, 'I don't think I want Dory christened. Let's have a naming ceremony instead.'

Amen to that!

Monday, 27 May 2019 – Moving Back Home

Shopping at IKEA on a bank holiday Monday is like drinking a pint of hydrochloric acid – it's ill-advised.

And yet, here we are, parking up at IKEA. Guess who's in charge of spearheading this one? The Matriarch.

Her reasons for forcing us to come here aren't devoid of logic, though. Tonight will be our first night back in our home.

Three years ago, Mummy and I sat down and mapped out the next stages of our life. There were three things on the list: travel, create a home and start a family. Owing to the nature of those goals, they had (at least, to us) a natural order of progression. Travel was first. To help fund the trip, we relocated ourselves into the smallest room in the house (what will be your nursery), so we could rent out the other bedrooms to lodgers. In our bedroom we had a floor space of a little over one square metre to stand in, and we also had five people living with us – with only one shared bathroom. But we saved up enough money.

In July 2017, we left the UK for Africa to begin our backpacking adventures. I've spoken to you before about our love of travelling, but one thing I didn't tell you is how tiring it is, especially as Mummy and Daddy aren't in their twenties any more. When you're constantly on the move through borders and time zones, living out of a backpack and staying in low-budget accommodation, you eventually burn out.

When we returned home, we hadn't finished unpacking our bags before we jumped right into the next goal: create a home. The original plan was to take things slowly, but an unexpected rodent problem accelerated our plans – a lot of rats were getting into our kitchen.

So, our unpacked bags were dragged straight back to Granny and Grandad's house, and we lived there for a year. We spent our evenings and weekends working on the house. If we thought travelling was hard, it was nothing compared to the renovation work that we undertook. This wasn't a painting and decorating job: we converted the loft and basement, added a downstairs utility room and downstairs toilet, lowered ceilings, added a staircase, removed a chimney, rewired and replumbed the entire house, added additional groundwork, bricked up old doorways and installed new windows. When we weren't doing the work ourselves, we were project-managing and reworking finances on an hourly basis.

I should add that we went into this with no experience. It was gruelling, it was frustrating and it tested our relationship to the limit at times. But we kept plugging away and putting in the work.

After ten long months, it's finally ready-ish.

I say 'ready-ish' because it's a home that's almost empty (your Granny Smurf notwithstanding), and so it needs filling with … stuff, hence our trip. By the way, I don't think Mummy realises that I'm only here for the meatballs.

And of course, while we were working on the house, we were also working towards goal number three: starting a family. But as you know, we were failing. I believed we were in for yet another period of instability: gearing up for hospital appointments, consultations, surgery and IVF treatments.

But we got lucky.

Now we're proud owners of a memory vault filled with travelling adventures, a home where you can still smell the new paint on the walls, and a Dory-bump that's getting bigger and bigger each day!

Not bad.

Tuesday, 28 May 2019 – Rocks And Hard Places

A friend of mine, Emily, works as a physiotherapist. She's breaking my heart with a work story. A father and his daughter have come over to the UK from the Middle East. The girl is not in great shape; she has complex health issues along with profound learning difficulties. To top it off, her ability to walk is becoming increasingly compromised – she may get to a stage where walking is no longer possible. Emily has been to check up on her today and has learned that it's her birthday. The little girl has no cards or toys, and there will be no party of any sort to celebrate her milestone.

I wonder if there is anything we can do. I've learnt that a tiny bit of kindness and the smallest of efforts can often seem like something special in the eyes of another.

I offer to send something over to the little girl, but it's illegal for Emily to give me any personal or identifiable information about her patients (obviously). I offer to have a whip-round with my mates to buy a gift and send it directly to Emily so that she can deliver it to the birthday girl. Wouldn't this mean no rules are broken? This 'effort' would take me less than thirty seconds to arrange.

Nope. That's a no-go as well. It crosses professional boundaries.

I'm not sure what the lesson here is, Dory, but I can't stop thinking about this all day. Laws are in place to protect people, and privacy is an entitlement that everyone should have access to. Yet this feels wrong. What would I be willing to do as a parent if you were in the same position?

Emily said that this girl's father is devoted to looking after her and he loves her unconditionally. How different and difficult is it being the parent of a child battling those types of health challenges?

It reminds me of the other day when we spoke about your screening results, and I reflect on what it's like for parents to be told their child will be born with a disability that will have a huge impact on the family's quality of life.

I imagine it's easier to be a more patient, loving and altogether 'better' parent to a child that is perfectly healthy, well grounded, intelligent and confident – not to mention having a partner who shares the parenting duties with you. This father has none of that, yet he shows up every day to love his daughter and to look after her. Is this a choice he's consciously made or are biological forces at play here?

I like to help others, but could I do what this father does every day without regret or resentment? I would like to think that I could, but I honestly don't know. These are questions that I hope I will never have to answer.

I'll never know this father's name or what he looks like, but he occupies my thoughts today – an unsung hero.

Wednesday, 29 May 2019 – Every Cloud

Mummy has been sick all day; she hasn't been able to hold any food or water down. Her main concern isn't her recovery, but that you're not getting enough food. She thinks she's a shit mother.

Ironically, this illustrates the opposite. Your Mummy is feeling so poorly that she's left work, headed home and crawled into bed; yet it's you she thinks of first.

My opinion may lean towards bias, but I believe you've selected an excellent Mummy. I tell her not to worry or put any pressure on herself, and to help her erase any fears of social services coming to take you away in November, I message Kat and ask if we should be worried.

Kat responds immediately, telling us to stand down from calling the emergency services.

Instead of heading home, Mummy's gone back to your Granny and Grandad's house because our place is still in a state of upheaval, since we've only been back two days and it's not a comfortable environment to be ill in.

There is a silver lining, though, Dory. Mummy's decision to go to Granny and Grandad's house provides me with an opportunity, as the television has suddenly been freed up for *Game of Thrones*.

It's not polite to judge.

Thursday, 30 May 2019 – Child Exploitation

You're sixteen weeks into your development, Dory. To celebrate, I will be exploiting you to maximum effect in the hope that you can help me overcome an obstacle.

You recall our recent issues with our remortgage? Well, they've got worse. Now, the building surveyor (acting on behalf of our potential new lender) is refusing to approve our remortgage, because he believes we've made all our home improvements without the correct approvals in place from the local authority.

In his defence, he's half-right. We went through the correct process and registered the project with the local authority, but I hadn't got round to getting it signed off now that it's been completed. Truthfully, it didn't occur to me that a mortgage surveyor would question it.

It also didn't occur to me that when we asked the building inspector to come over and sign off the project, he would say no. Which is exactly what he's saying. He won't sign off the project and give us the proper certification that we need for the new lender's surveyor.

Why won't he sign the house off? He feels that we don't have the right infrastructure in place to satisfy his fire-safety and evacuation concerns, and we need that to get the approval certificate.

In order to satisfy his concerns, I need to cough up five grand to install a particular fire alarm system. The fact that we already have fire alarms hardwired to the mains (don't get me started), all with battery-powered backup, is irrelevant – not to mention that he didn't raise this at the start of the fucking project before the walls had been plastered and painted.

We do not have the money, kiddo. We've maxed out our funds on the renovation. We need another option and we need it quickly. Time is ticking.

It is for that reason that an emergency meeting has been scheduled with the building inspector, our builder and your Mummy (I'm at work and can't attend) to have an open discussion about finding a way forward.

This is where you come in, Dory, and why your parents are shamefully preparing to exploit you. I've given Mummy strict instructions to play the part of the 'dumb little woman' who 'doesn't understand' these complicated men's rules and to lean heavily (I'm talking Del-Boy-at-the-bar heavy) on the fact that she's pregnant and stressed out. Our actions will do little for gender politics – your mother isn't a dumb little woman and she's certainly not ignorant of building regulations, but she does feel that her own interior design requirements should outrank theirs.

At half past two, I receive a call from the Matriarch.

'Hello. He's been,' says Mummy.

'And? Good news or bad news?'

'Well, at first he said he still wants to see the new alarm system in place, but then I kept rubbing my belly and he then said something else.'

'OK ...'

'He said that if he were still in his old job, he would be able to help us out. He said he would have recommended we speak to a fire evacuation officer – but as he was telling me this, he took out his phone and scrolled through his contacts so I could clearly see who he meant. Then he said, "I'm afraid I can't possibly advise you of this now, though, because I work for the council, but if I didn't, I would encourage you to note this number down right now, call it and ask to speak to Nigel, as he will be able to help put together a fire evacuation report – a report that will overrule my recommendations." Then he held his phone up to my face and found something interesting to look at over his shoulder.'

'What did you do?'

'I took the hint and took a picture of his phone.'

Hah. Dory, this conversation is going very well.

'I think he felt sorry for me,' says Mummy.

'Are we terrible people?' I ask.

'Possibly.'

'So, what now?'

'I guess I've got a phone call to make.'

Fast-forward ten minutes – we have an appointment booked in with Nigel.

Friday, 31 May 2019 – A Rare Event

I wake up to Mummy looking at me like I'm the most adorable man on the planet. After further investigation, I learn that I was talking in my sleep. I said to your mother, 'I love you and Dory very much.'

I'm shocked; not because what I said wasn't true, but because I said exactly the right thing to a pregnant woman.

June

Saturday, 1 June 2019 – Another Shit Day For Your Daddy

Somehow – defying physics and global expectations – your mother has made it out of bed before 8.00 a.m. on a Saturday. This would be an accomplishment in its own right, let alone with her being four months pregnant. I'm impressed.

Motivating Mummy for the early rise is the prospect of procuring a bargain at a local car boot sale.

Your Daddy is less than enthralled with today's plans. However, we both know I have little (absolutely zero) say in the matter.

Now, I do bloody well enjoy witnessing an arm-waver demonstrating his craft at designating parking slots to incoming vehicles, Dory. Traffic management at car boot sales is an important job, but do we need six people within a ten-metre radius to tell me to park next to the car in front?

Drudging our way through the fair has forced me to consider the saying: 'One man's junk is another man's treasure.' I think it should be amended to: 'Most men's junk is mostly junk'. You are unlikely ... holy fucking shit, Dory, is that an original X-wing starfighter toy?

It is, along with a treasure trove of other *Star Wars* toys. The sight sends a rush of nostalgia through my veins.

Hang on – why are Han and Chewie shrinking in the distance? Oh, it's because I've been dragged away by the joy-extinguisher – your mother!

But now we've stumbled upon a *Finding Dory* teddy, Dory. Can you believe it? How can we not buy that for you, our unborn child whom we already love unconditionally? I'll tell you exactly why we can't: 'Second-hand soft toys are smelly.' The words of your mother, who clearly thinks a sixty-degree cycle through the washing machine is futile.

Dory, I didn't want to go to this stupid car boot sale. But go I did, because I'm a supportive partner who will stop at nothing to please your mother. Is it too much to ask for a little of that back?

In the spirit-crippling two hours that we've been here, in addition to vetoing the *Finding Dory* teddy, your mother has said no to the following proposed purchases:

- Star Wars collectables that are crucial to your growth and development.
- Two lightsabers (see above rationale).
- A Lego fire-engine set (see above rationale).
- Two pogo sticks (see above rationale).

Today is the fucking worst!

Monday, 3 June 2019 – Perambulator

I love new words. My favourite word is the verb *defenestrate*, which means 'to throw someone out of a window'.

I stumbled on a new word today: the word is *perambulator*, which means 'pram'. I didn't realise 'pram' was short for anything.

Tuesday, 4 June 2019 – The Feels Just Keep On Coming

Tonight, we took another step in our father-child bonding journey. It started a few minutes ago. Your mother took my hand, and she placed it on an area of her tummy that was noticeably harder than the rest.

'That's Dory; that's our baby,' she said.

Once again, I lack the words to describe these moments, but I have discovered a theme. Aside from the day of discovery, the moments that cause the strongest reactions are linked to the senses. And by strong reactions I mean ecstatic, heightened emotions: feelings so strong that

I would describe them as being in the realm of spirituality; and a strong urge to question the nature of our existence.

First came sight (at the first scan); then came sound (your heartbeat). Now there's touch. I know it's not quite the same as holding you in my arms for the first time will be, but still – each and every one of those experiences touches me profoundly.

According to our development trackers, you are a little over fourteen centimetres and are roughly the size of an onion. You've come a long way from the ball of cells that we fell in love with almost three months ago.

Just keep swimming.

Wednesday, 5 June 2019 – Powdered Milk

I've discovered how powdered milk is created. It's an incredible process. Milk is added to something called a 'spray dryer', and then tiny milk droplets fall from the top of the dryer. The air they fall through is heated at a precise temperature, causing the liquid inside the droplets to evaporate – thus leaving dried, powdered milk.

Thursday, 6 June 2019 – The Next Anticipated Milestone

It could happen any day now – at least, for Mummy. I'm talking about movement, specifically your movement. I know you've already been doing a lot of that; I've seen CCTV footage of you moving on the ultrasound screen (I was very proud). But Mummy hasn't yet felt you move. This is what could happen any time from now. For the first time ever, Mummy will be able to feel the movements of her unborn child – you, Dory. It will be subtle at first. The experience is described by women as a feeling of 'flutters'.

I'll level with you right now; I haven't the foggiest what a 'flutter' feels like. Your cousin Haylee has a butterfly toy called Flutter. I wonder if it's like that – a butterfly flapping its wings against nerve receptors inside Mummy. Either way, the experience will be a major step forward in helping the two most important people in my life to bond.

Saturday 8 June – The Fast And The Furious (Pregnancy Edition)

We have a list. On that list are three items: a sofa, a dining table and a pair of bedside tables. Our mission today is to acquire every item on that list.

The mission gets off to a great start; it's lunchtime and we've already selected and paid for a new sofa and a table.

Two items down, one to go.

Only the bedside tables remain. But this is a piece of piss to cross off the list – we've already ordered them online. They're out for delivery as we speak; we expect them to arrive within the next two hours.

But the mission has hit a snag. While carrying out a risk assessment, I failed to consider that today is carnival day, and certain sections of a key road (Main Street) are inaccessible, because that same road plays host to the carnival parade. As luck would have it, it's closed for the next two hours. The same two hours in which our delivery is due to arrive.

Five minutes later, the delivery driver calls to announce he's almost here, but unfortunately, he's entered Northampton from the wrong direction, and now he's trapped on the other side of the parade. I'm on the phone to him trying to brainstorm a solution, but he's adamant that he cannot reach us. Our house is on one side of the road and our tables are on the other.

Foiled by something that happens once a year!

The driver says he wants to reschedule. I wince, and then I float the idea by your mother. Naturally, she blows a blood vessel in each eyeball.

I sense Miss Heidi in the wings.

'Absolutely no fucking way, I've waited weeks and weeks for these tables.'

If we're being critical, Dory, we've waited two weeks.

'What do you want me to do about this? I can't get through,' says the driver.

Mummy overhears this and our eyes lock; I know exactly what she's thinking.

'Stay where you are, we're coming to you,' she says.

And with that in mind, we put on our shoes, grab the keys and leave the house to commence a hopeless mission to navigate the closed-off streets of

Northampton and retrieve two lovely-looking bedside tables.

Phase 1 – The calm before the storm

I cannot deny that your mother is a confident driver. I think in part this is due to her being the world's biggest hypocrite. You see, the reason for your mother's (by now, well-documented) road rage is that she harbours the belief that no one on the planet, other than herself, is qualified to hold a driving licence. Additionally, her licence is special – it permits her certain luxuries, such as carrying out manoeuvres akin to those of an emergency-response police car. A hypocrite she may be, but there is no one better suited to what we're about to attempt. For my part, I need to focus on keeping us all alive and preventing an appearance from Miss Heidi – not easy.

We're approaching our car, Dory. It's a Peugeot named Phoebe.

Phase 2 – The pursuit

'The carnival hasn't started yet, so if we can get ahead of the parade, we should be able to cut across,' Mummy says.

Cut across? I admire her optimism. She turns the key in the ignition, slides into first gear and peels away from the kerb.

We're immediately in trouble; we're not the only ones who didn't anticipate road closures – it seems half the town didn't anticipate them either.

We approach the first junction only to meet an intersection full of cars. There is a gap, but it's the size of a pinhead. Mummy doesn't flinch. She squeezes the accelerator, reaching almost fourteen miles per hour, to slot through said gap past Azlan Road and continue along Billiard Street. We ignore the death stares from other drivers.

We approach the next junction. This time, there isn't a gap, so Mummy creates one, anyway, by ploughing ahead, out into the road, causing the driver of a Range Rover to brake suddenly. There's no time to dwell on her decision-making process, because I've been flung to the back of my seat as Mummy reaches twenty-two miles per hour in under five seconds.

The G-force is intense.

But before we reach supersonic speed and break the sound barrier, more congestion forces us to slow down and bring Phoebe to a stop.

Now Mummy is bobbing and weaving over and around the steering wheel, trying to see what's happening so she can devise a strategy. She looks like Muhammad Ali dodging attacks inside the ring – but with more hair and more snarling.

We're on the move again, Dory.

Mummy slews around a driver – referring to him as a 'slow, useless cunt' – who hasn't managed to do his own slewing in a manner that matches the Matriarch's expectations.

Don't worry about the other cars in front, Dory; Mummy has found space on the other side of the road – i.e. the wrong side of the road – to continue our pursuit.

We overtake both the useless cunt and the rest of the traffic and then barge our way back onto the right side of the road, taking the next right and arriving into the heart of carnival territory – Main Street.

The street is lined with people and candy floss, but I can't see any carnival floats – can we pass?

I can't see a road-closure sign – fuck, yes I can.

It gets worse. Other drivers have put their faith in Mummy's geographical knowledge – and she's unintentionally led a convoy of ten cars to the same dead end.

And now the sound of drums echoes in the distance; the carnival has begun and the parade is heading in our direction.

———

Phase 3 – Tension mounts
Ring.

'Fuck, it's the delivery driver. Answer and stall him.' Mummy chucks me the phone before commencing a three-point turn at Mach 4 to begin finding another route. My head bounces off the passenger door as if it's made of rubber (my head, not the door). Somehow, I remain conscious.

'Hello?'

To mask our frantic attempts to reach the delivery driver, I allow my voice to take on the persona of a middle-aged butler serving caviar to a party of aristocrats. Think Alfred from *Batman*.

'Where are you then?' the driver asks.

'My dear sir, be advised that we are almost with you; please be patient for a few more moments …'

SSCCREEEECH. That'll be the tyres, Dory.

'… I assure you that we have our heading,' I say, 'and the roadblock will in absolutely no way impede us.'

He's not convinced, but he mumbles that he'll wait a few more minutes.

And now Mummy is somehow driving through spaces that are too narrow for the car. It's as if we're driving the Knight Bus from *Harry Potter*.

Drivers smash their horns and pass judgements, but your mother is as cool as an igloo – she's doing a sterling job weaving in and out of the traffic.

Two minutes later, we're in a position to take yet another crack at passing Main Street. There's no road-closure sign in sight and the pavements are less congested too.

Maybe the parade doesn't come up this far.

But then a hi-vis-wearing woman appears with the road-closure sign. Dory, she looks like she's had the day from hell.

'I'm sorry,' she says, 'but this road is closed for the carnival.'

I don't know what it is, but something is not right with this woman. I think she's about to cry.

Fortunately for the mission, I live with a pregnant woman, and I've been operating (mostly in fear) in this complex emotional space for the past four months. It's time for me to play my part in the story. I can feel it. Up until now, I've largely been a supporting character, but my big moment has finally arrived.

I get out of the car and the first thing I do is smile and say, 'You don't look like you're having fun.'

'I've been spat at, sworn at and swerved at – no, I'm not having fun.'

Fuck. No wonder she's fed up, Dory.

'I'm not here to do any of those things to you and I don't hold you directly responsible for the road closures; if we can't get through then we'll sit here and watch the carnival.'

'I'm sorry, you can't pass.'

So much for my big moment.

I am generally empathetic – but at the same time, I'm scared because I now have to return to the car and update the Matriarch.

She has questions, Dory (obviously). 'What did she say? Can we pass? Can we pass right now? What's happening? Tell me.'

'The carnival has started. We can't pass.'

'Call the delivery driver and ask him to walk across the park with the tables,' says your mother, not missing a beat.

'Say what?'

She snatches the phone from me and dispatches her instructions to the delivery driver herself.

'Right, go and meet him somewhere in the middle of the park.'

'I think high-vis woman will commit suicide if anyone upsets her again.'

'She said you can't drive across; she didn't say anything about walking across.'

But Mummy hasn't seen the state of this poor woman, Dory.

Mummy looks me dead in the eyes and says, 'Find a way.'

I exit Phoebe and sidle up to the hi-vis woman – and make out I'm completely on her side. In one sense this is true: I'm going to go out on a limb and suggest that she probably doesn't deserve to be spat on for doing her job. However, I do have an ulterior motive, and the clock is ticking.

'Listen, I know the road is closed. Is that for cars only or can pedestrians pass?' Obviously, I already know pedestrians can't pass, Dory.

'No, they can't.'

The dream of a hot cuppa resting on my new bedside table diminishes.

But then … 'Why do you need to get across, anyway?'

A chance, Dory. A sliver of a chance.

'We have a delivery that can't reach us because of the carnival and I have a pregnant woman in the car who *really needs* to collect this delivery today, as it's for the baby.'

I'm not proud, Dory. Yet again, I've used you as a lie to get what I want, but what I want is for your mother to be happy (and therefore you to be happy) and for Miss Heidi not to show up – I can justify all the lies in the world for that.

Hi-vis woman sizes me up and assesses my character. This is the make-or-break moment. Have a few misbehaving scumbags upset her that much?

Her lips begin to move. She's made her decision, Dory.

'If you're quick, you can go right now.'

We are a *go* for table extraction.

I sprint across Main Street, vault the park wall and conduct my search for the delivery driver and our sacred tables. As far as parks go, it's big (forty-seven-hectares big). It's also busy. I call upon years of wordsearch-puzzle training and *Where's Wally?* books and I begin searching for a needle in a hayst—

Fuck, I've found him already: a young lad in hi-vis dragging a trolley with two table-sized boxes resting on it. That has to be him.

He's about 350 metres away. I now have to convince him to drag the tables across the park and through the blocked carnival parade and then load them into the car.

I check my wallet. I never usually have cash on me, but the table-gods are smiling down upon me; I have twenty quid tucked away – bingo!

Things run smoothly from then on: the delivery chap agrees to come to the car; he then agrees to load the cargo into the car; and he agrees to take twenty quid from me for his trouble.

The only problem I had in all of this was the bollocking I got from Mummy for parting with money we don't have.

But what we do have, though, is a pair of sexy bedside tables.

———

Mission epilogue

I'm back in the car with Mummy, and we're feeling pretty satisfied, all things considered. It's been one hell of a tense twenty minutes, but all Mummy's hard work and dogged determination have paid off. We won, Dory; we secured the cargo. And I got my big moment, after all.

We're cruising back home in leisurely style, unperturbed by the congestion and silently reflecting on our success, when an impatient driver honks his horn and overtakes Mummy. I await expletives, but they don't come. Instead, your mother turns to me with a smile and says, 'Some people get so angry while driving, don't they?'

I'm stunned, Dory. Unequivocally fucking stunned!

'What?' says Mummy, all wide eyes and false innocence.

POT FUCKING KETTLE!

Sunday, 9 June 2019 – Caffeinegate

According to the internet, expectant mothers shouldn't consume more than two hundred milligrams of caffeine a day.

Mummy has been adhering to the recommendation ever since she found out she was pregnant. She has one cup of tea each day (way below the limit), and she was saving up today's single cup to have now in bed. Mummy got into bed, as planned, but forgot her cup of tea. This was not planned. What do you think Mummy did, Dory?

A: She went and made herself a cup of tea.

B: She asked me to make her a cup of tea.

C: She needlessly burst into tears.

I'll give you a clue, Dory – it was C. Another confirmation that she's definitely expecting.

Monday, 10 June 2019 – Caffeinegate Continued

Mummy's in a much better mood tonight. She's got her cup of tea. I risk a light-hearted joke about how upset she got last night over the forgotten cup of tea. The joke goes down well, Dory; she's laughing.

And now she's stopped laughing and started crying …

Tuesday, 11 June 2019 – The 180-Degree Turn On The Trouser Situation

Mummy has reversed her decision to accept that her trousers no longer fit her. However, she's reached, what has to be said, a workable compromise – for now, at least. She's squeezed back into her trousers, but this time, she's left the buttons unfastened. To stop her trousers from falling down, she's employed the services of a rubber band. She's looped the band around the top button, threaded the other end through the buttonhole and then looped it back and around the button a second time, ensuring a semi-secure pair of trousers, with a little extra bandwidth around the waist – to allow you to breathe.

I'm impressed – Mummy gets a round of applause.

Remember, Dory, every piece of clothing that Mummy can no longer fit into brings us one step closer to your birth.

Wednesday, 12 June 2019 – Maternal Instincts

News just in concerning your gender: your mother has announced that she believes you are a boy. I attack her hypothesis from more angles than you'll see in a trick shot from Ronnie O'Sullivan. How do you know? How *can* you know? Have you made this up for attention or is there some maternal magic at play here?

She tells me that she doesn't know, but she has a 'feeling'. I'm skeptical. I'm calling bullshit.

Personally, I'm not swayed one way or the other. We've decided to wait until your birth to find out, so I've deliberately not thought about it too much. What's the point? Getting it right is a coin flip, anyway, so even if you do end up being a boy, I'm not subscribing to the idea that your mother could be a Jedi. She doesn't even like *Star Wars* (don't get me started).

The only thing I will say on the matter is that whenever I participate in a guess-the-gender game when a friend or work colleague is pregnant, I always guess whatever the Mummy thinks. I hate to say it, but I have a good track record with this method.

Come to think of it, your Granny Smurf says that when I was handed to her wrapped up in blankets, she didn't even check the tackle situation down below – she knew I was a boy. Again, I'm sceptical over something that's fifty-fifty.

Time will tell. I do know this: if you are a boy, Mummy will be adding 'gender clairvoyant' as a qualification to her CV.

Thursday, 13 June 2019 – First Movements

We're in bed when – 'Whoa, I think Dory just kicked me,' Mummy says.
'Fuck, really?'

She's not a hundred per cent, but she reports a unique feeling that she's never felt before. Dare I ask if it's a 'flutter'?

'It's happened again. I think it's Dory.'

It looks like you're now big enough and flexible enough to cause Mummy to feel … something. It's not hard to imagine; Mummy's Dory-bump is at a point where it's difficult not to know you're cooking. And now that Mummy has started to feel you kick, it's getting all the more exciting.

I'm not sure if you can hear me yet; I think we're still several weeks away from that, but I still like to talk to you every day. I have done so since my day of discovery.

I'm lying (lightly) on Mummy's tummy speaking to you right now. I praise you for kicking Mummy, and I ask how well you've been growing, if you're getting your five a day and if you're content. Mummy responds on your behalf (like she always does): you're growing lots, you have been getting all your fruit and veg and you're content.

I love all of this.

Friday, 14 June 2019 – The Beauty Of The Written Record

We've only been awake ten minutes and Mummy has already referred to you as a twat. She's bestowed this charming little word unto you because of the location you're currently lying in. It's apparently uncomfortable.

If you ever find yourself in a position whereby you need to choose a side, remember this moment, Dory. And before you start getting all dramatic, I'm not alluding to a parental break-up or anything like that. It's more in line with deciding what takeaway to have or what film to watch, or even what holiday destination to visit. In these instances, I trust that you'll side with Daddy, Dory.

It's a good job I'm here to record and recount all of these moments throughout the pregnancy. Otherwise today would have been lost forever in the void of forgotten memories. Thank God I've immortalised it on the page.

Saturday, 15 June 2019 – The Stethoscope Challenge

I went to see friends today, Dory; friends with children. That meant donations, hand-me-downs and offloads of old crap. Parenting is new to us, so we're saying yes to anything and everything that's offered. We can always move it on at a later date if it's of no use to us.

One item of particular interest was a stethoscope so we can listen to your heartbeat. The midwife specifically advised against this. Apparently, parents are woefully inadequate at picking up the sound of their babies' heartbeats compared to medically trained professionals, and the absence of any 'thud-thumping' sounds prompts panic alarms to go off, triggering those unnecessary trips down to A&E for emergency scans.

We've already had more of those than we would like, thank you very much. So, with that in mind, we opt to ignore the advice of the midwife, but vow not to panic should we hear nothing.

'I can't hear anything,' I say.

Your mother takes a turn, and she can't hear anything either.

I've dialled 999 in case it's an emergency.

Just kidding.

Sunday, 16 June 2019 – Father's Day

It's Father's Day, Dory. I wonder if this means I'll get any presents as I'm a soon-to-be father. I'm almost certain it does. My conclusions are thus: you got Mummy a card for Mother's Day, and I know your mother gets a grade three wide-on for sentimentality. This shit is like air to her.

It's 7.30 a.m. and I've returned from my first sit-down wee of the day; there is a bag waiting for me on my pillow with a card poking out. I knew it. I act calm but I'm excited to receive a gift from my unborn child who's temporarily named Dory.

On the front of the card is a picture of you; it's one of your scan pictures. Inside the bag are two cans of gin and tonic. I'm not a big drinker these days, but today is special, so I treat myself to one of the gins, regardless of the fact it's half past seven in the morning.

As it's Father's Day, I've taken Granny Smurf out for breakfast to say thanks for her Daddy duties over the years. I assume you find this statement confusing. This isn't a typo. To put the obvious question to bed, she hasn't had a sex change (at least, not to my knowledge). Your Daddy's Daddy has never been in our lives. He took off once he discovered I was in Granny Smurf's tummy, leaving her to pick up sole parenting duties. This is why you will only ever have one grandfather in your life (two, if you count your great-grandad).

Don't feel bad about this, kiddo, it isn't unusual. Parents don't always stay together, and sometimes they choose to be absent from their children's lives. I find this one difficult to accept given my position as a soon-to-be Daddy, but there are exceptions to every scenario in life. I try not to judge even my own father, who, by all accounts, has done me a solid by staying away. I mean, would you really want me in your life if I stole money from Mummy, or if I told child support services that I wasn't your father and forced Mummy to consider taking me to court to legally enforce a DNA test?

Granny Smurf didn't in the end go ahead with the test to establish my paternity, but she still suffered the trauma of being bullied into making an agonising decision. As it turned out, she was more than qualified to fulfil the duties of both parents. I'll tell you a quick story from my childhood that I value more as an adult now than I did when I was a child. One Christmas (I think I must have been around 6 or 7), I asked Santa for one thing more than anything else. That was the video game *Aladdin* for my Sega Mega Drive. I asked Santa for that game every day. When I woke up on Christmas morning, there in my stocking was the thing I coveted most: *Aladdin*.

Looking back, a couple of things stand out: first, when I was growing up, we had little money – almost zero disposable income (and I do mean almost zero). Yet somehow my Mummy found a way to get that game for me. I don't know how, but she did. I suspect she had to go without a few things. Second, Santa got all the credit for coming up with the goods, not

Mummy. She was as shocked and pleased as I was when I unwrapped it. I think about that every Christmas.

From breakfast, my day takes me to the discount store so that Mummy can stock up on cleaning products. This is a crucial chore, Dory, because at this rate, we're likely to run out of washing-up liquid within the next eight years. Mummy is unperturbed by my sarcasm, not to mention my overall lack of interest.

This is boring!

Things are no longer boring, Dory; I've discovered a plunger on aisle sixteen and now I'm chasing your mother and declaring that we cannot possibly wait until November to meet you and that I will deliver you right this instant with the aid of said plunger. My attempts to stick the plunger on Mummy's 'tummy entrance' attract curious glances from onlookers. If your mother lives for stockpiling cleaning products, then I live for causing scenes in public places. I believe we're 1–1.

In the end, we've agreed that it's best I perhaps don't interfere with nature. Sorry, kiddo. Blame your fun-killer mother.

I can't end Father's Day without going on a mini-rant about Father's Day cards – and indeed any other celebration-day cards that children might send to their parents. They almost always say something along the lines of 'You're the greatest parent ever.' I think this is a little insincere, despite the message they're purporting to convey.

For one thing, 99.9999 per cent of children who send that message are incorrect, owing to the hierarchical nature of being the best. One assumes there's a measurable metric to conform to. Unless all parents that receive a 'greatest-ever' accolade are jointly great. But then we stumble on to another problem: if every parent is great then surely none of them are.

Who calls the shots on defining the criteria for greatest parent, anyway? Is it the children themselves? If so, do they hold all the facts necessary to make that kind of decision? I'd argue that a lack of life experience answers that one. Is this process regulated, Dory? Are random spot checks and audits carried out to see if kids have been a bit liberal and free-flowing in showering Mummy and Daddy with 'greatest-ever' badges?

I'm potentially overthinking this. Perhaps it's just a way for children to show a bit of gratitude towards Mummy and Daddy for parenting them. Still, if you ask me, it seems a bit woolly.

We can return to this subject next year when you're here in person.

Monday, 17 June – Daddy's OS 1.0

Some days I wake up and the first thing I do is smile because I know that in November I'll be a Daddy. I recognise that this is a miracle and a privilege. Other days I wake up and I don't smile, because the thought of parenthood terrifies me. I'm scared about taking on a responsibility that is, at least to me, bigger than the planet Jupiter – and it's one that's rapidly heading my way.

I don't feel bad about having these feelings (although sometimes I do); I've listened to enough first-hand accounts from parents telling me that this is all perfectly natural.

Why do I feel this way? It's got little to do with me worrying about whether I'll be a good parent. I mean, that plays on my mind, but that's such a broad topic to quantify that it's asking for trouble even to try. So I don't.

Perhaps it's about making mistakes.

But I've already made peace with the knowledge that I'll be making plenty of those. Mistakes will form part of my education, and as long as they're not physically or mentally debilitating they'll be filed under 'parental learning and development'.

Maybe it's the 'debilitating' part of that statement that's to blame. If you play a video game and you come across a particularly tricky level, you keep trying until you succeed – or you give up. If you lose a hundred lives, you can reset the game, restart the level and have another crack at the goal. That mandate doesn't apply here. And I'm not only talking about keeping you alive (although that's one parental objective I'm deeply committed to); it would also be cool if your parents could avoid fucking up your mental health.

When you arrive, I'll be starting from scratch with no hands-on experience. On day one of your life I'll install version 1.0 of Daddy's operating system (OS). I'll have to cobble something basic together to get us through the first twenty-four hours. Then I'll review it, identify the learnings and build improvements ready for day two: version 1.1 of Daddy's OS. Mummy will have to do the same with her own OS.

I predict that some days I'll feel pretty good about where we're all at. The operating system will be equipped to deal with all expected Dory-scenarios, and there will be processes in place to prevent and mitigate tears and discomfort (from both parent and child). On other days, I foresee two lost and confused parents with operating systems that have crashed, malfunctioned and been abandoned.

At least we'll all be lost together, Dory. You, me and Mummy. Being lost in a dark space in the middle of the woods without a map is made all the more bearable with a hand to hold and someone to help figure out how you get back home. There isn't a hand in the world I would rather hold going into parenthood than your mother's.

Still – I do hope we don't fuck you up.

Tuesday, 18 June 2019 – Confirmed Kicking

If Mummy wasn't a hundred per cent sure she felt you kicking last week, she is today. She rings me from the Morrisons car park to tell me the news.

I'm envious, but it won't be long before I am able to feel you kicking myself.

You get a free pass at kicking your mother from now until ... I don't know. What age do you have to reach before kicking one of your parents (or anyone else) is considered disrespectful?

That's one for another day, I feel.

Getting back to kicking Mummy in the tummy, Daddy awards you one gold star for your first confirmed uterus kick. May these kicks continue right up until birth and then never be seen again unless in one of the following contexts: self-defence, sport, or role-playing adventures in a lost magical kingdom with Daddy.

Friday, 21 June 2019 – A Happy Childhood

When you look back and reflect on your childhood, I want it filled with happy memories. I can't imagine that's a sentiment that isn't shared by nearly every other parent on the planet. But how do I do that? What environment can I help create that will foster happiness, and what boundaries can I put in place to protect you?

I've been thinking about three areas in particular (I'm sure there are hundreds): affection, socialising, and toys. These are required, but in precise quantities. Stray too far and they could contribute to the very thing I want to avoid for you – an unhappy childhood.

Let's start with affection. Children need to have affection; it's as essential to life as water and air. Both Mummy and Daddy had an affectionate upbringing, and we're affectionate towards each other (most of the time).

Something that keeps cropping up in my reading is advice encouraging self-soothing and independence in children – i.e. don't run to the child's aid at the faintest sign of a whimper. I don't reject these protocols, because at this point I'm not qualified to reject anything, as I haven't done any parenting yet; but if my Dory wants a cuddle, you're going to get a cuddle.

But then there is that counterargument: should your parents appear by your side every time you fall over, with a bandage, blanket and dummy in hand, uttering pacifying phrases such as 'There, there' or 'Shh, shh'? I don't want to be one of those ardent protectors whose behaviour compromises your developing confidence and self-reliance. That's a nice way of saying I don't want you to be too soft.

Conversely, I don't want to reject you in a way that confuses you, as again this could hamper your confidence levels – and your happiness – when you're growing up. Your parents should be the first people you can rely on for affection.

Let's take a common childhood haunt – the playground. I believe the playground is an area where every small human embarks on a rite of passage. Social skills are formed; cognitive functions are tested; scrapes and bruises are worn as badges.

It begins slowly. Children take on a series of mini-risks or small developmental steps that build up to something bigger, such as the first time (and I'll never forget mine) they slide down a 'fireman's pole' unencumbered by the safety blanket of a guardian's arms to catch them.

We need to strike a fine balance between giving you affection and letting you get knocked around a bit to teach you those important lessons. After all, if you can't suffer a bit of pain, then I fear lightsaber duels are at risk – I will not be going easy on you!

Another question is that of socialising. I'm an only child, so perhaps I valued this more than your Mummy did, as she had Auntie Lisa around, not to mention a gazillion cousins. I didn't, and so those instances where I got to socialise as a child stand out in my mind. I have wonderful memories of being let loose with friends to test boundaries, go on adventures and play. I want you to socialise often and remember the adventures you have.

Mummy told me a story the other day of how she and her cousins had the 'come on kids, it's time to go home' system rigged. What would happen is the family would meet on a Sunday; if all the children behaved, there was a chance that the parents would have a few drinks. But Mummy and her cousins learnt that if they continued to keep quiet, behave and remain out of sight, the parents would have more than a few drinks until it got to a point where the kids knew no one could drive them home. This meant they would have to stay at whoever's house they were visiting, which also meant the holy grail – no school on a Monday.

I love that story.

You will be encouraged to socialise a lot, but I don't want you spending time with little dickheads and becoming one yourself. It's on Mummy and me to ensure that this doesn't happen, at least in the early years. After that, we'll have to trust you to make your own decisions about whom to spend your time with.

Toys are another area for which I can't find a map to navigate. People who get everything they want, when they want it, are rarely content – particularly children. If children get everything they want, then they baseline that as normal and kick off when their expectations aren't met immediately. This instils the wrong values in children and sets them up not just for an unhappy childhood, but for an unhappy life. I don't want you being a spoilt little wanker who takes everything for granted. Again, it's on us to ensure you are taught that lesson from a young age.

We will be imposing some boundaries when it comes to toys. This issue with consumption extends beyond parenting; we live on a planet that we're seriously fucking up, and consumption is a major problem – particularly consumption of plastic. And the majority of children's toys are made of plastic.

This leads me to assume two things. First, you will be getting a lot of second-hand toys, especially during the first few years of your life, when you won't care where they come from. Second, you're not getting a million toys for Christmas and birthdays. I've already told you that I don't mind you being spoilt with travel experiences, but I can't see us being those parents who spend a fortune on stuff you won't fully appreciate. Perhaps the answer is to spread gifts out throughout the year and give them to you as a reward for good behaviour.

That's about it for my musings today: we want to be affectionate and protective, but we don't want you to be so soft that it restricts confidence; we want you to socialise with the right people; and we want you to have fewer 'things' so that you appreciate more those you do get. Hopefully, these decisions will ensure that your childhood memories are deep and rich.

That's the goal, anyway.

Sunday, 23 June 2019 – Bloody Great Day

I'm not sure if it's the sugar from the dessert or the fact that Mummy is relaxed, but she says you are more active than ever. You've graduated from 'flutters' and enrolled in a full-frontal organ assault. I'm super-proud. As we drift off to sleep, I'm holding Mummy's hand, and she's lightly pressing it every time she feels you move. She's been doing this every few seconds for the last ten minutes.

What a bloody great day.

Monday, 24 June 2019 – New In Stock

Granny Smurf has completed her first task from her Mother's Day card: she's knitted you a blanket, and she's done an outstanding job. It's white and made from baby wool (which I didn't know was a thing until a few seconds ago), and it evokes lots of cute adjectives – adorable, sweet, wonderful … I think this will be the blanket we take you home in.

Actually, hold that thought. You're likely to have a lot of your mother's DNA on you right after your birth and it will be … well, gunky. Perhaps this blanket will be saved until we've hosed you down or for when you're a bit older. You might be cute, adorable and wonderful, but if your new white blanket is covered in afterbirth it might not make for the profile picture we're envisioning.

Tuesday, 25 June 2019 – Halfway

I told you to just keep swimming, and that's what you've done, Dory; we're at the twenty-week mark! I think that means we're halfway there. Outstanding stuff – I'm proud of you, kiddo.

And I'm proud of Mummy as well; she is doing a phenomenal job with the pregnancy so far. Don't forget, she carries the added burden of putting up with your Daddy, which she reports as being 'harder than the pregnancy itself'.

I honestly can't tell if that's a win for Daddy or not.

Fuck! I've totally just felt you kick for the first time. Yikes. This is amazing. I didn't think I'd tick this box off for a few weeks. I'm so, so proud.

What another bloody great day.

Daddy loves you tons.

Thursday, 27 June 2019 – Blink And It's Gone

We're at the hospital for the twenty-week scan and we're in and out inside fifteen minutes. Things went so well that I'm suspicious. Nothing in pregnancy goes this smoothly, does it?

You're fine by the way; you're doing great.

Friday, 28 June 2019 – Morning Routines And Walruses

Our morning routine used to look like this. The alarm would go off at 7.00 a.m. After snoozing it for ten minutes, I would politely inform your mother that she needed to get up and begin getting ready for work. She would naturally treat this as a direct personal attack and respond with a five-minute sulk.

After the sulk, she'd acknowledge that she did in fact need to get up, but not before negotiating a thirty-second cuddle. That was our routine.

You have impacted that routine in two ways.

First, I like to talk to you in the morning, and your mother recognises this as the perfect manipulation tactic. She uses a father's love for his unborn child to ensure a few more minutes of prolonging the inevitable – getting up.

The second impact is more unusual. In the 'old days', it would take your mother less than two seconds to turn from her side of the bed, roll over and come in for a cuddle. This morning, though, it didn't take her two seconds; it took considerably longer.

Furthermore, in the 'old days', your mother would execute the turn, roll and cuddle manoeuvre in one fluid movement. It's a manoeuvre she performed with grace, not quite meeting Russian ballet standards, but never far off. Judging from her actions and sounds this morning, I thought she was auditioning for the role of a walrus playing hopscotch into the wind.

'That took a bit longer than usual, didn't it?' says Mummy.

Yes; yes, it did. Neither of us could help but laugh.

It's probably a bit unfair to start making walrus observations while she's going through pregnancy, but I can't help but call things as I see them, Dory. At least I didn't say any of this to her face, which probably confirms that I'm a great guy.

I completely forgot – there was a point to all this, Dory. We're running late for work, and it's becoming a regular occurrence.

Saturday, 29 June 2019 – Names

We've taken our first stab at coming up with baby names. I've been keeping a haphazard list for weeks, but neither of us had committed any serious time or energy to it outside perusing a few lists online. But now that we've crossed the halfway point, we can start seriously considering what you'll be named when you can graduate from your pre-birth name of Dory.

We're reasonably confident on girls' names. We have several contenders listed, and one of those in particular is a favourite of ours. It stands a strong chance of being written on your birth certificate – should you be born a girl.

Until today, we had diddly-squat for boys' names. But that was until today. I've said out loud a potential boy's name, and we both love it.

I'm not going to tell you any of these names, for two reasons. First, we will no doubt go through this exercise a number of times before your birth, and what's on the list now may not be on the list as we approach the birth.

Second, we don't know what gender you'll be, and while we're not getting our hopes up, you never know what the future holds. One day you may have a brother or sister and we'll need to excavate something from the list again.

Still, take it from me, we've had a productive twenty minutes.

In other news, your mother has expanded her walrus-turning-over-in-bed act to include getting into the car, getting out of the car, sitting down at a table and plain old walking.

I'm proud of how quickly she's been able to scale up her little enterprise.

Sunday, 30 June 2019 – Parenting And Hangovers

Daddy doesn't feel at his best today, Dory. I'm nursing this thing grown-ups have; it's called a 'hangover'. I used to get hangovers regularly until I realised my brain cells didn't appreciate being treated that way. It's a bit like your mother's tolerance level for my bullshit: she can only abide so much before enough is enough.

Despite reducing in frequency, they still happen from time to time –

including right now. I usually plan these periods in advance so I can ensure I have zero commitments the following day, doing very little apart from wallowing around in self-pity, watching classic '80s movies all day and maybe ordering in pizza.

This is yet another area of my life that needs rethinking for when you arrive. I can't see you playing ball with my routine. Even if it is one I've had in place for nearly two decades.

Perhaps you'll be open to negotiations. What say we both sign up to a treaty of sorts where you agree to no crying? I'll allow you to bring a compromise to the table: maybe I'll sanction the slightest of whimpers, so long as it doesn't go beyond that. We'll save those whimpers (maximum of four) for when you're hungry or you need your nappy changing.

What say you, kiddo?

Joking aside – I need advice on this one. One of my options as a not-so-responsible parent is to rely on Mummy (if she's not hung-over herself) to take care of parenting duties so I can recover. This is workable, so long as I pay back the favour.

Or, I suck it up and get on with it ...

But thinking that in the state I'm in makes me want to burst into tears.

July

Monday, 1 July 2019 – It Was Never Just 'A Little Pump'

'Dory will explode,' says Mummy.

I wish she would be a bit more creative with her excuses. 'Just so I'm clear,' I say, 'you're saying that if you had held in that rancid, putrid gas ball that you've just unleashed from your intestines under the bedcovers, our child would be dead?'

'Yes,' says Mummy, who accompanies her answer with a smile and a nod.

'Good job you took the action you did and shit yourself, then. Otherwise Dory would be done for.'

'I did not shit myself – I did a little pump.'

Dory, Mummy's 'little pump' has singed the hairs off every living creature within a ten-mile radius. It tastes like a crematorium.

'Leave me alone. I'm sad,' she says.

My nostrils can relate to that, Dory.

I should give her some slack – Mummy had a whooping cough injection today, and it has left her arm in a lot of pain. The nurse says this is because the vaccination is administered directly into the muscle tissue. She has been told that the pain will last a few days and that she'll feel tired and run-down (over and above being pregnant).

But that's not why she's sad. Apparently, Dory, you'll have to have the same injection when you are six weeks old. It will be horrible – you will feel betrayed and abandoned, and you won't understand what's happening, or why. We have committed to providing round-the-clock comfort for when that day comes.

Please understand we only want to protect you, even if it means sticking a needle in your arm. The thought is enough to break our hearts, and it's for this reason that Mummy feels I need to cut her some slack about shitting herself. Sorry, I mean doing a little pump.

On a cheerier note, Mummy has created her own dance to rival my Baby Daddy Dance. She has named it 'The Baby Mama Dance'. I'll let the partial copyright infringement slide.

It's not half bad. She holds her Dory-bump in both hands and bobs along to a beat that she hums. Oh, she's bare-ass naked as well. I'm sure you can't wait to picture that one.

Tuesday, 2 July 2019 – The Sugar-Baby Hypothesis

We're about to head out the door to go to the cinema and watch *Spider-Man: Far From Home* when Mummy confesses that she hasn't felt you move in a couple of days. She's now starting to panic.

No shit – why did she not report this sooner?

Thankfully – and the importance of this to us as expecting parents cannot be overstated – we have Rebecca, our on-call midwife, to refer to in our time of need. Mummy sends her a message highlighting our concerns. Rebecca responds immediately, instructing us to come in for a check-up.

No reason to panic, but that doesn't mean we don't.

We park up and barely make it through the door before Rebecca greets us and ushers us into a room.

Thirty seconds later, Mummy is on a bed while Rebecca is preparing the CTG machine (something that can record your heartbeat). Ten seconds after that, we can hear your heartbeat, which dispels any concerns about your well-being.

Incredible. This whole process started and ended inside the twenty-minute mark. I can't help but compare the experience to the last time we had a scare. Why do the experiences differ so much? Yes, Rebecca is a friend, so we may perhaps have circumnavigated the 'correct procedure' at the front desk. But the comparison is nonetheless stark. The first scare lasted sixteen hours and featured conflicting information about what was happening, while we were pulling an all-nighter; the second scare was put to bed in twenty minutes. That's a big difference.

Rebecca says that this is all to do with how busy they are in certain wards and areas. If it's a quiet time, the Mummies get seen quickly, but if they're busy, they don't – unless there's a serious problem.

Despite the good news that you're OK, I should point out that you do like to keep Mummy and Daddy on their toes, don't you? If it were a competition between the scheduled and unscheduled scans we've had throughout this pregnancy, the score would stand at 2–2. No more of that, now.

Still, like I said, it's good news; you're alive and well.

The other thing to note is that Rebecca reckons she accidentally saw what you are – either a boy or a girl. That's fine; I'd rather that happen, but know you're OK. Let's hope she doesn't accidentally let it slip out!

Since we were in and out of the hospital in no time at all, guess where we're headed right this second? *Spider-Man: Far From Home* – here we come.

I love a win-win, Dory.

After the film, we get in the car and head home, where Mummy says that she believes your movements are linked to her sugar-consuming habits – a mint choc chip ice cream woke you up during *Spider-Man*.

I sense we've ended our evening with Mummy finding a new angle to justify eating sweets and ice cream every day.

Crafty, but well played.

Wednesday, 3 July 2019 – Sugar Theory Confirmed

I've felt three kicks in quick succession, which means your kickboxing skills are back to normal. Annoyingly, your mother inhaled a pack of Haribo fifteen minutes ago, which she is taking as overwhelming evidence that her sugar theory is correct.

She might have a point. I didn't realise babies get this stuff into their system that quickly. I remember when you weren't in the right position to be measured during your twelve-week scan, and we overcame that by feeding Mummy cake. I thought the sonographer sent Mummy to the café for said cake to get you moving around, not to give you a sugar-rush injection.

Friday, 5 July 2019 – The Day We Met

A mutual friend of ours is a woman named Taci (pronounced 'tah-see'). Taci is one of Mummy's closest friends and I used to work with her. Today she's celebrating her fifth wedding anniversary with her husband, Adam – and, on this day five years ago, Mummy met Daddy.

Our first encounter was far from conventional: I met your Mummy on a merry-go-round (the wedding had a fairground).

I remember it clearly: the snot-dribbling child of one of the guests had dragged me onto the ride. I was resentful, because I was about to head to the bar for beer number five. Anyhow, before the ride operator came around to conduct the usual lacklustre safety check, I heard the voice of a woman barking orders to several children all at once. I turned around to see one of the bridesmaids – the owner of the barking voice – telling the children to hold on to her hand as they climbed aboard the merry-go-round. I was struck by how well this woman was handling these micro-beings; they obeyed her every instruction.

Up to this point, the ride was occupied by me, my temporary companion (whom I was planning to ditch as soon as the ride was over) and the ride operator, meaning that the loud-speaking child-tamer had the full run of the merry-go-round deck to choose seats for her and the kids.

And yet, whether by coincidence or by fate or because she'd eyed your Daddy up as a potential mate, she chose to sit by me.

Fast-forward fifteen seconds and I'm crammed into a carriage with five random children and a woman whose vocal range could topple a mountain. She was loud, Dory; no wonder the children were listening to her – they were fucking terrified.

But it was another of her features that stood out the most for me: her smile. She had the perfect smile.

We made small talk about how we each knew the bride and groom while occasionally looking over to make sure the kids were alive. Shortly after, the ride was over, and as we were disembarking, we introduced ourselves.

We met several times again throughout the evening, and I felt an attraction between us. An attraction that soon evaporated!

I've told you before how Mummy has a reputation for the odd 'glass of bubbles' here and there, but I'm not sure if I've ever gone into detail about her alternate personalities – the ones that like to show up after she's eight ciders deep.

Mummy's alcohol consumption will invariably introduce one of two characters to the party; both are from the *Gremlins* movies. The first is Gizmo, the mogwai. Gizmo is a cute, playful little thing. Gizmo loves cuddles. Next, we have Stripe. Stripe is a gremlin who doesn't love cuddles. Stripe is a vicious, foul-tempered, spoilt bully of a creature, who lashes out aggressively towards others, especially if they try and take her drink away or say she's too drunk to have another one.

Stripe is a lot like Miss Heidi, and it's almost always Stripe who shows up in place of Gizmo, because Stripe is a bully.

It happened quickly, Dory; I was chatting to your Mummy and we were getting on well. I was even thinking of asking for her phone number when she vanished, leaving this Stripe character in her place. Stripe carried on our conversation but in a far more hostile fashion.

'I know you're expecting me to invite you back to my room but that ain't going to happen,' Stripe said.

As Stripe said that, my taxi showed up.

 Now, I won't pretend I wouldn't have accepted an invitation to continue getting to know each other, but I had revealed no such intentions or advances towards her. After all, I am a gentleman.

'Actually, my taxi has arrived,' I said.

Stripe didn't like this. Stripe thought this was a defence mechanism kicking in to cover up my wounded pride (I'm not saying Stripe got this a hundred per cent wrong, but still).

Stripe must have felt that I hadn't heard correctly, because Stripe repeated herself, but this time with more venom and contempt.

'You might be used to other girls behaving that way, but I will not be doing that,' Stripe said.

'You've made that clear. Anyhow, lovely to meet you. Goodbye.'

I left thinking that I would never see her again.

'You have no idea how wrong you've got this,' Taci said to me a few weeks later at work. 'She is the nicest, easiest-going person you could ever meet.'

I wasn't interested, Dory. The truth was that I had recently come out of a messy break-up, and I had made an iron-clad promise to myself not to get with anyone who wasn't drama-free (I've since learnt the futility of this approach: all relationships feature dramatic episodes, although their size and frequency can vary).

'Well, you're an idiot,' Taci continued.

In the end, she gave me Mummy's number and said that the least I could do was send her a message. It took me several months, but in the end, I caved.

I don't mean to be a twat when I said I caved, but that was honestly the truth. The reason I'm telling you this is so you know how close you came to not happening.

I've spent the last ten minutes scrolling back to my first ever message to Mummy. Here's what I wrote:

Evening. Despite you 'wounding my pride' at Taci's wedding by not letting me spend the night in your hotel room, I have decided to risk it all again and say hello x

Fast-forward to 8.00 p.m. on Wednesday, 26 November 2014. I was staring at my future. I knew it within twenty minutes of our first official date. I didn't quite see our future mapped out beat for beat, but, hand on heart, I knew within those twenty minutes that your mother and I would be together.

It's her smile, Dory. I'm convinced it has been bioengineered to perfection. It disarms Daddy more effectively than a team of highly trained Navy

Seals. It's my favourite feature, and it needs to take some of the credit for your existence.

If the only physical trait we pass on to you as parents is Mummy's smile, then you could be doing a lot worse. If you have it, you possess a ruthlessly effective weapon. Use it genuinely and honestly. Mummy does, and people are drawn to it. It breaks down social boundaries, it brings people together, and it gets Mummy out of trouble a lot more often than she deserves.

There you have it – the story of how your parents met. As far as places to meet the future mother of your child go, merry-go-rounds ain't bad!

Saturday, 6 July 2019 – There Be Tremors

Dory-kicks are now visible to the naked eye. Or at least the last one was. It was barely visible, but Mummy's tummy tremored ever so slightly; a bit like that scene in *Jurassic Park* when the cup of water ripples, announcing the arrival of the T-Rex. Another milestone, Dory – well done.

We're waiting to see if it happens again.

Waiting …

Waiting …

Boom.

And there it is. This is hitting all the high notes – it's made me come over all feely-like.

Boom.

Yikes! There you go again.

Tuesday, 9 July 2019 – To Buy Or Not To Buy A Changing Station

We've started looking for nursery furniture. Despite you owning a boatload of gear, everything has been donated or made or bought by other members of the family. The exception is Ruby, your red-headed unicorn, who came with the Easter egg I bought on the day of discovery. Other than that, we've bought you *nada*. In our defence, we still have four months to go.

Mummy has said that we can save a few quid by not buying a changing station. Her business case is that her natural nappy-changing capabilities, coupled with years of experience looking after other people's children, mean she could change a baby on a beer mat if she had to (a scenario I think she secretly wishes for). To buy a changing station is to make a mockery of her inherent maternal abilities.

I confess that my own skill levels are non-existent, apart from that one time I changed your cousin Haylee's nappy, when I ended up with shit up my arm.

She's not convinced. She's annoyed that I don't have much experience and that I want a changing station. I try another angle. 'If you don't want to get one, that's fine with me, but I'm not taking the responsibility for getting baby shit on our brand-new carpets.'

After careful review, your mother has reversed her decision.

For the record, just because we're getting a changing station, it doesn't mean there won't be baby shit on the carpets.

Wednesday, 10 July 2019 – Crusty Bread

Tonight, Mummy is playing a game. She is testing my parenting skills by throwing a tantrum.

I believe she's doing this so that when it comes to your more testing periods, I will be psychologically equipped to cope.

I'll set the scene for you: Mummy (who's 34 years of age) is currently lying face down on the bed kicking her feet.

'Why are you throwing a strop?' I ask.

'I want crusty bread … and cheese.'

I love this game, Dory; it's so much fun already.

'Well, why don't you go and make yourself some?' I say.

'We don't have any fucking bread, so I can't.'

'In that case, why don't you have something else tonight, and we can make sure we pick up some bread—'

'CRUSTY bread.'

'… crusty bread tomorrow.'

Like any parent should aim to do, I've remained calm throughout the exchange. I haven't outright said no either; I've offered a way for the child

– sorry, for Mummy – to get what she wants if she employs patience. A vitally important lesson that all 'children' must learn.

At this point, she remembers you're in her tummy and can no longer lie face down. She readjusts her position. As she does this, she glares at me the whole time. Her genius cannot be overlooked. The glare distracts me, the audience, from her bump, meaning I'm still firmly within the narrative of the parent-child scenario.

Back to the game. I say, 'I'll buy some tomorrow.'

'But I want my crusty bread now.'

'There isn't any, so you will need to choose something else,' I say, mirroring her tone of voice, but with reduced volume and added calmness.

'Fine. Can you go and make me some crackers?'

She's testing me, Dory, but I'm ready. 'What word would we normally use when we want something?'

'PLEASE!'

'Excuse me?' I say.

'Please would you go and make me some crackers and cheese.'

Victory. This game has been a complete success. I've learnt something about myself and about parenting.

I march downstairs and into the kitchen, and I open up the food cupboard – only to be greeted by the icing on the cake.

Can you guess what it is, Dory? It's only a loaf of CRUSTY bread.

Thursday, 11 July 2019 – Meet Baby Puncher

Mummy's at a friend's house and they're putting together a plan of attack for this weekend. This particular friend of Mummy's is going away, and we're on babysitting duties for her two girls.

Mummy later told me that the younger of the two girls (who, it has to be said, is a right character) told her, while laughing, to 'punch the baby'. She was referring to you, Dory.

Now, the girl is only 4 years old. She hasn't acquired enough wisdom in life to know that she probably shouldn't be encouraging violence towards anyone, let alone an unborn baby.

I'm not 4; I'm all grown up. I can see her comments for what they are: those of a child. I don't get offended. I brush her words off like fallen crumbs on the table and ignore them. I even manage a little chuckle. 'Ha, ha, little tyke,' I say in my mind.

I sure as hell don't feel the want or need to break the young lady's face with my elbow. I mean, she's only 4. It would be an overreaction for an adult to feel like that.

Kids, Dory. What are they like?

Friday, 12 July 2019 – Conflict Leads To Growth

Remember, conflict is an opportunity for growth. I visualise those words as I prepare for this weekend's monumental babysitting challenge.

Baby Puncher is 4 and Baby Puncher's sister is 6. Why did I agree to this? That's easy; I didn't. Mummy committed us to this little endeavour without Daddy's input.

To ensure we're maximising this opportunity for 'growth', it's been decided (by someone who isn't me) that the girls will remain in our care (they're staying at our house) from tonight, when we pick them up in a few minutes, allllllll the way through to Monday morning, when we drop the little darlings off at nursery and school.

If you've not been counting, that's three sleeps, Dory; three bedtime routines for me to traverse and three mornings to endure – not to mention the long parts in between. And let's not forget mealtimes, sibling warfare and all the adult vulnerabilities that children have a knack for exploiting. We'll be like lambs to the slaughter.

But like I said, conflict is an opportunity for growth. As soon-to-be parents, we'll learn a lot. We've both looked after children before, but we haven't done so while knowing we've got one of our own on the way. Our perspective and framing will be different and, hopefully, valuable.

We've parked up. We're now walking to the door. There's just enough time for one last internal repetition of my mantra: 'Conflict equals growth, conflict equals growth, conf—'

Christ, I can hear them screaming already. The countdown has begun.

I'm trying to remember if I've ever looked forward to going to work on a Monday as much as I am right now.

But I can't complain yet, Dory. I've just been handed a Friday-night hall pass. Your Mummy, who I've always said is a splendid and terrific woman, has agreed to let me visit a friend who's moving to Ireland next week. He sent me a 'I know it's short notice, but do you want to come over for a bit' text. And Mummy said it was OK. I don't think this is even a backhanded, pregnant-hormonal, passive-aggressive sign-off; she genuinely means it. *Get in.*

I hit the road before she changes her mind. With any luck, the little ladies will be in bed by the time I get home.

One sleep routine avoided, two to go.

Saturday, 13 July 2019 – So Many Fucking Questions

This parenting stuff is a doddle, Dory; I don't know why I was worried. We're having a lovely morning in bed chatting, watching cartoons and messing around. The only thing I would say is that the verbal tempo doesn't seem to let up. Words fall out of their mouths quicker than bullets exit a trigger-squeezed assault rifle, but I'm confident that's because they're staying with us; it's somewhere new and it's exciting. I suspect the novelty will soon wear off.

There is cereal all over my brand-new dining-room table. I'd never purchased a brand-new table before … I suppose this is just mealtime collateral damage and overexcitement. The little princesses seem more focused on getting the in-depth lowdown on this weekend's itinerary and less on table-manner etiquette.

But it's difficult to answer a question when three more hit you before you've uttered more than a syllable responding to the first.

Let's all take a deep breath and calm down.

But they don't calm down. Not one bit. They have so many questions, Dory. I need to escape. I search for solace, and I find it in the bathroom.

One of the reasons why I'm a huge advocate of the sit-down wee is that it gives me a few precious seconds to myself where I don't even need to concentrate on aiming. I value these micro-breaks.

'Where are you?' I hear, from two young female voices simultaneously. I'm still mid-urination, so I'm surprised I'm having to field this type of enquiry after being out of the picture for less than ten seconds.

'I'm on the toilet. I'll be out in a sec.'

There. Now back to my micro-br—

'What are you doing on the toilet?'

I'm honestly not sure how to respond. Should I say I'm going to the toilet and leave it that? Should I be specific about exactly what I'm doing on the toilet? Or should I ignore them?

The girls arrived with a suitcase packed with clothes, toiletries and toys; I wonder if their parents included their operations guides and FAQ documents.

Somehow, we've reached the midday mark. Just keep swimming, Dory.

Speaking of swimming, we've taken the girls to the local pool so they can offload some of their excitement and energy. We're employing a classic dog-owner's trick whereby you take your dogs to the park for a runaround and by the time you get home they're exhausted, and all they want to do is sleep. Children are the same, right?

Everything is going OK in the pool, but Baby Puncher seems a little bit wary of me, and she keeps looking at me strangely. It takes me a while to figure out why that is, and the reason does nothing for my self-confidence.

You see, for the last decade I've been battling with a receding hairline and some thinning on top. Fortunately, it's been a slow battle, and my current hair-loss status isn't by any means as terrible as it could be. But a dip in the pool reveals an entirely different story; one that's packed to the rafters with tragedy. In short, once my head is submerged below water it magnifies the problem and I look, for want of a better phrase, like a complete and utter weirdo. I look like I'm wearing a swim-cap with a few glued-on hairs. No wonder I'm getting strange looks – one glance in the mirror and even I'm yelling: 'Stranger danger!'

It's an hour later and I've rectified this embarrassing little drama with a hairdryer. Baby Puncher is no longer looking at me as if I need to be on 'that register'.

Is it nap time yet?

'They don't nap,' states Mummy.

What a wonderful fucking revelation that one is.

Baby Puncher's sister is partial to the odd white lie. I say odd; she's been fibbing on an hourly basis. It's innocent enough. Like the time she fell down the stairs and broke her leg.

After we challenge some details of the story, like the part where we know this definitely didn't happen, she changes the broken limb from a leg to an arm. This version doesn't hold up any better and neither do the rest.

Mummy tells her that she shouldn't tell fibs and her admittedly reasonable response to this is to ask why. I take the lead on this one and answer in the form of a classic piece of literature: *The Boy Who Cried Wolf*. I stumble over recalling some of the finer details, but I know the story well enough to improvise and get the message across.

I'm hoping that using a story to explain why you shouldn't do something will help provide real context that they can each understand and reflect on. I see this as actual parenting, instead of going with the classic 'because I said so' response.

I finish the story, and we move into the obligatory Q&A session. My word – don't they make the most out of this opportunity! How big was the wolf? What happened to the boy? What colour eyes did the wolf have? What was the wolf's name? Why didn't the villagers help?

Their verbal output is relentless, Dory.

I take their questions from the top. 'The wolf was big, the boy died because he got eaten by the wolf, the wolf had yellowish eyes with a twang of opal sunrise, the wolf's name was Derrick and if you had listened to the story you would know why the villagers didn't come and help!'

And breathe.

It's 3.00 p.m. They usually go to sleep at 7.00 p.m. We have four hours left.

We shoot over to Sean and Rebecca's house for a BBQ. This serves as a reprieve, Dory.

Sean and Rebecca have a big garden and a daughter (so toys) and none of their furniture belongs to me – so if the girls trash it, it's unfortunate, but not as unfortunate as if it were something of Daddy's.

We're having a lovely time, the food is great, the kids are self-solving for stuff to do (a first for the weekend), and the weather isn't too bad either. It's going well. At least, it was – Baby Puncher's sister has decided that she's not getting enough attention, so she's stuck her entire right hand into the butter.

And just like that, I understand why parents are always apologising for their children.

We're almost done for the day. The girls have been bathed and are ready for bed. But then Mummy notices that Baby Puncher's sister's towel is covered in something red. Understandably, she's worried she's hurt herself.

'What's this on the towel?' says Mummy.

'I don't know,' says Baby Puncher's sister.

Hmmm. A closer inspection reveals it's not blood. Phew, Dory.

It turns out it's berry juice. She sneaked downstairs and scoffed a load of strawberries despite being told she couldn't.

I'm secretly impressed by that one, Dory. The kid's got balls.

We put the girls to bed and have a few minutes to ourselves.

Fuck, I'm tired. It's 10.00 p.m. We've got through the day. I kiss you goodnight but forgo the usual Daddy-and-child bonding time as I'm shattered.

Sunday, 14 July 2019 – The Concept Of Time

We've decided to outsource parenting duties to the local cinema this morning. It's perfect. The cinema is dead, meaning we won't have to constantly shush the girls for talking. I've already seen the film so there will be no missing out on key plot points, and Mummy has bought popcorn.

We're midway through the film. It's just me and Baby Puncher; Mummy has taken Baby Puncher's sister to the toilet. Baby Puncher turns to me and says, 'I need the toilet as well.'

That's an easy one for me. I tell her that Mummy will take her when she gets back.

'Can't you take me?' she says.

'Of course I can,' I agree, but I've not thought things through at all. As I walk the twenty or so metres to the exit, I begin to panic. I do not know what the protocol is for taking a 4-year-old girl to the toilet. Do I take her to the men's toilet or the women's toilet? Do I go into the cubicle with her or wait outside? Does she need a number one or a number two? If it's a number two, what is my role – what the fuck do I do? I'm sweating now, Dory. Why don't I know any of this? I know why; I don't have any bloody kids yet!

I'm about to slit my own throat with my house keys when a guardian angel swoops down to save me. It's the Matriarch, Dory; my reprieve, my saviour, my guiding light. I love this woman more than anything in the world.

'Thank fuck you've come back into my life,' I whisper to Mummy.

'What's the matter?'

She saves me, Dory. I return to my seat and begin my breathing exercises.

———————

By popular request, I've retold *The Boy Who Cried Wolf* four times. What's more, Baby Puncher's sister has decreed that whoever wins a game of rock, paper, scissors will be allowed to tell as many lies as they want. I have no idea what's going on here psychologically, but I reckon I've caused something to stir in her little mind.

Interesting.

In the last two days, I've developed a fascination for child psychology.

Final activity of the day – cake baking. The weekend is almost over, Dory! The girls are behaving wonderfully. They stir the mixture as taught, and they listen well to Mummy's guidance as she takes them through the process. It's a joy to watch; what a lovely way to round off the weekend.

'When are we going to the park?' says Baby Puncher.

I look at your mother, confused. 'The park?' we both say.

Now Puncher's sister moves in to abate any confusion. 'Yes, you said we could go to the park today.'

Fuck, Dory, we did say that. But it's now 4.30 p.m., and we need to think about dinner, bath and bed. I'm sure they'll understand. We can use the weekend's accomplished activities to manipulate a concession on their part.

No dice, Dory.

'But you promised,' they both say.

The lips of two young girls begin to quiver, and it's no wonder. They've been lied to by adults – adults, who don't lie; especially those same adults who have been telling them a story all weekend about not fucking lying!

They've got us by the short and curlies. I contemplate sticking my head under the shower and asking if they still want to go, but I know the stubbornness of children will always prevail over my best-laid plans.

I guess we're going to the park then.

Mummy explains to me that it takes a while for children to understand the nuances of time and how it works. This enables us to do the very thing we told them not to do – lie. But lie without them realising – the best kind of lying.

We promised them that we would spend thirty minutes in the park, right? And as far as they're concerned, we're adhering to that. What we're not adhering to is the rules of time. Our lie is to triple the speed of time. So, when ten minutes is up, we add on the triple-speed rate of interest and hey presto – 'Girls, your thirty minutes is up.'

I don't feel bad about this, Dory.

Fast-forward a few hours and the girls are in bed. It will be a photo finish between them and your parents as to who falls asleep first.

Monday, 15 July 2019 – A Chance To Reflect

I do not want to get up this morning. I've seen planks of wood move through their morning routine quicker than me. But I battle through; I get the girls up with your mother, and I ensure they're dressed and into the car on time. We drop them off at school and nursery.

Your parents get back into the car, and we let out an unnecessarily exaggerated sigh.

How is looking after children this hard? All things considered, they behaved remarkably well. Sure, they tested a few boundaries, but no more than any kid. They went to bed when they were told; they didn't fight or argue. I feel as if I've trekked Everest carrying a family of hippos (each with type 2 diabetes).

If I've learnt anything from this weekend, it's that I would love it if your mother didn't die on me any time soon. I would struggle with single parenting.

Wednesday, 17 July 2019 – Kick

Kick.

Pregnancy is a joy to behold. I'm lying on Mummy's tummy and you're kicking me. It's beautiful. Each kick represents a feeling or a thought.

Kick – Not long now till we meet.

Kick – Fuck, fuck, fuck, it's not long now till we meet.

Kick – I will love you unconditionally.

Kick – It will be hard.

Kick – I will question my right to parent you on more than one occasion.

Kick – I will put your safety before anything else on every occasion.

Kick – We're both growing.

Kick – You, Dory, are growing physically.

Kick – Daddy is growing mentally.

Kick – Mummy has clearly had far too much sugar this evening.

Thursday, 18 July 2019 – What's That You Hear?

I have the best of news, Dory. Your mother tells me you are now at a point in your development where you can distinguish sounds outside her tummy. There are three major reasons why this is just the best news.

First, I can get to work on that music playlist for you. Obviously, we need to include 'Shells'. The *Guardians of the Galaxy* soundtrack is another no-brainer. What else? This is exciting. Second, I can ramp up our Daddy-and-Dory conversations. I know they will still be one-sided, but knowing you can hear my voice is wonderful. Third, I can read to you. Yikes. You know how Daddy gets when it comes to books. He gets an erection strong enough to rival the shoulders of Atlas.

But this excitement is not without dilemma: how do I know what your first story should be? Granny Smurf has bought you some books, but I haven't been all that impressed with them, if I'm honest. I will devote much of my time today to reflecting on how to proceed. The importance of this matter cannot be overstated.

I've messaged your mother asking her to say the following sentence out loud: 'Would you like a story, Dory?'

Obviously, she started crying, but these were good pregnancy tears – for a change.

Sunday, 21 July 2019 – What Part Of Shut The Fuck Up Can't You Comprehend?

As a general rule, I don't believe in violence towards others. But there are exceptions to every rule in life, Dory, and laying a smackdown on someone is no different. Daddy came close to one of those exceptions this morning.

It all started when we went to see Taci (our relationship broker). At some point, the conversation veered to babies. We admitted to Taci that we're not finding out your gender, and what a magical experience we anticipate the moment will be when we do find out – on the day of your birth. But I also let slip that Rebecca thinks she accidentally saw what gender you were during our last emergency scan.

'If she accidentally saw it, it can only be a—' began Taci.

'Shut your mouth now,' I said, reacting quicker than a viper strike.

I wasn't expecting that, Dory.

It gets worse. When I told Taci to shut her mouth, I felt my intention and meaning were clear. My instructions were limited to a mere four words, eliminating the risk of confusion.

But alas, I must have missed something when formulating my strategy; I clearly overlooked some variable because Taci has decided to continue speaking – about the same fucking subject.

'Honestly, I'm telling you, if—'

I interjected again.

Now, what I wanted to say (and would have said had time permitted) was something like this: 'Look, Taci, it's great that you know something about this baby-development stuff that we don't; you have three beautiful children, and we're both happy for you. But we're having our first child now, and we know nothing about it all, except that Dory means everything and more to us. That's why we want the gender to be a nice surprise. Surely you can relate to that, and respect the wishes of your best friend, by being a bit more aware of this current moment and finding it within yourself to support our decision – and read the fucking room?'

But I didn't have time for bunting and flowers, so I went for something more akin to my initial response – this time with an added question: 'Shut up right now and stop talking. What part of "We don't want to know" do you not understand?'

Taci altered the subject of the conversation immediately without showing any sign of offence.

You might be thinking that if a midwife accidentally saw something, then it would have to be a willy, right? This means you're a boy. But it's not the case, apparently; Rebecca says it's not as simple as that when identifying the gender. She's also told me several conflicting pieces of information on purpose – to confuse us. And it's worked; truthfully, we have no idea. That's why Taci needed to shut up.

In retrospect, we shouldn't get too hung up on this. The number one priority is that you're OK. But to find out if you're a baby boy or a baby girl when we hold you in our arms for the first time will be the gold standard of life experiences.

We've had a lucky escape, Dory, but we must be cautious, particularly around Taci. If I have to throat-punch her to get her to shut up about her child-development insights – so be it. That goes for anyone else too.

Monday, 22 July 2019 – Yawn

Mummy is showing her highest levels of exhaustion yet. She's wiped out – and she feels dizzy. I'm in the game of linking every spell of dizziness to low iron levels, so my response is to make her a spinach smoothie. Just call me 'Doctor Daddy' – a name I could warm to if it didn't sound like the lead in an adult entertainment movie set in a run-down private medical centre (with a production budget of a tenner).

The smoothie hasn't worked. Neither has a daytime nap, nor a bath – nor the eight ice creams that she's scoffed inside an hour.

There isn't much we can do. Part of pregnancy is exhaustion. The fact that it's dialled up a notch tells me that we're another step closer to the birth. Increased levels of exhaustion must mean more of Mummy's nutrients are diverted to the placenta to nourish you and aid in your growth and development. This is one of many major sacrifices that your mother will make for you: a sacrifice she doesn't regret at all – and one for which you will never need to thank her.

As for the metaphorical elephant in the room: eating eight ice creams in quick succession would put even a non-metaphorical elephant at risk of a sugar coma.

Tuesday, 23 July 2019 – Giddy Up

We have two pregnancy products in our bedroom that are both useless. The first is Mummy's maternity pillow. She says it's not helping her because she's not sleeping (valid thinking). The second is a stethoscope which, as you know, should enable us to hear your heartbeat. We've still to find any success – I can't pick up my own heartbeat, let alone yours.

I usually discard anything that adds no value to our lives, as Mummy and I dislike clutter, and I am about to suggest as much to Mummy when genius strikes me like a Newton's-apple-shaped lightning bolt.

The two useless products can be combined to form a useful one. If I tie the stethoscope around one end of the pillow, I effectively have something that looks like a horse with reins on it. And if I gallop around the bedroom at 7.00 a.m. making neighing sounds, Mummy will be distracted from the fact that she's tired. It's yet another example of the infinite levels of altruism I'm willing to channel for your mother.

'Neigh, neigh.' My performance is of such a high standard that I don't even require coconut shells.

Thursday, 25 July 2019 – Let's Get Deep For A Second (But Only For A Second)

Yesterday a combination of medical science and the law could prevent your life from continuing. Today it can't (barring extreme circumstances).

Mental, huh?

From what I can gather, the twenty-four-week line in the sand has been agreed by those in the know because the odds of you surviving are favourable, should you be born any time from now. It's also been decided by those in the know that at twenty-four weeks you begin to feel pain (although I've read many conflicting reports on this point).

I wonder at the process involved in deciding on these life-and-death matters. I don't envy any committee member whose job it is to translate philosophy and science into policy. How do you get your teeth into that one? I hope everyone involved in the process was a parent.

I don't know your gender, what colour hair you will have, what your name will be, if you will excel at sport or if you will fall in love. I know none of those things, yet you are real to me. To think that we could have had you aborted yesterday is a hard notion for me to wrap my head around philosophically.

During this pregnancy, my mind has often travelled far and wide to some of the deepest and most exotic rabbit holes I've ever discovered – and today is no exception.

I don't often contemplate the meaning of life – in a spiritual sense, I mean. I figure our existence is incredibly unlikely, but not impossible (clearly), and that life has evolved to what it is today because of a combination of science, timing and astronomical odds. Nothing more. Instead of questioning that, I'm just thankful for it, and I'll continue to approach it that way. I'm ready to revisit my position any time we learn more facts.

But then I wake up, and I learn that the country I live in has a policy that means it's illegal for my child to be aborted today – but it wasn't illegal yesterday.

And now I find myself on a voyage, drifting towards impossible questions that I've not shown any interest in for a long time. What is life's great purpose? If the universe started out because of a 'big bang', then what came before the bang? And if something came before the bang, then what came before that? Was time invented or discovered? We can't understand the concept that time doesn't have a beginning – are there beings out there that can? And if there is some cosmic godlike being that can add time and other dimensions to our reality as if they're ingredients in a pasta dish, then who created this force – and can they tell shit jokes better than I can?

While we're at it, try and define humour. Where the fuck does that actually come from?

I need to stop this right now before I destroy my mind. Instead, I should probably get back to making dinner.

Something else has occurred to me. If you can now feel pain, we probably need to stop poking Mummy's tummy every evening to make you move and kick for our besotted enjoyment.

Full disclaimer, Dory: we do this – every day.

Friday, 26 July 2019 – Another Bad Decision

The temperature is thirty-seven degrees today. I don't know how you're coping being cooped up indoors without a fan; it must be like swimming laps in an active volcano.

Mummy's not loving the heat situation either; she's had to up her talcum powder usage, which should illustrate the severity of the situation. I should add also that she's changed her choice of night-time underwear from big knickers to massively big knickers. It goes without saying that her new garment selection elicits a mature and helpful response from Daddy.

Still, being annoying and unhelpful isn't a full-time gig. I have a more important job, which is to look after you both, so I've taken us to the cinema so we can all enjoy a couple of hours in a room cooled by air conditioning – at least, that's how I've sold it …

But I've failed to consider an important variable. The film we're watching is the live-action remake of *The Lion King*, which happens to include one of the most traumatic death scenes ever captured on camera, and now this scene has been recreated in live action using the latest photorealistic technology. I doubt even Sir David Attenborough could tell the difference between what's real and what isn't.

Mufasa is not living his best life. A confusion of wildebeest (thanks, Google) is stampeding its way through a canyon – a canyon in the middle of which Mufasa is standing. He's had eighty per cent of his vital organs punctured by their horns, and now the wildebeest are treating his face as if it's the Shibuya Crossing – his entire body falls under their hooves as he's dragged down and under, again and again.

A few moments later, he somehow makes it out. *Christ, that Mufasa is one tough bastard.*

One glance at your mother confirms what my ears suspected – Mummy is sobbing.

Mufasa's day isn't getting any cheerier either; his brother betrays him and sends him hurtling back down the cliffside and into the canyon for another bout with the trample-train express.

Poor Mufasa.

Mummy turns to me, tear-stricken. 'Why did we come to see this?' she says.

Probably to give my lungs a break from ingesting all the talcum powder.

Saturday, 27 July 2019 – Hang On, Haven't We Been Here Before?

Mummy receives a call from the doctor to tell her that her iron and B12 levels are low. No shit – she's exhausted.

They're not low enough to win the 2019 limbo world championship, but low enough nonetheless to require medical intervention. As you know by now, Dory, the problem is that Mummy has digestive organs that are prone to sub-par operational performances, and any supplements that can reverse these deficiencies will fuck her up quicker than the cold fucks up the elderly in winter.

The doctor is giving her some expert advice on how to improve the situation. Unfortunately, we're in all-too-familiar territory.

'I recommend lots of red meat,' instructs the doctor.

'I can't eat red meat; I have Crohn's disease,' Mummy says.

'Hmm. I see,' says the doctor. 'In that case, lots of lentils and beans.'

'I can't eat lentils or beans; I have Crohn's disease,' Mummy says monotonously.

And so it continues.

This is frustrating; not only does this verbal exchange occur during every doctor, midwife and hospital appointment we attend, but her condition has been documented (both digitally and in handwriting) hundreds of times. Why does no one know this in advance of an appointment? This happens regularly, despite claims that her notes have been thoroughly reviewed beforehand.

The doctor has decided to give the matter some thought and will be reaching out to us in due course.

Monday, 29 July 2019 – Saying The Wrong Thing

I'm in big trouble. It started a few seconds ago when I met Mummy after work and affectionately referred to her as 'Big Bird'. According to her, this was the wrong thing to say.

In hindsight, I recognise that one probably doesn't need to have lived with a pregnant woman to realise this was a mistake. But I did it in such a playful and adorable way that I thought Mummy would decode it in the right spirit.

She didn't. And now I'm a gnat's nutsack away from Miss Heidi breaking my face. I must tread carefully, Dory.

I have an idea. Why don't we downgrade Mummy's status from 'Big Bird' to 'Medium-Sized Bird'? That's got successful turnaround written all over it, right?

Wrong. Your mother doesn't fancy compromising this evening, Dory. She's being very unreasonable.

I suppose I'm asking for trouble if I point out that her steps-per-minute ratio has plummeted since last week?

Tuesday, 30 July 2019 – Let There Be Light, And Then Follow That Light

You're responding to light. At least, you seem to be. We've been using the torches on our phones and shining them on Mummy's tummy, and you seem to be reacting with Dory-kicks.

I should note that I attribute any movement you make to a kick. The reaction to light could equally be you using your fists or administering a headbutt – I don't know.

Wednesday, 31 July 2019 – Music Round

As yesterday's light experiment worked, we've decided to graduate you from sight to sound – or more accurately, melodies. Melodies that are age-appropriate, of course.

Mummy selects Nirvana's 'Smells Like Teen Spirit' for the first test. This elicits movement from you. By using an equation that I've just made up (MTM = ETM: movement to music equals enjoyment to music), we can take this as absolute confirmation that you like Nirvana.

Daddy's up next. I've selected an auditory sensation that I'm convinced will not fail: Frank Sinatra's 'Fly Me to the Moon'.

Nothing. Not a shudder; not a whisper. For fuck's sake, Dory. Mummy is smiling and looking all smug, which now means a bit of harmless bump-time fun has transformed into a contest. A contest that Daddy is losing 1–0.

It's on.

Mummy scores again with Madonna's 'Vogue'. She's now two for two. Shit.

My next move is Gene Kelly's 'Singin' in the Rain'. Once again, you decide to stab your old man in the back by doing the opposite of moving – cheers, pal.

Your mother continues her winning streak with a song from Pink, but I'm claiming bullshit as I can't feel the kicks, so she can fuck off.

Mummy now wants to call it a day and let you rest, but I refuse. I need one more crack at this, and so I play my final card and select from the

Guardians of the Galaxy soundtrack.

If you don't know what success sounds like, I'll tell you. It sounds like 'Hooked on a Feeling', 'Come and Get Your Love' and 'Spirit in the Sky'. You've responded to all of these songs. It has everything to do with the melody and nothing to do with me cranking up the volume.

MTM = ETM, motherfucker!

August

Thursday, 1 August 2019 – Do We Swear Too Much?

Mummy says that your kicks have become more powerful. She says sometimes it's like being on a rollercoaster when the ride suddenly drops, sending your insides somersaulting. Other times, her Dory-bump feels more tender.

'Dory's just cunt-punted me, and it hurt,' Mummy says.

I think both of your parents need to review how often they swear.

Don't feel bad about the kicking; we're proud. You're getting stronger, and that's all that matters.

Friday, 2 August 2019 – Bedroom Rules

Nursery preparation has begun. We've measured up for your cot, wardrobe and chest of drawers. Your nursery's snug – but big enough.

You won't go in there immediately; you'll be in with us for the first few months. I'm OK with this, as long as you agree to follow the rules:

- No snoring.
- No derogatory comments about R-rated cartoons, for which Netflix offers a wide variety of top-class content. FYI, Moronic Mummy thinks Rick and Morty isn't very good. She is mistaken.

- No interrupting a programme, particularly when Sir David Attenborough is narrating, to show Daddy pointless, irrelevant crap on social media that he couldn't give two shinies about.

What do you reckon, kiddo – you good with all of that?

At least someone is.

Saturday, 3 August 2019 – I'm Not Going Down Without A Fight

Daddy is hung-over to hell. All I want to do is build a fort in bed and spend the day watching Marvel films. Only I can't, because that torturing psychopath (your mother) has decreed that my assistance is required for the weekly food shop.

I know, Dory – this is horseshit.

But I'm not submitting to that witch's demands without a fight. I'll go along, but my best behaviour will not be accompanying us.

Twenty minutes later and we're in the supermarket. I've already been told off three times for pacing up the aisles as quickly as possible. When will this end? I feel sick, and the smell of food is not helping.

I'm compelled to misbehave.

Mummy has a stain on her dress. I think it's from a Bakewell tart she ate this morning. Excellent. Just the opener I need. With all the innocence I can muster, I say (loudly), 'Darling, has that discharge on your dress arrived from your vagina?'

Success. At least four people heard me. Your mother is marching away in protest.

This is what I like to call a multi-layered success. First, Mummy will think ahead next time before forcing me at gunpoint to go trudging down the aisles with her on a shopping trip when I'm hung-over. Second, she's begun shopping a lot quicker.

Every time Mummy slows down, I start pretending I'm a cheerleader on finals day, shouting, 'Give me a V! Give me a D! What does it mean? Whhhoooaaa, vaginal discharge!'

I don't think it's just me, Dory; I believe supermarkets have something in the air con system that encourages misbehaviour in men.

Mummy is now refusing to talk to me, so I've decided to lay off being an arsehole for ten minutes (but not a second more, God damn it).

Now we're at the checkout and Mummy turns to me and says that the stain on her dress is from when she went down into the cellar.

'The cellar?' I say. *The comedy gods aren't this generous, are they?*

'Yes, the cellar.'

'But I've been telling you that for the past ten minutes!'

There's a common rule among children and their parents that no matter how much of a little bastard the child is being, if it can make its parents laugh, then it cannot be told off for its behaviour. That wonderfully written piece of legislation has got Daddy his ticket out of the doghouse.

Monday, 5 August 2019 – Night-Feed Training

We've begun night-feed training. Our training programme is straightforward and simple, like all good training programmes should be. It starts with Daddy falling asleep, which happens approximately eight seconds after his head hits the pillow. Because of her added Dory-growing responsibilities, Mummy takes considerably longer. But eventually she'll drift off as well.

Then we wait for you to decide how things play out. Last night, for instance, I don't know what organ you pressed down on, but it was one of the more tender ones; it caused Mummy to launch herself out of bed (no mean feat for someone who's almost six months pregnant) and in the process wake me up.

It's critical that both parents are woken simultaneously as we need to mirror as best we can what it will be like when you wake up in the night and want … whatever it is that you will want: changing, feeding, a cuddle.

It then falls to us to settle you back down. In training mode, we achieve this by walking you up and down the landing. Well, Mummy does the walking part while Daddy enjoys a relaxed sit-down wee, but with the door open, so he can encourage Mummy with some sympathetic staring –

which I swear doesn't look creepy.

At some point (there's no hard and fast rule as far as timings are concerned), you decide your parents have completed the training module for the night – you readjust your limbs, taking the pressure off the tender area, and allow Mummy to relax.

Finally, we begin the process of getting back to sleep, and the cycle resets. Simple and effective. Great work, Dory.

Out of interest, when are our rest days?

Tuesday, 6 August 2019 – Please, Please, Please Start Crying

I'm freaking out about the birth; it's the first time it's happened to me during the pregnancy. I blame your mother – she's making me watch some stupid programme on television that's set in a labour ward.

One small female human has just been welcomed into the world; she's breathing but she's not crying, and that's cause for concern. The midwives are looking into the problem; a minute passes, then another and another.

Still no crying.

It's now been ten minutes without a peep from the baba. The midwives continue to reassure both the parents and the viewing public that everything is OK, but neither the parents nor the viewing public believe them.

The problem with programmes of this type is that they double down on the dramatic elements, which is fine if you have no way of directly relating to what's on the screen – but I do (I do now, anyway), so can they please hurry up and tell me if the baby is OK and put these terrified parents out of their misery?

My wishes have gone ignored – the producers are letting this one play out.

I should add that the Mummy is haemorrhaging blood, but you wouldn't know that from her facial expression, which is frozen in carbonite. Her attention isn't on the crash team scattered around her trying to stem the flow of blood, and it's not on the Daddy. Instead, she fixes her gaze on her silent baby and on the hands of the midwife, who's working desperately to push the plot of this story forward in a happy direction.

She's watching and hoping, hoping that her baby is OK. That's all she can do. Fuck.

'Wahhhhh!'

Finally, Dory – the baby is crying.

I wonder how many people in the UK just issued a collective sigh of relief.

Wednesday, 7 August 2019 – May The Odds Forever Be In Your Favour

You're now twenty-six weeks into your development – a massive milestone, Dory. Last week you had a fifty to eighty per cent chance of surviving a premature birth; this week you have an eighty to ninety per cent chance. A week is such a short time, yet in those seven days the odds have swung astronomically in your favour.

They will continue to improve. Next week, the odds of you surviving jump to ninety per cent and above. At week thirty, they're at ninety-five per cent and over; and there is a ninety-eight per cent chance of survival at week thirty-four.

Just keep swimming, Dory.

Thursday, 8 August 2019 – Happy Birthday, Mummy

It's Mummy's last birthday as a non-Mummy.

This year was a tough one for Daddy. Birthdays are usually a straightforward affair; I have a go-to box of tricks I can call upon featuring tickets to the theatre, afternoon tea (never fails), clothes, a holiday or a day out adventuring.

This year is different. Mummy is six months pregnant. I can't get tickets to anything before or after your birth. Pre-birth treats are out because Mummy needs to pee every eight seconds, and post-birth ones don't make any sense until we know how you like to operate – and it's a bit much to start lining up the babysitters at this stage. That said, I know a couple of grandmothers who would strongly disagree.

Afternoon tea is out because Mummy did that last week. Clothes are out for obvious reasons – I don't think maternity garb will qualify as a satisfactory birthday gift. Finally, going out on a day's adventure is out because your mother's stamina and dexterity levels couldn't rival those of a dead panda with muscular dystrophy.

In the end, I've decided to buy her a stupid plastic bottle from a reality TV show that she likes and a pregnancy massage. I've also outsourced the entire day to other people and created a series of mini-surprises (if I can pull it off). This demands almost zero effort from Daddy while allowing him to take a hundred per cent of the credit.

Let's see how we do.

7.00 a.m. We wake up and I wish Mummy a happy birthday. Mummy has the day off work to enjoy her special day. She thinks I don't have the day off. I previously told her that I need to save up all of my holiday leave for when you're here. So, when I ask her what she fancies doing today, it takes her a moment to twig that I'm off work as well. She's pleased – a good start, as I was worried she would be disappointed with the news that she'd be spending her birthday with me.

8.00 a.m. Mini-surprise number two unfolds as I had hoped. Taci turns up for tea and toast.

10.50 a.m. My next trick is to give her a card from you. Good work, kiddo. Remember that you will exploit us a lot more than we'll exploit you. Actually, let's park that one for now.

11.00 a.m. Quick history lesson. Over the years, I've taken your mother to some of the best musicals ever to have graced the West End stages of London; I've taken her all over the world travelling; and there have been countless other times where I've strived to create something memorable for her. But never have I seen her as happy as I see her now, after I've given her the stupid water bottle with her name written on it. What the actual fuckery? It's like when you spend hundreds of pounds on toys for children and all they want to do is play in the box – bonkers.

11.05 a.m. And now I've had to deploy the wet-floor safety signs because I've just given her a similar bottle, only this one is a lot smaller; it has two handles on it, and the name on it is 'Dory'. Can someone pass me the mop?

1.00 p.m. Lunch with the family at a beautiful little pub overlooking a canal. Granny Feeder is living up to her name and feeding your cousin Haylee everything she can get her hands on. Haylee is barely seven months old. Granny Feeder will need to be watched at all times, Dory. She is not to be trusted.

7.30 p.m. The final surprise is a meal out for the two of us – except it's not just the two of us, it's with her friends, who are already seated in the restaurant, waiting. We walk through the door, and the reaction from Mummy says that she suspected nothing. That's a surprise hit-rate of one hundred per cent, Dory!

9.30 p.m. You don't want to know this bit.

9.31 p.m. That's another year done, Dory. You'll be with us next year – and you'll be around nine months old. Scary.

Mummy has thanked me for a lovely day. It's nice to be thanked, and it's nice that Mummy feels that way, but there is a huge lesson here, Dory, and it's one I want you to learn. Are you listening?

I've done very little today in terms of effort. I reckon I spent under five minutes sending messages to her friends, ten minutes making her card from you and then fifteen minutes buying her presents (all online). Total time spent was under an hour. The lesson is that it takes a minimal amount of effort to show someone you give a shit. In my opinion, that's a great return on investment – especially if it also gets you laid.

Friday, 9 August 2019 – Getting Ready

Mummy has bought you a present: it's your first item of clothing purchased using our own money. It's funny, your nursery is replete with bags of clothes and all manner of gizmos and gadgets, but it's all been regifted.

Not only is this the first item of clothing that we've bought you; it's also the first time we've spent a single penny on you. That's if you discount Ruby, your unicorn, and the silly Dory water bottle for Mummy's birthday.

At first glance, you may be thinking you have a pair of tight-arsed parents, but this signifies a psychological shift in our preparation for parenthood.

We're getting ready. Next week we move into the third and final trimester. We have set an early-October deadline for having everything prepared in case you should show up ahead of time. Equipment includes Daddy's emergency delivery kit that I absolutely don't want to use (but a little bit of me secretly does).

Tuesday, 13 August 2019 – I Can't Win This One … Or Maybe I Can

I've woken up to the face of your Mummy, a face packed with rage. I sense Miss Heidi. I presume Mummy has not slept well.

'Rough night?' I ask.

'I didn't sleep at all. I had a bad dream, and we were arguing in it.'

I thought this perhaps wasn't the best time to point out that if Mummy was dreaming, she must at least have got some sleep – even a quick forty. But I don't provoke; I ask after your welfare instead.

You're doing OK, kiddo; lots of movement. During her report, Mummy lets slip that she nipped downstairs to the kitchen at midnight to scoff a few biscuits and a pack of Haribo. Mummy assures me, despite my suspicion, that her actions cannot possibly have any bearing on the way she feels – or the lack of sleep.

I lean in for a kiss. It's not rejected, but the reaction is laced with anger.

Now, I'm good at getting into trouble with your mother (especially these days), but I'm not that good. All I've done is wake up.

There must be something I'm miss—

Ah, I think I've got it.

'Are you angry at me because you had a dream that we were arguing and you blame me?'

Her silence and her refusal to make eye contact answer the question. God damn it, Dory. I'm in the doghouse because of something I said in a dream.

I suppose that means I won the argument, though.

Wednesday, 14 August 2019 – On Your Marks, Get Set, GO!

While you've been swimming, I've been running. I've been running for six months straight. I've tripped, stumbled and lost my way at times, but I've never stopped moving. I've maintained my heading and stayed the course. I'm tired, but not exhausted. I have enough left in the tank for what comes next – the third trimester.

I can see the curve straightening out to reveal the finishing line. It materialises right before my eyes. At least, I think it does – it's barely visible, like the horizon on a stormy day or a blade of grass in the wind. It's fragile, and it's brittle. I dare not celebrate the possibility of reaching it yet. But it is there; can you see it?

I only have time for a quick glance up, but it's enough to reveal what I'm up against: birthing plans, emergency plans, baby names, equipment to buy, midwife appointments, mineral deficiencies to restore in Mummy, HR forms to fill out at work, feeding plans, nappy strategies, NCT classes to complete and baby first aid to learn. That's only what I can think of today. The road to labour is fraught with obstacles.

How do you prepare for something you've never done before, something you only get one shot at doing? If potholes represent my lack of knowledge, then the road we're on looks like it's been without local funding for a century – it's littered with voids.

It's enough to overwhelm anyone, but it doesn't overwhelm me (not yet) – because I'm not alone.

I risk a second glance, this time to my right. Your Mummy fills my vision. She's running too – she looks strong; no small achievement, given that her side of the road has more obstacles than my side of the road. She's carried you for six months, and she'll carry you for three more. The delivery will be painful, and the changes to her hormone levels have been brutal, both mentally and physically, without any sign of slowing. In fact, they're winding up for a dramatic finish. But she takes it all in her stride. She looks amazing – she is amazing; I'm proud of her.

She looks at me, smiling. Then she reaches over and takes my hand. A big kick from you acts as the starting gun. It signals the start of the final lap. Three months left, Dory. If you keep swimming, Mummy and Daddy will keep running.

Friday, 16 August 2019 – Nappy Rant

Environmental sustainability is a topic I've been increasingly drawn to ever since I fell in love with travelling (and, ergo, the planet), and my interest in it has only become keener since I learnt I'm to become a father. I cannot in good conscience live my life ignoring the many environmental challenges we face. The plastic epidemic is one of those challenges, and it's an epidemic to which I don't want to contribute by letting a baby serve as an excuse for choosing convenience at the expense of the planet – it takes five hundred years for a disposable nappy to biodegrade.

Granny Feeder must have heard me talk about this at some point because she's presented us with our first set of reusable nappies. This means a lot to me.

When all is said and done, I'm going to be covered in shit at some point, anyway, so why should it matter if it occurs more frequently? A lot of people cite expense as a reason not to climb aboard, and while I'm not discounting that as a genuine consideration (for a few), I would challenge most people on this point; it seems to me to be more of an excuse than a genuine financial concern. We're talking pennies, Dory; maybe a few pounds here and there. Actually, reusables are supposed to save money over time. It's the upfront cost that's problematic.

I'm ranting today but I'm not sorry; did I mention that a typical disposable nappy that's thrown away today won't biodegrade until around 2519?

That's fucking insane!

Sunday, 18 August 2019 – A Day I've Long Waited For

Today is going to be glorious; a bold claim, seeing that all I'm doing is assembling flat-pack furniture with your Mummy. That's it. Usually, a job like that wouldn't summon any feelings of gloriousness – it would barely qualify as average. But this job is special. Why? Because the furniture we're building is your bedroom furniture and it marks another symbolic step in our journey to parenthood.

I've set the camera up so we can film a time-lapse of the journey.

Now all there is to do is get stuck in.

Despite a few instruction-manual reading errors, two hours later we stand immersed in victory, surveying a job well done: one cot, one chest of drawers (with changing mat), one wardrobe and a truckload of hand-me-downs regifted by friends and family. A proud moment for your parents and a perfect moment that cannot possibly be ruined ...

Your mother has dropped a gas ball the size of London from her backside and she smells like a power cut at the morgue.

She's not sorry, Dory. She never is.

Monday, 19 August 2019 – How Many Types of Baby Shit Are There, Dory?

Mummy has decided that we need to brush up on our knowledge of baby shit – seems reasonable to me. And by baby shit, I mean exactly that – baby shit. She's found an online video that uses a catchy rhythm, some cute animation and a mesmerising colour scheme to capture and maintain our attention. It then proceeds to break down the different varieties of baby poop that we're likely to come up against. Here we go.

- Meconium. Your first of many toilet episodes begins with a meconium offering. Apparently, it's made up of fluids, cells and other bits and bobs that you ingest while in utero. Wait, what's utero? Oh, it's Latin for 'womb'. Say womb then! Colours range from dark green to black. It's sticky, but it doesn't smell bad – every cloud, Dory.

- Transitional. Still operating in the green-poop colour range, this poop isn't quite meconium, but neither is it ... normal. It slots nicely into the in-between stage, hence the name 'transitional'. Aroma levels are once again manageable.

- Breastfed poop. No way. Is that the correct medical terminology?

Breastfed poop? Then again, who am I to question the internet, Dory? The video content tells us this stuff is more on the lighter side: pale green or perhaps even yellow. It can be mushy.

- Frothy green poop. This is a joke, right? I barely bought breastfed poop; now I'm supposed to believe that frothy green poop is a thing. Is Mummy playing a joke on me? But it turns out it is a thing, Dory – unless everyone online is in on the joke. The frothy green stuff materialises when there has been a user error, either in the baby operating the boob or in the boob-owner, who has probably withdrawn her services ahead of time. If this shows up, you need more booby action. I wonder – if I tell your mother that Daddy's poop is frothy and green will she extend me the same courtesy?

- Black-flecked poop. This one sounds nasty, and it is nasty – but mainly for the Mummies. The black-flecked stuff is caused by swallowing blood from a bleeding nipple. Ouch. Mummies get the rough end of the stick in all of this baby-making stuff, don't they?

- Formula-fed poop, solid-fed poop, and hard and pebbly poop. I've grouped these together because, to be honest, there's only so much attention a video on baby poop can capture – regardless of the high production value of the visuals. Formula-fed poop looks like peanut butter, solid-fed poop is dark and stinky, and you get the hard and pebbly stuff when you're constipated.

- Explosive poop. Now this is one I am familiar with – all the Mummies at work talk about it. It can be elusive, but it will happen at some point. If you've not taken a point-blank round of explosive poop to the chest and face then you shouldn't even be calling yourself a parent. I can't wait.

- Slimy green poop. This one could be a sign of infection – we need to call the doctor for advice.

- Red poop. The worst kind of poop, as red means blood. I'm guessing that's another call to the doctor.

Well, I've certainly learnt something today, I'll admit that much.

Tuesday, 20 August 2019 – All The Daddies Know

I've received a message from a (male) friend. It says:

> How are you getting on living with a pregnant lady? I think it's like living with a wild animal – you have to keep it fed and watered and show it love – but also respect, because sometimes, for absolutely no reason at all, it will rip up your sofa and scratch your face. You never know what you'll get!

This is the voice of someone who has met Miss Heidi. He knows what it's like; all the Daddies know. I dare not show this to your mother. Beware Miss Heidi, Dory.

Wednesday, 21 August 2019 – Hiccups

Hiccups, Dory! Your first ones. It's beautiful. I put my ear to Mummy's tummy and listen. *Hiccup. Hiccup. Hiccup.*

They're sounding off with surprising regularity – every few seconds. If that doesn't bring a smile to any expecting parent's face, then I'd posit that they regret some of their more recent lifestyle choices.

Aside from baby hiccups being cute and adorable, there's good news, developmentally speaking. Baby hiccups (the internet tells me they're called 'foetal hiccups') are a sign that you're developing your diaphragm by practising breathing.

Right now, you're breathing in amniotic fluid rather than air, and that causes hiccups.

I read one article that suggests this can be taken as confirmation that your brain and spinal cord are working. Both of your parents enthusiastically agree that this is a good thing.

Another listen. *Hiccup. Hiccup. Hiccup.* My heart melts.

Thursday, 22 August 2019 – Shared Parental Leave

I've spent the afternoon reading up on Shared Parental Leave (SPL). Even if I had ten Rosetta Stones and Elon Musk's uninterrupted assistance for one afternoon this area of government policy would still confuse me.

Let's start with what I think I understand. At the time of writing, Mummies have fifty-two weeks of maternity support from the government, which means they can choose to take up to one year off work to look after their babies. The UK government will provide financial support for some of that time.

It's less complicated for Daddies. Traditionally, they get two weeks off when the baby is born. After that, they return to the workforce full time.

I'm not interested in taking two weeks' paternity leave – I want longer.

Fortunately, there has been some sensible discussion down at Westminster: in 2015, the government took a stab at improving equality as far as Daddies are concerned. Their efforts resulted in the Shared Parental Leave policy – a policy that allows Mummies to give some of their fifty-two weeks' maternity support over to the Daddies.

How brilliant is that, Dory? For the first time ever, Daddies have the option of staying at home with their newborns longer than the standard two weeks.

It's no secret that the role of a Daddy has undergone a definition overhaul in recent years – to be honest, I'm not sure myself of what the expectations of Daddies are today. Your Grandad Tools never changed a single nappy. But, like every other father of his generation, he was never expected to.

Still, the SPL policy acknowledges that times are changing – and I want in.

It's not all rainbows and end-credit Marvel-movie stingers, though – there are trade-offs to consider. For every week that the Mummy gives the Daddy, she has one week fewer before she has to go back to work. There are multi-tiered financial implications to consider. And not all employee benefits are created equal. We need to weigh everything up.

Which is what we have done; we've considered all of the above, and we want to take advantage of the Shared Parental Leave option. I want extra time at home to bond with you and I want to help Mummy out as much as possible, particularly during the early stages, as she'll be nursing her front-bottom ouchie. Or she might be recovering from a C-section, where the average recovery time is six to eight weeks. Not to mention having a brand-new baby to look after.

Lovely stuff – where do I sign?

But it's not that simple. I can't send an email to my employer to say I'm taking eleven weeks' SPL. I need to complete an application. And that's the kicker, Dory. The SPL application policy has not been designed for simpletons like your father.

I'm not sure what the stats are on parents taking advantage of the SPL, but I can guarantee the figures would improve if the policy were easier to understand. I've read through the policy documents a dozen times, and I'm still getting confused. Can someone please make the process user-friendly? It's giving me a bloody headache.

Friday, 23 August 2019 – Karma

Mummy has been watching one of those programmes that show clips of people having accidents or being the victims of practical jokes. She is pissing herself laughing at their misfortune. Literally – she has actually pissed herself.

I believe this is known in pregnancy terms as a 'thing'.

Saturday, 24 August 2019 – What's Left To Get?

According to Mummy, this is what we have left to acquire ahead of your arrival: buggy; sling; nappy bag; more reusable nappies; disposable nappies – the eco-friendliest ones we can find; coming-home outfit – very important (according to you know who), despite us already having enough baby clothes to fill Santa's sleigh twice over; mattress for cot; mattress for Moses basket; Ewan the Dream Sheep (even I've heard of these white-noise angels that go baa); Gro-egg thermometer; baby monitor; formula (just in case the boob doesn't work out); swaddle blankets; changing mat; two sets of crib sheets (why aren't these called 'bed sheets'?); and a bulb syringe – I've heard about this from one of the Daddies at work: it's great for excavating snotty debris from nasal passages.

As you can see, we still have a fair bit to acquire, but at least we have a well-planned list. Life is a lot easier to navigate when you have one of those.

Sunday, 25 August 2019 – Why Do We Have Babies?

While we're chatting over homemade burgers, it transpires that Mummy, Granny Smurf and I are guilty of visiting your nursery on occasion and standing in the middle of the room to spend a few seconds looking around. I'm not sure why we do this.

It makes me question why we have babies in the first place. Is it an innate biological desire to continue the human race? Is it a survival instinct, as we know that one day we'll get old and feeble and will need our children to look after us? Or is it a longing for human contact that is difficult to replicate with non-family members?

The answers to these questions may seem self-evident, but right now we're at a strange point in time – in uncharted waters, if you will. The population is growing dangerously large, to the extent that it's reportedly threatening the prospects for our long-term survival on the planet.

Care for the elderly is available. The services aren't always as advertised and there are some well-documented shoddy providers out there, but the point is that, in the UK at least, there exist systems and services to cater for the needs of the elderly; they're not wholly dependent on the (biological) next generation to help them live out their twilight years.

What about all the children in the world that are without a Mummy or a Daddy – or even a home? Their only hope is for a family to take them in and adopt them.

But adoption is usually seen as a last resort when couples are starting a family. Why? Why spend potentially thousands of pounds on uncomfortable IVF treatments that offer no guarantee of success when you can call the adoption agency and be sure of finding a child in need? Or what about circumnavigating labour for women? Parents go to such lengths to pass on their genetic code at a time in history when we should perhaps back up and question whether we need to do that.

Is conscious choice responsible for the decisions we make about having children? I ask, because despite the above convincing reasons not to have babies, we have them, anyway.

Both your parents are guilty of this (obviously). We didn't go through IVF because, as you know, we got lucky. But we were prepared to do so.

We've talked about adoption many times in the past, even before we thought about trying to make a baby, and it's something I hope we'll revisit in the future, but that shouldn't hide the fact that we both want to experience the feeling of having our own biological child.

I think about all of this while standing in your nursery. I feel guilty, but my guilt isn't powerful enough to override whatever innate biological forces have come into play to take me to where I am now: waiting for the arrival of my first-born child.

Monday, 26 August 2019 – The Jaws Photo

Tonight, I'm flying solo as an evening guest at a wedding. Mummy is citing a third-trimester energy deficiency as her excuse for not attending.

People ask me questions about you. It's sweet; everyone is excited for us. They want to know what our birth plan is, if we know what we're having and how Mummy is coping. They offer advice: what to do, what not to do, what might happen, how to cope with a 'fill-in-the-blank' scenario. Most of our close friends have children; they've all been through it before (some recently), and they know what we're about to face. They reminisce about their own experiences, which is strangely comforting. Everything will be OK.

After the eleventh labour story comes to a close, I think about heading to the bar. But then one of my mates says to his wife, 'Are you comfortable showing him the *Jaws* photo?'

'Sure.'

The Jaws *photo?* Do I want the see this, Dory? Probably. She takes out her phone, finds the photo and shows it to me. I'm looking at a picture of her in a birthing pool. She's beaming with love and pride as she cradles her newborn baby boy, having delivered him a few seconds ago. It's beautiful, and it's empowering.

I don't understand why it's called the *Jaws* pho—

Oh. Now I do. A closer look at the pool reveals the colour of the water. It's red, Dory. Blood red. And the volume of water in the pool is slightly larger than the volume needed to fill your average kettle.

It's time for that drink, Dory.

I can't get the *Jaws* photo out of my mind; the picture of the smiling Mummy doesn't match up with the loss of blood revealed in the pool. Wasn't she in agony? But the pain is secondary; outranking pain, at least in this example, is love.

One of the many things I've learnt about women and babies recently is that there is no such thing as a boring or uneventful birth. I've listened to many women give detailed (not to mention graphic) accounts of their experiences, and every single one of them has a different narrative. But they all follow a similar pattern of dramatic episodes: birth plans going out of the window, complications with the delivery, consultants unexpectedly called in, long labours, surgery and much more. And that doesn't even take into consideration the pain that Mummies endure. It's tough. I guess all parents have their own versions of a *Jaws* photo saved in the albums of their lives.

Women are the true warriors of our species.

Next up is the unconditional love you're rewarded with when you hold your baby for the first time, having gone through all of that drama and suffering. The *Jaws* photo illustrates this. Every Mummy I've spoken to tells me that the special moment when you hold your baby is worth all the agonising ones that came before.

As a man who will never experience what it's like to go through labour, I find that mind-blowing. Admittedly, I'm saying this before I've witnessed the experience up close, but I can't think of anything in the world that is worth that much pain, that much suffering and all those potentially life-altering physical changes to your body. Yet every Mummy says childbirth is worth all of that.

Incredible.

And many Mummies opt to go through the experience again and again. It's one thing to have a baby not knowing what the process entails, but to put yourself through that experience knowing what it takes – that's something else.

I wonder what our version of the *Jaws* photo will look like.

Tuesday, 27 August 2019 – There She Blows

I empathise with the man standing in front of me. It's not his fault. He can't be responsible for the manufacturing standards of every single product that the company he works for sells. He's just a customer-service advisor who takes payments for goods. It's bad luck that he's working his shift right now. I look into his eyes, Dory; they're the eyes of a kind man – one with forbearance. Good job, because I know someone who's about to test-drive the shit out of his patience.

'I need to return this fan!'

No prizes for guessing whose voice that is, Dory.

'Oh, OK. What seems to be the problem?'

It was a blink-and-you'll-miss-it moment, but the advisor checked out your bump, Dory. He knows he's treading on wafer-thin ice.

'It's missing all the parts to put it together, which wasn't helpful last night when it was roasting hot,' Mummy says.

Time slows down for me and the advisor, Dory, and I watch as he retreats into his mind to work through an appropriate response to a heavily-pregnant woman. I can see the cogs rotating and the gears churning. His slightly raised right eyebrow suggests to me that he doubts the validity of Mummy's claims, but he knows what he risks (his life) if he brazenly dares to challenge a woman in her third trimester.

After a few moments, he concludes his analysis of the situation. He exits the solitude of his mind and begins to respond to Mummy – his raised eyebrow drops, and he affects a sympathetic smile. The survival instincts of this man are strong.

'Well then, we'd better get that replaced for you immediately. Please help yourself to an alternative.'

'Oh, OK … thanks,' Mummy says.

I think your mother is secretly disappointed that he didn't give her an excuse to get the claws out. Or worse, morph into you-know-who.

We're back at the car, in possession of a replacement fan. 'Is it worth taking a look in the box,' I say, 'in case the fan is part of a bad batch, and the bits are missing again?'

Between the two of us, we unbox all the parts and take a quick inventory of what we've got, using the instruction manual as a reference point.

'I don't fucking believe this; they're not here again.'

Mummy's gone – Miss Heidi is here. Shit.

'Bastards. Where are the fucking screws?'

It gets worse, Dory – it gets stratospherically worse. I've realised exactly what's going on here. First of all, Mummy is incorrect. The parts are here, and I am almost certain they were there in the fan we returned.

Her confusion is understandable, though. She was looking for a bag of screws, which is standard in this type of product. But not in this instance. In an attempt to make life easier, the manufacturers have pre-fitted screws to all the parts. This means that you the consumer unscrew them, assemble the parts and retighten the screws, but with the right parts joined together. Not the worst idea in the world – the right screws are in the right holes so you can't mistakenly select the wrong ones from the pack.

I'm about to point that out to Miss Heidi, but I squeeze the brakes just in time. Like the customer-service chap before me, I retreat into the depths of my mind and have a conversation with myself about a response strategy that won't aggravate the situation.

I conclude that it's not smart to point out that Miss Heidi has made a mistake; I need a different approach, and so I pretend I've not noticed anything – for now.

Instead, I deliver an Oscar-winning performance of inspecting the parts, playing the role of Sherlock Holmes looking for clues to help unravel the mystery of the missing screws.

After an appropriate amount of time passes – enough to convince Miss Heidi that I'm as angry and grief-stricken as she is – I make my move. 'What's that?' I say.

'What's what?'

'I think there's a tiny screw in one of those parts.' The exaggeration I'm pulling here cannot be overstated. I make like I'm in a desert and have seen a glint in the far distance. Is it real? Is it a mirage? Do my eyes deceive me?

'Well, I can't see a screw.'

I point to it while at the same time reiterating how small and difficult this piece of metal is to see. I ignore the fact that the screw is silver and the fan is white: ergo, it's easy to see – even without glasses.

Miss Heidi spends a long-drawn-out thirty seconds looking back and forth between the silver screw and the instruction manual.

'OK, well that's one screw, what about the rest of the parts?'

'I'm sure they're all here,' I say. Which I am, Dory; I checked while Miss Heidi was devouring the instruction manual.

'What about this part here?' she says, stabbing a finger at the manual.

'It's right here,' I say, pointing it out.

'What about this one?'

'Right here.' I repeat the above action.

'That one then?'

'Below your left hand.'

We go through this exercise for every single fucking part.

I assume you'll take my word for it when I tell you that I was later blamed for this entire episode and that we exchanged a word count of zero on the car trip back home.

Wednesday, 28 August 2019 – Trigonometry

I've not thought about trigonometry since I was at school. And I wouldn't exactly call it a passion of mine, even then. Yet I find myself returning to it this evening, courtesy of your mother.

I'll explain what we're doing first, and then I'll tell you why, Dory.

All triangles have three points: A, B and C. We are examining the relationship between those three points in one particular triangle located in our bedroom. Point A is me, your Daddy; point B is the Matriarch; and point C represents a fan (the type that blows air). It's the same fan we procured yesterday. The fan is in our bedroom, and it's operating at maximum speed, oscillating and blowing cool air in the direction of points A and B by turns.

Point B of the triangle (the Matriarch) has had one of her not-unusual rear-end chemistry accidents, expelling a gas cloud with enough force that it finds its way into the path of point C, the fan – which sends it back my way (point A) quicker than a return of serve from Roger Federer.

The cloud-particles permeate the air with rapid efficiency, as if all the orcs and goblins of Middle Earth had come together to invade an unattended allotment plot.

It tastes worse than shit – in fact, I'd love the taste of shit right now.

And that is the reason trigonometry has re-entered my life after a two-decade hiatus.

Friday, 30 August 2019 – Adding Up The Numbers

After months of delays and additional works (involving a lot more money), our remortgage is complete. This means I can again review our finances.

Remember, Dory, we were told our chances of making a baby were slim. No matter what financial struggles life throws at us, I will try never to lose sight of that.

After running the numbers, it's tight. We don't have a lot of wiggle room for anything other than the bills. But it fits. Considering we're about to go from a two-income household to a one-income home with a baby (and a house-renovation loan), I don't think that's too bad for day one. As long as we put thought into everything we're buying and ask ourselves if we need it, I think we'll be OK.

I'm travelling back home with Mummy, and I've been discussing the outputs of my financial calculations. She agrees wholeheartedly that we need to put more thought behind what we spend. It's nice to see she's on board.

'So how was your day?' I say.

'Good. I met a gypsy, and she made me buy some lucky heather and a crystal.'

'Right,' I say. 'She *made* you buy that?'

'Well, she didn't make me, but it's bad luck not to buy lucky heather from a gypsy, and my Mum would have had a heart attack if I'd refused.'

'How much was it?'

'A tenner, but I haggled her down to a fiver.'

'…'

Saturday, 31 August 2019 – Rules For Social Gatherings When Attending With Children

We're at a child-friendly christening party. I've learnt the following:

- If you attend a social gathering with your children, the most you can hope for is up to three minutes of uninterrupted conversation with your friends before parenting needs swoop in and hijack your attention.
- Babies get heavy quickly. I tried to bottle-feed my mate's four-month-old standing up and had to excuse myself after five minutes to go and sit on the stairs.
- If parents attend these things together, you will witness some of the masterful and creative strategies that they have devised for offloading children on to one another. It's like watching a professional table tennis rally: 'I bet you can't find Daddy', 'Quick, Mummy will leave you forever if you don't go and find her,' and 'I think Daddy will die if you don't give him a cuddle for at least twenty minutes – that's adult minutes, not the bullshit you think is a minute.'

I'm taking notes, Dory.

September

Sunday, 1 September 2019 – I'm Busy

'Do you want to come to IKEA with me to look around?' your mother says.

'Oh, I would love to,' I say, 'except I can't. I'm busy ... with the new nail gun that I've this exact second reserved online to go and collect in-store. I'm planning to introduce it to the back of my throat and my eyeballs. Thanks for the invitation, though.'

Monday, 2 September 2019 – I Know What That's Like

A woman in my team explained to me today that she spent her entire weekend hating her husband for no reason. But there is a reason. A perfectly good reason. One that I wouldn't have had the foggiest idea about seven months ago. She's pregnant, Dory. And that means Miss Heidi. Beware Miss Heidi, Dory.

This marks the first time I have participated in a pregnancy conversation where my experience means I can relate to what's being said.

Tuesday, 3 September 2019 – Hacking And Slashing

Thrust.

Block.

Swing.

Clang.

The force of Link's sword meeting the enemy's shield causes his balance to abandon him temporarily. The sound of the weapons clashing explodes through the television speaker – this is gripping stuff, Dory.

Link recovers his balance with a split second to spare, which might not seem like much, but in the heat of battle a split second can be the difference between a vanquished foe and a restart from the last save point.

Come on Link, you gangly, pointy-eared, gorgeous creature. We've got goblins to smite; let's fucking have it!

I can now select an attack from a long list of options, but I've barely mastered the basics, and my neurons are firing too quickly for me to get a handle on things. I recall my childhood computer-gaming years. If in doubt, hit every button on the controller as many times as you can and hope for the right outcome. I commence randomised button-bashing. Meanwhile, Link somersaults backwards, but then immediately launches forwards with a devastating melee attack.

Poof.

The goblin has vanished in a literal puff of smoke.

'Any more of you fuckheads wanna go at it, cos I'm ready!' I mean it, Dory; I'm having a lot of fun. I'm really fired up.

Zelda is my all-time favourite computer game. Mummy bought the latest version for me as a Christmas present, and it's remained in the wrapper for eight months.

I kept promising myself I'd play it, but then something always got in the way. Or at least, that's the excuse I tell myself. It's an excuse I know by heart.

The truth is, I'm guilty of not taking enough time for myself to do things for the sheer pleasure of it. I admit this is a weakness of mine. It's one that I need to work on, but I'm also hoping you will help Daddy here.

Something I'm conscious of, going into fatherhood, is remaining present and living in the moment to watch you grow up. I know how quickly it will happen. I've not met a single parent who claims otherwise. Some nights will be impossibly long, but I know the years will pass by quicker than the flapping wings of a hummingbird.

Maintaining presence of mind is something I want to practise; even if the first step is unwrapping a computer game that's been sitting on the shelf for eight months. This is where you will help Daddy. You'll help make me accountable for every single one of my choices, whether you realise it or not.

There are more goblins arriving onscreen, Dory. They look pissed off. In their defence, I have just decapitated one of their pals. I'd be a bit peeved if I were in their position. But I'm not in their position – I'm in Link's position, and I will be for at least another thirty minutes. I'm not going to worry about my to-do list, any household chores or personal development goals. I'm going to fuck some shit up with a sword.

And I'm going to enjoy doing it.

Wednesday, 4 September 2019 – Names, Names And More Names

Coming up with names is hard, Dory. It's taken us months to create a modest list for boys' and girls' names, because we've binned most of them off. We're finding boys' names are the hardest. Anything we liked previously we're now not keen on, and anything new that we like gets rejected when we come to the stress-testing phase (more on that below).

It feels as though we're climbing a mountain, but picking a name that Mummy and Daddy both like only gets us halfway up. Once we have a name, we need to ensure it holds up against the pressures of spoken syntax, rhythm and school-playground bullying potential. For every name we add to our list, we lose four others.

Let's look at stress testing. The first stress test is to add my surname to the end of any possible first name, and then say it out loud. My surname is not a 'one size fits all' one, and because of this we ask many first-name contenders to return back down the mountain. They are rejects.

Our next stress test is to step into the shoes of every playground-roaming arsehole that you can imagine and try to anticipate any potential bullying taunts they might hurl at you. It would break my heart if you came home from school one day and told me that a bully had come up with a nasty way to make fun of you because of a poor name choice on the part of your parents. Even Mummy and Daddy find unfortunate naming choices funny, odd or terrible.

My favourite naming faux pas is 'Anna Sassin'. At what point did Anna's parents realise her name sounded like 'an assassin'? Although as naming mistakes go, you could do a lot worse than having a name that sounds like 'an assassin'. What about some of these classics? Carrie Oakey, Stan Still, Barb Dwyer, Jenny Taylor … there are trap doors everywhere, Dory.

It gets worse, as it's not only first names we need to consider – it's middle names as well. I did question why we needed a middle name, but Mummy responded by telling me that we have to have one because we do.

Always nice to have these intellectual discussions with your mother.

We've decided not to name you after any of your extended family. On one hand, this affords us additional creative freedom, but then on the other, we have yet another naming decision to make, which doubles the workload of an already time-consuming task.

Once we settle on a middle name, we repeat the above stress-testing steps, saying your potential full name out loud.

Putting the above into practice reveals that most of our name choices either have too many syllables or are over-stuffed with vowels that fall in the wrong order, so that when you say them, they sound clunky, and the speaker has to work a lot harder than they should.

If we're struggling to say some of our name choices without verbally tripping up, then what chance does a supply teacher taking the register at school have? The other kids will strike.

Part of me thinks that this exercise is pointless and that I shouldn't be worried about what one little arsehole at school might say to you. But that opinion merely reflects my age and my ignorance of how things are at school nowadays. That said, I'm sure things have changed since I was at school. But if I cast my mind back, the memories come flooding back

– painfully. Some of the kids in my class were little cunts, Dory. Children don't realise how hurtful their words can be. If a bully receives a pleasing crowd reaction to a nasty joke about someone's name, he's going to keep doing it. I'll be damned if I'm going to be the one to give the bully a leg up and make my kid easy pickings.

Having that many obstacles to overcome, although exhausting, has benefits, because we are now left with a shortlist (and I do mean short). We have one girl's name that we have liked since our first naming session. It remains a favourite. And now we have a middle name to match it; one that gets over the stress-test hurdles. I think it will be the one we go with, but I'm not telling you what it is, in case it isn't the final choice.

We have two boys' names on our list that we like. Mummy prefers one of them, and I prefer the other, but we don't have any middle names yet.

The naming journey continues.

I will say this – I thought picking names would be one of the more enjoyable elements of the pregnancy. I was wrong – it's about as enjoyable as getting a blow job from a vampire.

Thursday, 5 September 2019 – I Ask The Same Questions Every Day

Mummy is thirty weeks pregnant today. Congratulations to all of us, but especially to Mummy. Dory, this could mean that seventy-five per cent of our pregnancy journey is complete. Or it could mean that we're eighty-five per cent of the way – or only seventy per cent. Since my day of discovery, we've been on a parental timeline, each day taking us closer to your birth.

Every second of every day I ask myself questions. Are you OK? Is Mummy OK? Will the birth be OK? Will Mummy cope? Is everything ready at home? Do we have what we need? What have I not thought of? Will work approve my Shared Parental Leave application? Am I a selfish prick for wanting an extra Sky box in the spare bedroom? Do we need a new car? How will I cope, being a Daddy? Do I have what it takes to give you what you need? Does Mummy? Will we work well together as parents? Will our relationship grow and develop as a result of having a baby? Am

I doing enough to prepare? When should I book a baby first-aid course? What if I can't remember everything from the baby first-aid course and something happens to you? Do I deserve the opportunity to be a parent?

I think about those questions and a million more every day and all the time: when I feel you kick, when I don't feel you kick, when Mummy turns over and makes one of her farm-animal-noise impressions to indicate she's in pain, when I'm brushing my teeth, when I'm looking at my bank balance, when I stand in your nursery, when I write to you, when I don't write to you.

I love the fact we call you 'Dory', and I love the fact that there is a piece of music called 'Shells' about a child searching for its parents. Its poignancy is unequalled, and it helps me stay sane while these questions cycle through my mind, because it provides the answers. You're OK. Mummy is doing better than OK; she's doing great. The birth will be fine; Mummy will be surrounded by professionals who have done this hundreds of times. Mummy won't cope; she will soar. We will have everything we need at home, and what we don't have, we can get. Bringing you home is all that we need to do. There are a million things I've not thought of, but so what? I will learn. Work will approve my Shared Parental Leave application. No, I'm not a selfish prick; it's smart to have a spare room that's comfortable for all of us to use. No, we don't need a new car. Fuck knows how I will cope, but I will. Yes, I do have what it takes. So does Mummy. We are a team; not an unshakeable one – we're human – but we have roots that go deep, and they will not fail us. We will grow. Nothing will prepare me for what I'm about to face, so I have to stop trying so hard and chill out. And I'll speak to the midwife about the baby first-aid course. I won't forget. Fuck, yes; I deserve this opportunity.

Thirty weeks today, kiddo. You might not be knocking on the door yet, but you've passed the front gate, and you're crawling up the garden path. I can hear the faint crunch of disturbed gravel. Not long to go – you know what to do.

Friday, 6 September 2019 – Dory's Kicking Schedule

Your daily movements have fallen into a routine. I asked Mummy to write them down for the day.

6.45 a.m. Woke up to Dory kicking.

8.45 a.m. Started moving after I had eaten breakfast.

11.20 a.m. Big movement and a big push outwards.

12.21 p.m. General movement.

2.30 p.m. General movement.

3.33 p.m. General movement.

4.15 p.m. Hiccups.

6.00 p.m. General movement.

7.30 p.m. General movement.

10.00 p.m. Raving time. Lots of movement when we got into bed (our favourite moment to have family time talking to you and playing music for you).

Saturday, 7 September 2019 – Our First NCT Class

Today is our first National Childbirth Trust (NCT) class, Dory. It's a paid-for service. Couples living in the same area who are expecting their first child come together to learn about what to expect during labour and the first few weeks of parenthood – and lots of other useful bits, I'm sure. We can form new friendships, and we can access helpful resources.

There are eight other couples in total. The Daddies don't look thrilled to be here; most of them look as if their participation was a result of a direct order from their partners.

The course is being run by a lady named Katie. Katie has three children so she's familiar with the joys of childbirth. After the course introduction, we get right down to it. The first section covers making decisions in labour, and it features case studies and acronyms like BRAIN: benefits, risks, alternatives, intuition, nothing – which is a model to help with the decision-making process during labour.

Next, we're separated into two groups: Mummies and Daddies. We Daddies are given two tasks, each designed to encourage empathy with our partners by providing us with an understanding of what it's like for the Mummies to carry and birth a baby.

Our first task is to fit a ten-centimetre ball through a model of the female pelvis. The ball represents an average-sized baby's head. I'm up first, Dory. I hold the pelvis upright and prepare to wrestle with the ball. I expect a tussle.

But there's no tussle – and no empathy. No wrestling is required; the ball falls straight through. All of us Daddies are confused. Maybe it was a fluke. Let's see how the others fare.

It wasn't a fluke; the ball falls through the pelvis each time and this has now become rather amusing. We're about to start throwing the ball through the pelvis from a distance when Katie steps in and politely invites us to begin task number two.

Task two sees the Daddies having to sort through a selection of objects. We need to figure out which objects are of the same weight as the following: the baby, the placenta, the amniotic fluid and the amniotic sac. *What about the extra ten pounds of added boob weight?* Once we've worked our way through the list, we put everything in a rucksack and wear it in a front-facing position. The aim here is to replicate what it's like to carry a baby.

There are two reasons why this exercise is flawed. First, we're all grown men, and so we're unlikely to experience the same strain as women do if the weight we're lifting is not adjusted for our body structures. Second, we've been asked to carry the rucksack for a few seconds – women carry babies for a little longer than that (I know at least that much about pregnancy).

Once again, no empathy is elicited. The Daddies pass the 'baby' around and shrug. None of us sees what the problem is. We quickly become bored, and so I harmlessly enquire of the guys how long it takes for their partners to roll over in bed these days, noting that it takes mine so long that she has to book time off from work.

I feel like we're really bonding here.

But this isn't a boys' club, Dory; we're here to learn, and we're here to support our partners – so I ask one of the Daddies to lie down with the bag attached, and we begin timing how long it takes him to roll over.

Spoiler alert: he is considerably quicker than Mummy.

Fuck – our activities have attracted the interest of the Mummies – especially your own, Dory, who takes one look at me and knows I'm the man responsible for the rollover exercise.

We're back sitting around the circle and the course leader asks all us Daddies to give feedback about the rucksack exercise. We glance at each other, and in a split second we realise that the formulation of our collective response will need careful handling. Our story needs to be straight; after all, we're in this together. We work on our answers, and we agree to support one another no matter what. We achieve all of this in absolute silence, and in under two seconds.

'Not only was it heavy, but it was awkward as well,' says one of the Daddies.

As planned, the rest of us nod excessively in agreement – like politicians backing up a colleague proposing a new bill in the House of Commons.

'I can't imagine what that's like for nine months,' says another.

I'm desperate to point out that carrying the full weight of the baby only comes at the end of the pregnancy, but I don't. Instead, I stick to the script and back up the Daddies with my own comments – which are fully aligned with the plan.

The Mummies are suspicious; they're not buying it. But we've given them nothing to grasp at. There are no flaws in our story; no misalignments. The Daddies live to fight another day.

And now Katie takes us through a mindfulness-meditation routine. This is one for the Mummies; it's to help them work through contractions. The course leader is using metaphor and comparing contractions to a hurricane. She describes it as devastating and brutal, which wouldn't be my opening line if I were trying to reduce the anxiety levels of any woman who's not got long to go before experiencing labour.

But new information is coming to light, Dory: the devastation and brutality is everything outside the contraction. The contraction is at the centre of the hurricane. It's calm and peaceful. I'm not quite following, but most of the Mummies are in the zone, so I suppose it's working for them – but surely contractions are anything but peaceful, right?

Still, I slowly feel myself getting pulled in; I'm relaxed. I achieve a few seconds of complete mindfulness where I'm entirely present – a moment which comes to an abrupt end when one of the Daddies almost falls off his partner's birthing ball.

And now we're back in a space where this is all quite funny, and I'm wondering when we can take a break so I can eat biscuits.

Sunday, 8 September 2019 – Parent Boot Camp

Today marks the start of an intense week of parental training for Mummy and me. It will be the nearest we will get to observing parenthood up close for an extended period of time.

Our training takes place just outside Barcelona – we're off on our holidays with four other couples and their kids: four babies, a toddler and a 3-year-old. The Daddies in this group are all old uni mates. You will spend a lot of time with their children, growing up.

This holiday will give us a much richer experience than, say, babysitting Haylee for a few hours. This isn't only about learning how to look after babies, Dory; this is about how Mummies and Daddies function together as a team, and we're aiming to distil what works and what doesn't, so that we can borrow what we'll need for our parenting journey.

Mummy is over thirty weeks pregnant; we're told to expect you any time from week thirty-seven. Despite an early arrival being unlikely, I need to prepare for one nevertheless. I've taken the following precautions: packed Mummy's pregnancy notes and rubber gloves (I'm not joking); noted down where the nearest hospitals to our resort are; translated several phrases into Spanish* for medical staff, explaining how far gone Mummy is, that she has Crohn's and that we have insurance; downloaded local maps and a Spanish-language resource for offline use.

We're at the airport, having just met up with everybody. There's excitement, but no one can fully relax. It's immediately apparent to me how different this holiday will be compared to previous ones. Mummies

---

* It was later pointed out to me that Catalan is the dominant language in Barcelona.

and Daddies are on the lookout for potential threats and for poor decisions their children might make, and they all seem to have an anxious awareness of the unknown.

Amy has taken her nine-month-old daughter for a nappy change. Her husband, James, thinks she's taking too long. Then again, he always thinks she takes too long.

'You watch, mate, she'll come back and make out she's returned from a double tour in Afghanistan,' he says.

Amy returns battle-worn and weary from the front line. She needs support. Her first choice is James, her husband, and father of their daughter. James is the one she can always count on.

'You would not believe what I've gone through in there,' she says.

It's an easy one for James; he doesn't need to do much at all – listen, nod in the right places and make sympathetic noises.

Instead, he travels down another path: he responds by bursting out laughing, and then says, 'See? See? What did I tell you?'

He says this to me within earshot of Amy ... and everyone else in our group.

I'm conflicted, Dory; James is one of Daddy's closest friends. I've known him for fifteen years. He's funny and ruthlessly quick at coming up with amusing perspectives on life, right on the spot, reacting to events as they are unfolding before his eyes. So, my default response is to laugh. After all, it is funny.

But there are other considerations, Dory. Amy does not see the funny side of the situation. Not only has she had to deal with a screaming baby, but she has had to do that in public. She's also understandably resentful towards James, who has no right to assume he knows what went on during this particular nappy change – he wasn't there.

Finally, I've also got your Mummy giving me 'the look' – as if to say, 'Don't you dare encourage this. Don't you fucking dare!'

I didn't dare (or I did, but I turned around so no one could see me).

An hour later and we're boarding our flight. The airline seems to have stuck all the families with young children at the back of the aircraft (along with you, Mummy and me). All the parents look as if they're about to be burnt at the stake. They tell themselves it will all be worth it when they get there.

There's a mother and her toddler (not part of our group) sitting in James and Amy's seats. James notices and politely points this out to the woman, who takes a dread-filled look at her toddler. You can read it in her eyes, Dory. She looks like she's about to have her liver removed with a steak knife – without anaesthetic.

She takes a deep breath and explains to her son that they're in the wrong seats and that they need to move. The toddler's reaction is instantaneous and ferocious: he screams so loudly that I fear for the structural integrity of the aircraft.

Such a drama, just to move seats.

The correct seats are only two metres away, but in many ways, the journey this mother must take is like the one Leonardo DiCaprio took in *The Revenant.*

The Mummy wrestles with her screaming toddler and eventually traverses the two-metre distance to the correct seats. She doesn't apologise, Dory. Nor does she need to. She's in the company of those who know. The aircraft takes off and it's not long before the captain gives the all-clear for passengers to unfasten their seatbelts. Children are quick to climb onto their seats and adopt giraffe postures, craning their heads over the backs of their seats to investigate their surroundings and satisfy their curiosity. Parents deploy quick hands and stern words to stop them from invading the space of other passengers. When quick hands and stern words fail, sweets and treats do the trick.

Our friend Jess is breastfeeding her youngest boy. All of a sudden, she winces. 'Daniel, don't bite Mummy,' she says. I wince too, Dory, because I know that, despite Daniel only being a few months old, his bottom two teeth have come through already.

Ouch.

'Honestly, it's not that painful any more; it just takes me by surprise,' says Jess. 'After having two kids in quick succession, I've got nipples like toughened leather.'

There is no moment during the flight that doesn't feature at least one child partaking in one of the following: crying, sulking, arguing, climbing, fighting, making a mess or being a nuisance.

It's funny how I'm noticing this stuff in the way that I am. I've taken many flights in my life, often in the company of children that aren't associated with me. But I've never taken a trip with other people's children knowing that I'm about to become a father. Before, if a child sat near me and decided to scream at his sister and tell her how much he hated her, I would see it as a temporary annoyance, and eliminate it with a set of noise-cancelling headphones.

But not on this trip, Dory. Right now, I'm trying to figure out what I would do in these situations. It's tough – some children are relentlessly efficient at focusing all their attention on one goal, such as acquiring an extra packet of crisps.

My headphones remain in my bag. Like I said at the start, this trip calls for a sharpened pencil and a blank page. I am a student, Dory, and I'd be wise not to skip lectures.

It's evening. We've arrived at our villa, and all the kids are asleep – for now. The villa we're staying in is right on the money. It has an outdoor patio that's blanketed in astroturf. Trees frame the patio's outside edges, ready to fend off tomorrow's sunlight. It's perfect, especially if you're a shade-seeker with a baby. Rounding out the amenities we have a hammock, a pool table, a tennis court, a swimming pool, six bedrooms, five bathrooms and blackout blinds in every room.

So far, so good.

Monday, 9 September 2019 – Field Research

Babies are joyful company in the morning, Dory. A night's sleep, punctuated by feeds, has armed them with enough smile ammunition to make me question why anyone wouldn't want children. These are the moments parents savour; the ones that make carting the extra ten pieces of baby-related luggage through airport security worthwhile.

I do an almost perfect job of dismantling the mood by announcing to the group that I enjoyed eight hours of uninterrupted sleep.

169

'Just you wait,' they say, wiping the venom from their chins.

Even Mummy glares at me – it seems you're responsible for keeping her awake in the night. Don't feel bad; Mummy loves you.

We have a day of on-the-job parenting and relaxation in the villa ahead of us – or is that an oxymoron; parenting and relaxing? Anyway, I have the opportunity to conduct some of the field research I'd planned to do on this trip.

I ask lots of questions, Dory. I ask about routines, feeding, what works and what doesn't work. There is a consensus among everyone that the most detailed and meticulous plans can be blown out of the water by a non-compliant infant. It reminds me of a Mike Tyson quote: 'Everyone has a plan until they get punched in the mouth.'

Something that might sound silly is a concern I have about watching TV in bed when you're here. I worry about the light and noise stimulation provoking bad habits that become hard to break when it comes to relocating you to the nursery. But everyone tells me my fears are unwarranted – you will slot nicely into my evening routine of watching *Archer* on Netflix before bed.

It's such a silly concern, but the fact I've written it down suggests it's important to me. Which it is – I bloody love *Archer*.

Tuesday, 10 September 2019 – Perhaps The Greatest Quiz-Team Name Ever

It's raining. The weather forecast says that the rain will continue all day, so we can't play outside in the pool. Instead, we've decided to head out and explore the local area for something to do. But every time we're about to leave the villa, one of the babies needs something – feeding, changing or a nap. After the fourth failed escape attempt, we decide to resign ourselves to a day indoors.

There's another lesson here, Dory. Travelling with one baby means you can work around its schedule, but when you have multiple small humans on different schedules, group activities become difficult to choreograph.

The day isn't wasted, though; I've been introduced to a wonderful children's book called *The Wonky Donkey*. I didn't realise how much joy an adult could derive from a book intended for children. It's great fun.

There are others: *Oi Frog!*, *That's Not My Penguin*, *Hairy Maclary*, and *The Gruffalo*, which I had heard of but never read. I'm compiling a list for you; we've already identified an area in your nursery for bookshelves.

While I've been getting up to speed with children's books, James has spent a large part of his day putting together a quiz for the group. It's Mummies versus Daddies, and there's a bonus point for the team with the best quiz name. The Mummies knock it out of the park: inspired by *The Wonky Donkey*, they've called themselves 'The Milky, Manky, Grumpy, Frumpy, Sleepy, Weepy, Saggy, Baggy, Scrummy Mummies'. Take a bow, Mummies!

All the babies are asleep and the quiz begins; the Daddies definitely don't use their smartphones to cheat …

The baby monitors are huddled together at the end of a nearby table, like emperor penguins in Antarctica. One of them goes off, sounding the alarm: 'Parents, come quickly – infant in distress!' Several anxiety-ridden faces switch their attention away from their quiz sheets and towards the group of monitors. After a few moments, all but one set of parents slump their shoulders in relief.

This happens several times throughout the evening.

———

I'm pleased to report, Dory, that at the end of the quiz, it's the Daddies who bask in victory. We don't have time to marvel at our performance, though, as for some reason we all need to charge up our phones.

Wednesday, 11 September 2019 – Day Trip To Barcelona

Today's mission is a day trip to Barcelona city. No one is excluded; all parents and children have been conscripted for a day of sightseeing. If yesterday's failed attempt to leave the villa is anything to go by, I anticipate heavy resistance.

We will be going by train, so all we need to do is drive to the station. The mission is a go.

Hold up – one of the babies needs changing. The mission is not a go.

Ten minutes later, we're ready for another crack at departing the villa. Three, two, one, the mission is—

Wait! Another one of the babies needs changing.

A further twelve minutes elapse (two minutes more than the first time; either the nappy-changing hands weren't as dextrous as the first pair, or this nappy was considerably fuller than the last). Finally, we're driving to the train station.

Fast-forward ten minutes, and we've parked up. Parents are deploying lightweight transportation buggies for the mini-infantrymen. They secure the straps, apply camouflage cream (a.k.a. sun cream) and pull down buggy visors for extra UV protection. We reach the train-station checkpoint – two hours behind schedule.

Tickets are acquired, and we board the train. Some of our mini-infantry soldiers require feeding, but that's OK – the train is moving.

Thirty minutes later, we're walking the streets of Barcelona. We've grouped ourselves in tourist formation, and we're admiring the architecture and smiling politely as we decline the advances of on-foot retailers selling sunglasses. Finally, we're slowing down our walking pace because life has slowed down, Dory; we're living in the present and absorbing the small details of our surroundings, which we wouldn't normally get to do. This is why we come on holiday in the first place.

But such moments rarely last, and we're reminded of their transience by wailing babies. It seems we've taken our eye off the needs of our mini-infantry members. Our focus is redirected – it's time to find a base for lunch so that nappies can be changed and milk can be provided. Historical stone structures and pretty church spires are merely glimpsed as we attend to the needs of the babies.

Once our entire party has eaten, drunk, visited the bathroom and squared the bill, we're ready to resume the day. Hopefully, we can recapture some of that mood we had before lunch. Our next checkpoint is Barcelona harbour. Ten minutes later, the crying begins again. Our ranks are under strain, disunited and fracturing quicker than Evel Knievel's bones did when he landed (or didn't land) the Caesars Palace jump in '67. Despite all of that, we arrive at the harbour – the sight of which is a postcard contender, for sure.

We agree to split up and take care of everyone's needs separately: the babies want fuck knows what; the toddlers want ice cream; the adults also want ice cream and to hear less crying from their babies; and your Mummy wants a wee. I don't want anything, Dory, but coffee is offered, so I accept it – after all, I don't want to miss out on wanting something.

Forty-five minutes later, we're once again pushing the battalion forward. There must be a better way to do the whole 'day out' thing; we just haven't figured out what that is yet. Or perhaps there isn't a better way to do it, and trying to coerce babies into fitting into a shared schedule is like attempting to fit a bowling ball into a keyhole – it doesn't work.

Finally, we make it to Montjuïc Castle, which I don't recommend (at least on foot) to anyone who is seven months pregnant. Getting to it is an uphill climb, and at this time of year it's bloody hot. However, surprising no one, your mother refuses to stay behind with me, despite me promising her sweets.

Before we can explore the castle, the babies need everything: feeding, changing, cuddling, more sun cream and general attention.

After that's done, we get a good chunk of time (twenty to thirty minutes) to explore at our leisure, before we think about heading home.

We're on the train travelling back, and everyone is tired. Looking back at the day, we reckon we've achieved three things that can be filed away under sightseeing: a stroll around the city, a visit to the harbour and a tour of Montjuïc Castle. Big-group city breaks with multiple babies do not work – at least, not in the way we've tried to make it work today. Today has been a great day for learning.

Thursday, 12 September 2019 – The Next Generation

One of the Mummies is sitting upright breastfeeding her baby. She's so tired that she has fallen asleep. She's putting into practice the old adage that with babies you should sleep whenever you get a chance. Fair play.

I'm watching the other babies, and I'm having a hard time processing the notion that you will all grow up together. You might not understand this until you have children of your own, but this is a wonderful privilege. And it's a privilege that extends beyond your creation. To see you in an environment where the best of me – that's you – bonds with the best of those I hold most dear is a real passing of the torch moment for us, collectively.

Friday, 13 September 2019 – Well Played, Young Sir

I've changed few nappies in my time, and the babies I have changed were close to the newborn stage, meaning their leg movements were a lot more subdued than those of the little chap I'm looking at right now. His name is Daniel.

He can't form words yet, but he doesn't need to. It's all in his facial expressions and sporadic leg-kicking movements. This will not be easy, Dory. Daniel's expression is sadistically calm. He's challenging me with his adorable smiles. He wants me to fail – I can sense it.

The reason I'm in this position is because the other parents think it will make for a delightful little training exercise. Mummy doesn't need any training because she's had ten years' experience working in a nursery – she's changed thousands of nappies.

Your Daddy has not.

OK, Dory, from the top. Clean nappy? Check. Wipes? Check. Changing mat? Partial check. I have one, but it's the size of a napkin. Will I be OK? A quick look at the sofa confirms that its colour is a lightish brown. The gods haven't abandoned me yet.

I also have James in my corner. Good ol' James. He once nearly got arrested not far from where we're staying, for breaking into a swimming pool for a dare. He was 19 at the time and we were on a university lacrosse tour. Now he's a family man who knows more about changing nappies than I do.

'Remember, as soon as you take the nappy off, the cold air is your enemy and it's likely to stimulate another wee, and if you aren't ready to contain it, chances are he'll piss in your face, in his own face or on the sofa – so the number one rule is to hold the front of the dirty nappy upright to catch anything that comes out during the changeover.'

'He might piss in my face …? They don't have that kind of range, do they?'

'Or something worse might happen,' says James.

'Worse?'

James nods. 'It can happen.'

Then I remember the video that your mother showed me a few weeks ago about the different types of baby poop – one of them was the explosive sort. Damn.

OK. I'm ready, Dory. On my marks, get set, go!

I release both tabs of the nappy and unfold it frontwards for a look under the hood. 'What seems to be the problem, young man?' I say to Daniel, who's lying suspiciously still. He smiles. I told you he was a sadist.

A quick inspection tells me we've got a number one, but not a number two. This is looking good, Dory; I anticipate the operation will run smoothly from here on out.

I try to quickly procure a wet wipe, but it won't come out of the fucking packet. It's become a two-handed task, but as soon as I go to retract the cavalry (my left hand), I sense James in my ear reminding me not to spread my forces too thinly: 'Remember rule number one.'

I need to think, Dory, and think quickly. What can Daddy do?

I know the answer – I hold on to the wet wipe like I would the safety bar of a theme-park roller coaster and give it a shake. The pack falls to the floor, leaving me with a wet wipe in hand. Success. My other hand remains in place to hold the barrier up to catch any wee that young Daniel might feel compelled to disperse.

'Now, you want to clean his willy first, then around his balls and then give his bum a quick wipe.'

Every new Daddy could do with a James in his corner, Dory.

I move in to begin the clean-up operation, but I'm met with instant resistance from little Daniel, who's decided it's time to start flailing his legs around. *I swear he was waiting for this exact moment.*

It's now become virtually impossible to use one hand to clean Daniel and the other to hold the dirty nappy in place. Should I risk it and drop the old nappy flap to free up a spare hand to hold down his legs? One look from James says I don't want to go there.

I've gone from calm, collected and focused to a man on the edge in under two seconds. I somehow manage to get a couple of dabs in with the wipe, but his leg-flailing is so distracting that I forget what bits I've cleaned and what I haven't, and I don't know what part of the wipe I've dirtied and what part I haven't.

I need another wet wipe! Possibly another hundred wet wipes.

Luckily, the pack is still within reaching distance.

A clumsy thirty seconds ensues, and Daniel is now clean and ready for his fresh nappy.

'What side is the front?' I say desperately, looking at the fresh nappy, but with my energy levels almost fully depleted.

James is there instantly. My guardian angel. He confirms with a quick check that it's the right way round. He even helps me get it ready by peeling back the tabs.

And just when I think this ordeal is about to come to an end, Daniel decides to start crying while at the same time ramping up the leg spasms.

'OK, Daniel, just a few more seconds, buddy,' I say aloud. *If you stop kicking your fucking legs, I can get this over and done with a lot quicker.* But he keeps waving his legs like an orchestral conductor with two batons.

After a scrimmage, I get the nappy on and the tabs fastened. They're loose, but good enough. Next, I reapply his Babygro and click the poppers in place. His crying is getting intense, and his leg-flailing makes me misfire with the poppers on several occasions.

Finally, I've done it, Dory. What an ordeal it's been for your poor Daddy.

I pick Daniel up, and he stops crying immediately. He even has the fucking audacity to smile at me.

Happy Friday the thirteenth to you too, Daniel – well played!

Sunday, 15 September 2019 – What I Learnt From Our Holiday

Our holiday is over, Dory. Next time we go on holiday with Mummy it will be as a family of three.

I've learnt a lot this week, not just about parenting, but also about travelling and group dynamics with children – particularly babies.

I'm lucky to have had this experience as an observer and hands-on childcare assistant instead of an ignorant parent of a newborn, who thinks he can travel in the same way with a baby as without one. I can design our trips around what I've learnt this week.

The key takeaway for me this week is that travelling with friends and young families can work – albeit with a lot of trade-offs.

First, you can't accomplish anywhere near as much as you plan to do when looking after a baby. This might seem obvious, but even with our group factoring in extra time for looking after the babies we still miscalculated and overspent on our time budget. Our miscalculations were compounded by the presence of multiple babies – all on their own schedules. They eat and need entertaining at different times, not to mention changing, napping, settling, cuddling, and so forth.

I've always been guilty of trying to fit too much in when I travel (despite considerable experience). If I hadn't had the learning opportunities I've had this week, travelling with you and Mummy for the first time would have been a real jolt to the system.

The other currency we overspent this week was effort. The effort it takes to do something as simple as go to the beach with children is considerable. Therefore, going forward, I believe it's worth having a checklist to run through before making a decision to go somewhere. How badly do I want to do this thing? Is the effort it will take worth it? Is there an alternative that has a better cost-benefit return as far as effort is concerned? Do I have everything I need, and if not, are there resources or amenities nearby that I can call on for help? These are questions I've never had to ask myself when travelling because I've only had myself and your Mummy to worry about. But now I know that having a mental checklist will help me make better decisions and be more organised.

Overspending on effort extends beyond looking after babies. It includes day-to-day decisions that need to be made, such as what we're going to eat, who's going shopping and who will do the cooking. Understand this, Dory: a parent's energy reserves are almost always running on the reserve tank, so it can be exhausting making multiple decisions about who wants to do what, and who's going to play what role to ensure that happens. And just when you're close to making a decision, the baby needs something, and the group is thrown off its trajectory. It's tough.

But none of these problems are insoluble; they're still just obstacles to overcome. The secret to success is having amazing teamwork within the group. Everyone needs to do their bit. Whatever that is. If you're not great at cooking but you're happy to clean up, fine. Clean up every day instead of cooking a single meal. Offer to do the shopping, or entertain more than your own children for half an hour.

It's clear to me that my days of spending a week relaxing by the pool reading fiction (not that we did much of that, anyway – but you take my point) are about to leave me behind. This is something I will have to get used to. It's one of the many new norms that come with parenthood.

But let's not forget some of the other news norms, like the amount of fun that's to be had playing with children around the pool, or the efforts you put into drawing out smiles from a baby – the results always delightful. I cannot wait to do this with you.

When you spend time living life through the eyes of a child, you don't need to climb Everest for an adventure. An hour building a fort and playing hide-and-seek can be adventure enough. I say that having spent an hour playing a game with 3-year-old Harry, where fallen leaves from a tree are 'real people' who live in a cave; a cave that has an awesome, gigantic waterfall that's full of special magic and powers.

I can't wait for these new norms to take shape for our family.

Monday, 16 September 2019 – Big Stretch, Dory

Your movements have increased in both vigour and regularity. When you move, Mummy's tummy looks and feels like a massage pillow with internal rotating ball bearings moving in a randomised pattern. I love watching this. There's an intimacy in watching your partner's body ripple, move and contort – all because a tiny human that I helped create is residing in the centre, growing and developing, with its vitality increasing each day. It's nothing short of phenomenal.

When the movements stop, I wait and wonder to see if you've gone to sleep, or if the tiny little cogs in your tiny little brain are turning and churning, helping you decide on what you'll do next. Will you be performing any more movements for the audience of one in the front row, or have you had enough for one night?

We're at one of those moments right now. Mummy's tummy is still, but it wasn't a few seconds ago. Have you gone to sleep?

I think you have.

But as I'm about to leave the theatre and divert my attention to the television, you come back out on stage for the encore – it's … not a kick, it's a stretch. A big stretch, as something is sticking out of Mummy. I think I'm holding your foot. It's definitely a limb, and it's more foot-shaped than hand-shaped. It's sticking out far enough for me to justify saying that I'm holding it rather than feeling it. And it doesn't move for a few seconds so I don't think it's a kick – it must be a stretch.

This is just … wow!

Mummy says that she's happy I'm having this experience, but she would like for you to stop now so that she can turn over. Apparently, having a limb sticking out far enough for me to hold it is causing great discomfort.

Tuesday, 17 September 2019 – Elevated Emotional Changes

Mummy's 'needy' level has risen – significantly. The internet tells me this is to be expected, and that elevated emotional changes during the third trimester are completely normal and nothing to worry about.

I disagree on both counts, Dory; there's nothing normal about the situation I'm in at the moment, and it is something to worry about, because you-know-who could show up and tear me a new one. As we speak, I'm in the middle of a live incident that demonstrates what an elevated emotional change looks like.

It started a few minutes ago when I responded to a group message before I responded to a message from Mummy. Unbeknown to me, Mummy went ahead and carried out a little investigation to research the order in which I'd sent my responses. Her findings concluded that I had seen her message first and the group message second. But I chose to respond to the group message first, and not to hers. In the eyes of a seven-month-pregnant woman … that was a mistake.

It's taken me a lot of work to de-escalate her hatred of me. I've had to reiterate how much I love her, how much I can't wait for us all to be a family and how my attention to detail has clearly taken a day off, because I would never normally respond to a group message ahead of responding to the woman carrying my child.

I've lost count of the times I've had to repeat myself in the last five minutes, to get her to believe me. As wonderful as the female body is during pregnancy, I can't help but feel it can be its own worst enemy at times.

Maybe a premature appearance from you wouldn't be the end of the world.

Wednesday, 18 September 2019 – The Magical Properties Of LED Tea Lights

We're at another of our NCT classes. Once again, the Mummies and Daddies are separated into groups. The Mummies are looking at different birthing options while the Daddies are asked to create a 'calming environment' for the Mummies on a makeshift labour ward.

The exercise is a farce. Our NCT meetings take place in a community centre and replicating anything that remotely resembles a labour ward is difficult. To compensate for the lack of realism, we're given flameless LED tea lights. These are for us Daddies to utilise when decorating the 'space'. Apparently, excellent lighting conditions will help the Mummies with labour.

Will it help, though, Dory? I know I've not witnessed labour yet, but I've heard enough stories to convince me that a few LED tea lights won't make much of a difference. Also, when we go to the labour ward, it will be because Mummy is in considerable pain. At what point am I to carry out these temporary labour-ward renovations – during contractions or in between them?

It's not all pessimism, though; all us Daddies have managed to polish off our second packet of Jaffa cakes.

Thursday, 19 September 2019 – Daddy's Last Immaturity Blowout

I'm on my way to Ibiza on a stag weekend. Expect to hear very little from me.

I've outsourced pregnancy updates to your mother for the next few days. She's begun already by sending me the outputs from this morning's visit to the midwife. In short, everything is on track. Your heartbeat is good, as is your size. You're currently weighing 4.2 lbs, which I'm told is also good, though I am curious to understand how exactly they can determine your weight.

Following on from our last NCT class, Mummy discussed her birth-plan preferences – she wants to have you in the birthing suite. That can only happen if it's available, and also only if Mummy is reclassified as low-risk (she's currently high-risk because of Crohn's and the ongoing drama with her iron levels).

Together, Mummy and Kat have locked down a plan: a follow-up appointment has been scheduled with the consultant towards the end of October; if Mummy's iron levels are still too low, then the consultant will consider an intravenous iron infusion, which should allow staff to downgrade Mummy from high-risk to low-risk, as the injection should bring the levels up to an acceptable standard.

This is comforting to read as I board my flight. I'm looking forward to this weekend, but I'm leaving behind the two people I care most about in the world at a time when they're vulnerable. I would ask the other

Daddies if they ever felt like this with their partners, but that would be an unforgivable infringement of stag-do etiquette. It's an unwritten rule not to discuss such deep and meaningful questions (while sober, at least). Instead, I should work on getting un-sober, and making clever quips to acquire points that can be used to improve my social ranking among the group – I get triple points if quips are aimed at the weakest members of the pack.

Friday, 20 September 2019 – Too Hung-Over To Talk

Daddy is too hung-over to talk – sorry. However, my day is made a little less painful because of a photo that your mother has sent me of her tummy. She's written the words 'We love you, Daddy' on it. I'm smitten.

Saturday, 21 September 2019 – Still Too Hung-Over To Talk

Daddy is still too hung-over to talk – and I'm still sorry.

Sunday, 22 September 2019 – Jealous Mummy

I'm back home; our family is reunited – I've missed you guys a lot. And you've missed me too, apparently. Mummy is reporting that your movements are much more frequent and lively as soon as I start talking to you. I don't think she's making this up either; she's jealous. Now she's berating you about why you've all of a sudden decided to wake up now Daddy is home.

I tell her she's imagining things, but I can't describe how happy this makes Daddy feel, Dory.

Monday, 23 September 2019 – Everyone Needs An Avocado Smasher

Mummy is delivering the usual vibrant commentary to my ears this evening; in no particular order, the following utterances have departed from her lips:

'I've been experiencing some super-aggressive farts tonight.'

'I can't wait to go for a wee and feel satisfyingly empty.'

'When are you going to sharpen our fucking knives?'

'Our child is a jackass and keeps elbowing me in the ribs.' Incidentally, this comment marks the first time Mummy has criticised you in a non-joking manner.

'What we need in life is an avocado smasher.'

Your mother never ceases to amuse and entertain.

Tuesday, 24 September 2019 – The Score Is 3-3

By my count, it's 3–3 in tonight's championship match between Mummy and Daddy on how many times they've each been woken up.

Who's doing the waking? Mummy's snoring. She's woken me up three times now, and in the time I lie awake trying to nod back off, your mother has also woken herself up three times.

Wednesday, 25 September 2019 – Anyone For Italian Food?

We're at another NCT class and the Mummies and Daddies have yet again been split up to complete a task. Seriously, Dory, when will the NCT charity learn that they need to rethink how they divide us up for group activities?

Our Daddy-task is to write down what we think the post-birth physical and emotional changes will be in our partners. We start with the physical. No one says anything at first, but a few nervous glances confirm that we're all thinking about the physical damage that labour often causes – particularly to the front-door areas of our loving partners. After a few minutes, one of the Daddies offers this: 'It might look a bit like smashed Italian cuisine.' The imagery is graphic and amusing. Naturally, we guffaw at the gag, like a group of schoolboys at the back of the bus on a non-uniform day out. After the laughter dies away, we have a conversation about whether we should write it down. There is a hesitancy among us –

we're worried that the Mummies will scold us for being silly and idiotic, not to mention a teensy-weensy bit insensitive.

After much deliberation, I agree to write down the comment, but with one exception: if it doesn't land well with the Mummies (which we know it won't), then we go down in the ship together, and no one is to say anything about who wrote it. If interrogated, the presenter of the comment will say, 'Hey, don't shoot the messenger, I'm just reading out what someone else wrote.' It will be a real #DadsUnited moment, Dory. It will consolidate our new brotherhood.

It's presentation time, Dory, and one of the Daddies is elaborating on what we mean by 'smashed Italian cuisine'. As soon as we hear the first non-amused tut from one of the Mummies, your poor Daddy is thrown right under the bus. The entire operation is blamed on me because I was the one who wrote down the comment. So much for #DadsUnited.

But the joke's on all of them – I'm happy to take the credit for such post-birth vaginal imagery as 'smashed Italian cuisine'.

Thursday, 26 September 2019 – Grey Or Black?

You are thirty-three weeks today, Dory. To celebrate, we've bought you your buggy. There was a price difference of fifty pounds between the black version of the buggy and the grey one. The grey one was the more expensive. I should point out that, apart from the colour, both buggies were identical.

Obviously, I don't need to tell you which one the Matriarch insisted on us getting.

Fifty fucking quid for a different colour? I can buy a second-hand book on Amazon for about three quid. This includes delivery. That's just shy of seventeen pieces of richly educational literature that I've forsaken, to have a grey-coloured buggy instead of a black one.

Fuck my life, Dory!

Friday, 27 September 2019 – Dreams Or Premonitions?

Mummy has woken up in an I'm-not-your-friend-you-piece-of-shit mood with me because of a dream she had last night. In her dream, I apparently left you and Mummy, and she's concluded that her dream is a premonition of sorts (I'm sure she had a similar one a few months back).

Honestly, what the fuck am I supposed to do, Dory? Your mother is 35 years old, yet I'm having to lobby for my innocence, which has been called into question because of a dream. You can imagine the court proceedings in her head.

'What crimes is the defendant accused of?' says the judge (Mummy).

'Infidelity, your honour,' responds the prosecution (also Mummy).

'I trust you have evidence to support your claim.'

'You betcha I do. I dreamt the whole thing.'

'A dream, you say? Well, I see no reason to delay. Guards, shoot this guilty man at once, and start by aiming at his testicles and be sure to use the rusty bullets.'

In case it's not clear – if you dream something, Dory, it's not true. You may dream about past events that have happened, or you may dream about things that you would like to happen, or indeed make happen – but dreams themselves are not necessarily a portrayal of anything factual. Will you please find a way to make your mother learn that?

Saturday, 28 September 2019 – Lightning Doesn't Strike Twice, They Say

I don't fucking believe this. She's had the same cunting dream again! I'm back in court, standing in the witness box. This time there are more details. First, the woman I've been sneaking around with is called Stacey Solomon. Not the TV personality Stacey Solomon; dream Stacey is Asian with jet-black hair (Mummy's words).

It gets worse. Apparently, I threw Mummy out of our house and refused to pay my share of a personal loan that was in her name – in short, I've been a real arsehole. Once again, I remind the Matriarch that it's a dream, that I've been in the same bed as her all night and that there's been no sneaking around. She's not buying it. What's more, every time she decides she's 'not my friend', it's never just her that isn't talking to me, it's apparently both of you. She'll say something like 'Me and Dory aren't talking to you', or 'Me and Dory don't find that funny.'

Mummy and Dory also don't find it funny when I play Mummy's voice memo about her not really hating me; she says that the contents of the memo are now null and void – owing to me being a cheating scumbag.

Will you please hurry up and be born, kiddo – I can't take much more of this!

Sunday, 29 September 2019 – Still So Much To Do

We still have a long-arse to-do list to work through. I know I've said it before, but it feels like we're on the final straight of the pregnancy – for real, this time. You could be here in as little as four weeks' time (or sooner), and we're not prepared. We need to change that. We need to be in a position where we can sit around watching *Star Wars* or Marvel films and wait for you to show up.

We've made excellent inroads this weekend into shortening the list. We've purchased a love seat (nicknamed 'the feeding chair'), painted a new side table to house potential feeding equipment (we still don't know if you will be boob- or bottle-fed), finished painting your cot, and bought you a cloud-shaped lampshade. The lampshade was top of Mummy's priority list this weekend.

Mummy is happy with the progress we've made, and I'm not taking that for granted, seeing as I cheated on her and left her twice this week in her dreams.

Monday, 30 September 2019 – Population Control

Up until now, I questioned whether having one's own children was adding to what I thought was a serious global problem – overpopulation. But according to Hans Rosling, and as detailed in his fantastic book *Factfulness*, the global population of children has remained steady in recent years at around the two-billion mark, and it will continue in that way (according to UN experts) until the year 2100 and thereafter – meaning the increase in population is not caused by us having babies. It's because adults are living longer, infant mortality has improved, and there has been progress in tackling extreme poverty. Healthcare and technology infrastructure have developed significantly, and there have been increases in GDP (gross domestic product). The population increase will continue for a short time, but by the time we reach 2060 each new generation of two billion people will be replaced by another generation of two billion people. The growth will stop and the circle of human life will be in balance.

My takeaway from this is that we don't need to tell people to stop having children; we need to build sustainable solutions to the challenge of housing a population of approximately eleven billion people. I have no idea what those solutions look like, but at least we have a number to work with, Dory.

October

Tuesday, 1 October 2019 – Premature Baby Statistics

There is a possibility that October could be your birth month. In the UK, approximately seven per cent of babies are born prematurely, or preterm. That's sixty thousand babies, Dory. Of those sixty thousand babies, eighty per cent are classed as 'moderately' preterm; in other words, born between thirty-two and thirty-seven weeks. That equates to fifty-one thousand babies. You would qualify as moderately preterm if you were born any time from now. I wonder if you'll be one of 2019's preterm babies.

Wednesday, 2 October 2019 – Fish Bait

We're at our final NCT class. Once again, the Mummies and Daddies are split into two groups in the usual thoughtless way. The Daddies are to note down a list of things we can do for our partners to make their lives easier during the first few weeks of parenthood. At the top of the list I write: 'Babysit for Mummy every so often.'

This is a test to see how well your mother knows me. I often drop the 'Daddy will babysit' comment around Mummy when I'm bored or she's being a twat (or both), as she's consistently quick to take the bait. She likes to remind me that you don't babysit your own children; you parent them. I do know this, Dory, but I manage to get a rise out of her every time, which amuses and entertains me. Why hasn't your silly Mummy learnt this yet? You extinguish a fire by starving it of oxygen, not by feeding it an

188

unlimited supply.

Let's see how she reacts in a group situation.

We're back around the circle and the Daddies are asked to present their answers. Naturally, I've been dragooned into presenting. It was only last week I was thrown under the bus for the 'smashed Italian cuisine' comment – this time, I've made peace with the fact that I won't get any support.

I begin my ambush. 'One thing that the Daddies can do is perhaps offer to babysit the baby so Mummy can take some—'

That's as far as I get, Dory.

'How many times do I have to tell you? You don't babysit your own kids,' Mummy says.

Excellent – that is what you call a bite, Dory. A big bite. Sometimes it can happen that way. You throw a little bit of something out there to see if you get a nibble; sometimes you catch nothing, other times you land an absolute whopper! But as noted earlier, the fish normally learn to recognise the bait after being caught out a few hundred times.

Not this fish.

Thursday, 3 October 2019 – Thirty-Four Weeks

Mummy is thirty-four weeks pregnant. At this stage, your chances of surviving a premature birth are ninety-five per cent. This was the final milestone I had marked out before Mummy reaches thirty-seven weeks, where she'll be considered full term. That's despite your due date landing in week forty – confusing, I know.

Just keep swimming, Dory – you little legend.

Friday, 4 October 2019 – Mummy's Last Day Of Employment

Today was Mummy's last day at work. As of now, she's on maternity leave. She arrived home with some lovely gifts from her work colleagues, including a pair of beige slippers in the style of some cute, fluffy wittle bunny-wabbits.

Her plan is to wear these in the hospital for labour. I pointed out that if she does that, the chances of them staying cute and fluffy are less than one per cent. Instead, they're likely to resemble something out of a scene from one of the *Saw* films.

Sunday, 6 October 2019 – Baby Shower

Today is Mummy's baby shower. She's been looking forward to it for weeks. She's wearing a red and black leopard-print dress. She looks stunning for someone who's almost eight months pregnant.

This whole baby-shower business is an absolute win for your Daddy. It's taking place at Granny Feeder's house, and it's an occasion that I'm prohibited from attending (it's a girls-only do). Yet I still benefit from all the presents and gifts that go hand in hand with baby showers. Technically speaking, it's you who will benefit, but the more you get given, the less I have to buy. My one regret is that invitations went out to close family and friends only, whereas we should have sent them out to every citizen on the planet.

———

It's the end of the day, and I've arrived to pick your mother up. It's taken me three trips to the car to pack up all your presents. Dory, you have been spoilt.

One of the gifts you've received is a Baby Dory teddy. I've wanted one for you for months, but I haven't bought you one, as I've been sulking ever since Mummy stopped me buying the one I found at that car boot sale we went to in the summer.

All your cards and gift tags are addressed to 'Baby Dory'. Some of the baby-shower games that the girls played today were Baby Dory themed.

It's been an exceptionally special day for Mummy, and I'm happy that it's exceeded her expectations. Earlier, I joked about this being a good opportunity to cash in on gifts, but I'm touched by people's generosity. I think I've caught some of Mummy's pregnancy hormones. I mean, it's not as if she doesn't have enough to go around.

Tuesday, 8 October 2019 – Potential Birthmark

Mummy has walked into a door.

That's not strictly true; she employed a sideways manoeuvre to shift past an open door, but she miscalculated because you've apparently grown again. Her miscalculation caused the latch to leave a dent in her tummy. The dent has now morphed into a bruise.

While examining the bruise up close, she says to me in absolute seriousness, 'Do you think this will leave Dory with a birthmark?'

Never a dull moment, Dory. Never.

Thursday, 10 October 2019 – It Must Suck To Be Pregnant At Times

You are thirty-five weeks today. To celebrate, you kicked your mother with such force that the impact caused her entire body to jerk spasmodically.

Friday, 11 October 2019 – Happy Birthday To Me

It's my birthday, Dory. I've woken up to this message from James:

> Happy birthday, mate – it's probably the last one anyone will remember or acknowledge.

Saturday, 12 October 2019 – I Still Got Dem Smooth Moves

I need to apologise, Dory. After Ibiza, I promised myself, you and Mummy that I wouldn't touch alcohol (at least, excessively) until after the birth. In my mind, that was an easy promise to make.

However, I find myself in breach of the conditions I self-imposed; I'm about to sink my fifth shot of the night.

This evening's brain-cell damaging activity hasn't been scheduled or planned. A few friends of mine have a rare hall pass from their partners, and their good fortune just happens to coincide with my birthday weekend.

I headed out with the intention of having a few pints and a few laughs and then returning home. But then some idiot started getting carried away with buying shots for a group of tired old men who can't hack it. And because it's my birthday, everyone is offloading all their unwanted shots on to me. I know better, but I don't have the strength to rebel against such peer pressure.

I now find myself in a position where I need to stumble home and execute a level-ten stealth mission to get through the door and up the stairs, undress and then get into bed without Mummy realising that my alcohol breath would melt a breathalyser.

But I've failed in my mission already, because Mummy has sent me a message to see if I'm having fun, which means she's still awake. Damn it! This one's on you, Dory; Mummy doesn't sleep much these days.

My mission brief has now changed. I need to return home knowing that the Matriarch will be awake. So, I'll have to act casually, as if I've walked in from work, but not so casually as to arouse suspicion. It's a delicate balance, but one I'm confident I can strike.

I begin my mission by responding to Mummy's message. I say that I'm having fun and that I'm at least three drinks away from being tipsy.

Perfect.

She won't suspect a damn thing, not with a response like that; I even spent five minutes reviewing my one-sentence reply to ensure my grammar was of the highest standard.

Do me a favour, kiddo, don't send Mummy into labour tonight, OK?

I thank my mates for my birthday drinks and begin the easy part of my mission: stumbling home. Ten minutes later, I'm standing outside my front door, ready for the next phase – making it through that door. I'm thankful that Mummy has left the hall light on for me.

I correctly turn the key on my first attempt and mentally set a reminder to pat myself on the back. This is going very well. Next, I creep along the hallway and gingerly poke my head into the lounge for a quick recce. Mummy is not in sight. Perfect. This is a fucking cakewalk, Dory.

THUD.

Crap, I've dropped my phone. Has my error caught her attention?

I wait. Nothing from the Matriarch – I'm in the clear. I begin one of the hardest parts of the mission – ascending the stairs. I know I must hang on to the banister and ascend one step at a time. Sometimes I wait and listen for a few seconds before taking my next step. If silence was in my job description, then I would be deserving of a top-performer bonus; I doubt even the BFG could hear me. I reach the top of the landing after only twelve minutes and then I slide into the bathroom for a well-deserved sit-down wee. I debate whether to get undressed now or wait until I get into the bedroom.

Creak.

What was that, Dory? Oh no, the bathroom door is opening. *It's the fucking Matriarch!*

Red alert, Dory – we have a red alert. OK. Act cool and stay calm.

'Hello baby, what are you doing up at this ungodly hour?'

I say this in a casually neutral tone, to make my fake sobriety seem more plausible.

'What was that crashing downstairs?'

Damn. OK, so maybe the BFG could in fact hear me, which means no bonus. 'That was my phone,' I say. 'It … slipped.'

'You're drunk, aren't you?'

'Outrageous, woman. How very dare you. I am at least three drinks away from being tipsy.'

'Hmmm, OK. Can you get up so I can go for a wee?'

'Of course. I'm in complete control of my actions, and I'm not even drunk, so you're a stupid silly-head for saying that I am.'

We switch places, and I'm weighing up the pros and cons of attempting to clean my teeth, when your mother announces that she feels sick. And now she's throwing up.

To be honest, if you had asked me which of the two of us would be throwing up tonight, even eight seconds ago, I would have put a fiver on myself. I'm not sure what to do; I can't clean my teeth or slink off to bed while the mother of my child is in distress. Then again, I can't do anything to help with the actual vomiting.

This needs careful thought and consideration.

In the end, I settle on the action that will provide the maximum value, given the situation I'm in – I decide to romance the love of my life. By romance, I mean seduce. That's two pats on the back I need to give myself, Dory.

I mean, my timing is impeccable when you think about it; Mummy is eight months pregnant, it's the middle of the night and she's throwing up. On paper, that would be the worst time to make a pass at her, but it's *precisely because* it's the worse time that it's the perfect time! I assume you agree, despite the uncomfortable subject matter.

If I'm interested in her when she's in this state then that must mean I really do love her more than anything. It's another example where challenging the norms rewards – as it's about to reward both of your parents with passion.

I move in to begin the magic.

'Get off; that's not helping me,' Mummy says.

'What's not helping?' I say, even though I know this is all part of the game.

'Pulling down my shorts while I'm throwing up.'

Ah – when she puts it like that, I admit she has a semi-valid argument. Rather than face complete rejection, I style out my moves, sublimating them from mind-blowing love and unity to a half-arsed attempt at a back rub instead, which I'm sure she's appreciating, even if she does seem to be shrugging my hands away.

On the way back from the bathroom, I have a long and honest conversation with myself and admit that perhaps I'm not three drinks away from being tipsy.

The reason it is a long conversation is because it takes me some time to walk from the bathroom to the bedroom – despite the distance being less than five metres.

Sunday, 13 October 2019 – Not Helpful, Ruby

Ouch.

Dory, Daddy has an ouchie head. Shots are the devil. I'm going to try and open my eyes and see if I can bear it.

The first thing I see is a red-headed unicorn smiling back at me as if to say, 'I bet you're feeling rough, aren't you?' No shit, Ruby!

Ruby and Dory (not you; the soft toy from Mummy's baby shower) have been sleeping in with us for the last week so that they smell like your parents – apparently, it can help to comfort you if we're not there. I'm not sure if it's true, but I do know that Ruby is of no fucking use to me at this precise moment in time.

Opening my eyes was a terrible decision – I'm going back to sleep.

Monday, 14 October 2019 – The Birth Plan

Mummy and I are at Rebecca and Sean's house for dinner. I've brought with me an agenda: I want to discuss Mummy's birth plan. Next week, she'll be thirty-seven weeks (full term).

I won't lie: writing 'thirty-seven' is scary. We're so close.

Originally, Mummy had visions of a home birth, but she quickly re-evaluated her position when I recounted a labour story from one of the Mummies at work, who catapulted some of her … fluids from her front bottom onto the face of one of the doctors. The lesson being: if you value the walls, carpets and upholstery in your home, think carefully about a home birth. In any case, Mummy is high-risk, so it was never truly an option for us.

That's when she revised her preference to having you in the birthing suite, and that's what she's been working towards with Kat, who has put a plan in place to tackle any unfavourable iron-level results by means of an intravenous infusion.

However, the success of Kat's plan isn't guaranteed. Mummy won't necessarily be downgraded to low-risk. And even if she is, the birthing-suite facilities are not always available. Christmas-conceived babies are the most common throughout the year, but there are other spikes – Valentine's

Day babies being one of them. That's when we think you were made.

Rebecca also advises us to think about medical staff having access to you and Mummy during the birth. She pointed out that it's safer in terms of access to be on a labour ward where the midwives and doctors are close by if you need them, instead of them having to hoist you out of the pool, or trying to carry out any medical manoeuvres in the pool itself. Her points are well made.

Ultimately, she says, it's up to us – or rather, it's up to Mummy, who decides the labour ward will be fine. Mummy is comforted by Rebecca's advice and reassurance. So am I. Rebecca also promises to ensure that our midwife (whoever it is) knows that we're friends with Rebecca, and that Dory's Mummy and Daddy are to be treated like royalty.

Perfect.

Next, I want to know what will happen the moment you arrive. Many people have tried to explain to me what it's like, the moment after your child is born, but by their own admissions they fail to do the experience justice with words alone. I'm predicting that both Mummy and Daddy will be overcome with emotion and exhaustion – not to mention that Mummy will be in pain.

We might not have time to emotionally transition from focusing on the birth to holding you for the first time. This is why I want to try and gauge what to expect – so I can prepare to enjoy every microsecond of the experience when it happens.

Now, we have some easy questions to answer. Will Daddy want to cut the cord? Fuck yes; Daddy absolutely wants to cut the cord. How will your gender be revealed? I will take a peek under the hood and introduce you to Mummy as our brand-new baby boy or baby girl (I'm welling up writing this). What is Mummy's feeding preference? Mummy will try booby first and see how she gets on.

One final consideration is what we do if things don't go according to plan and Mummy needs surgery. If that happens, Mummy wants me to stay with you at all costs, but call Granny Feeder for air support.

That's about it, kiddo. We've not discussed any scenario where things go seriously wrong – what's the point? We'll assume they won't, and we'll deal with whatever comes our way together, as a family.

Now, what's for pudding? Apple pie – lovely.

Tuesday, 15 October 2019 – Baby-Clothes Hangers

Tonight, we've hung all your clothes up in your nursery. An open wardrobe with your baby clothes on display, organised from newborn to six months, is a beautiful sight.

There were certain things in this pregnancy that I knew would be memorable, but I didn't expect to hit such a high note by looking at an open wardrobe.

It wasn't all emotional bliss, though. Mummy got angry at Daddy on more than one occasion – three, if we're being specific: me trying on your hats, me alternating the direction in which the hangers face and, finally, me calling her a stressy twat. There's no pleasing some people, Dory.

If we forget Mummy's criticisms of me, it's been a perfect evening – one we round out by packing your hospital bag.

Wednesday, 16 October 2019 – Breastfeeding Dilemma

One of the parental decisions we previously agreed on was that there was absolutely no pressure on Mummy to breastfeed. We both felt (and still do) that part of looking after your well-being means looking after our own well-being, and especially Mummy's. The pressure on Mummies to breastfeed often leads to stress, particularly when the baby chooses not to comply, or when there are issues with the Mummy's milk, or if she's having trouble bonding with the baby. I'm sure there are hundreds of other reasons.

The point is, avoiding stress is something every new parent should be working towards. And so, my views on breastfeeding have remained unchanged.

Until now.

I've been reading about the human body's microbiome. There is a lot of convincing research out there that highlights not just the health benefits of breastfeeding, but also the health risks of not doing so. The research makes the same case for natural delivery as against C-section delivery, and concludes that natural delivery is better for babies. Having babies naturally and then breastfeeding them provides them with the beneficial bacteria they need to create a healthy microbiome – something that has been discovered to be extremely important.

So, here's my dilemma, Dory: I want Mummy to read the same research I've read so that she knows what I know, instead of hearing it from me (as my voice sends her to sleep). Her top priority is your well-being, so anything that helps her to make informed decisions is welcome.

But it's not without risks: I believe that if she reads the research, she'll think she has to breastfeed, and if for any reason she can't she'll feel guilty and think I'm disappointed in her. This would be the last thing I want her to think, especially after she's done a fantastic job of growing you over the last (almost) nine months.

I have no idea how to navigate this one. Studies show that formula-fed babies have higher risks of susceptibility to allergies and to digestion-related diseases and other twenty-first century illnesses. All of these have links to both feeding choices and the individual's microbiome.

I now find myself in a position where I want to encourage breastfeeding, because I want you to have the best start in life. I wholeheartedly believe that to do nothing with this information would be to neglect my duties as a father. But what if I endanger Mummy's well-being by forcing us to revisit this issue a few weeks before you're born?

Then I remember I'm a bloke and can never truly understand what it's like for a woman in this position. I certainly don't claim to have any right to dictate what Mummy does with her body. That said, I do have to step in occasionally and limit her sweet consumption.

I could be worrying about nothing. You might arrive on time by natural delivery. You might love a bit of the boob and Mummy might love feeding you that way. The only one who misses out is Daddy, because, not having boobs, he doesn't get to feed you. But I'm sure Mummy will be all too happy to express milk and let me take some of the night shifts.

As things stand, that is now the best-case scenario in my mind.

What about a worst-case scenario? You arrive into the world via the sunroof, bypassing a lot of the healthy bacteria that Mummy would otherwise pass on to you, and then you go straight on to formula. What then? Well, it's not like that's uncommon. I'll just have to make sure you eat good food when it comes to solids. Granny Feeder will need to be watched closely. I'm sure she moonlights as a lobbyist for confectionery companies – just ask your cousin Haylee about her chocolate-button stash.

There might be other ways to introduce healthy bacteria into your system at a young age: baby probiotics, perhaps. I should probably remind myself I'm no scientist and seek out professional guidance.

Dory, you're entitled to blame your parents for anything that goes wrong in your life. But please note that we are trying to make the right decisions. Unfortunately, hardly any of them appear to be black and white.

On a brighter note, my Shared Parental Leave has been approved. This means I will be off work for the best part of four months. I'll be able to look after you and your Mummy and start getting to grips with my new job – being a Daddy.

This is yet another item on the to-do list that I can cross off. It's a good thing too, as we've noticed your position has dropped down – a clear indication that you are gearing up to hatch.

Thursday, 17 October 2019 – Nesting Mode

Thirty-six weeks today.

Fuck, that's four weeks until your due date, but only one week to go until Mummy is considered full term.

We still have a lot to do, but I need Mummy to take it easy. She disagrees. Instead, she's decided to move into full nesting mode – beginning with painting one of the walls in your nursery. Your nursery doesn't need painting; it's already been painted as part of our house-renovation project.

But she reminds me of a key consideration: 'If we don't paint at least one of the walls grey, then we can't use our cloud transfers.' Clouds feature heavily in your nursery, so as you can see, painting that one wall grey is a top priority.

Until a few minutes ago, we didn't have a car seat, but now your superstar

Mother has found you one on Facebook, and she's managed to source a car seat, Isofix and rain cover – all for thirty quid.

Top marks for Mummy.

By the way, I did look up what Isofix means, but reading the Wikipedia explanation brought on a big bout of snore-festivity, so I closed the page down. An Isofix is essentially a bit of kit that holds the car seat in place, so we don't have to use seat belts.

Friday, 18 October 2019 – Low Iron Levels

We're at another midwife appointment, and Kat has confirmed that Mummy's iron levels have dropped again. This means she will most likely need an infusion.

It also means that she's unlikely to be allowed to give birth anywhere other than on the labour ward, so it's a good job we revised our birth plans with Rebecca. Mummy's fine with this, and so am I. As long as you're both OK – that's all that matters.

———

In other news, one of the NCT Mummies has given birth. She's the first from our group. We were expecting at least one NCT baby today – one of the Mummies is now two weeks overdue and has gone into hospital to be induced.

But it wasn't her baby that was born; it was another couple's baby, whose due date wasn't until 18 November. The baby has turned up four weeks early, Dory.

Four weeks!

Understandably, they were caught off guard and so they hadn't packed the baby's bag, or their own bags. Luckily, all is well. Their baby is a little boy; he's on the small side, but he's doing OK – and so is his Mummy.

Phew. One couple down, Dory!

I'm now about to spend some time bonding with your mother, packing our bags.

Saturday, 19 October 2019 – Getting Prepared

Aside from snacks, everything is packed and ready to go. There's nothing like the shock announcement of the four-week-early arrival of a baby to shake soon-to-be parents into action. Judging by the NCT-group chat today, we're not the only ones.

We have everything Mummy needs for a stay in hospital of up to forty-eight hours. If you're not with us by then, I can always return home and grab supplies. We only live a few minutes away from the hospital. Failing that, I can dispatch one of your Grannies.

My next job is to install the car seat and Isofix in the back of the car. My training for this operation is being overseen by the Matriarch, who should be just as much in the dark about such matters as I am – she's never had her own children either. Yet somehow, she's an expert. She knows what bits go where, what buttons to press. For once, I'm not being sarcastic, Dory – she knows exactly what she's talking about.

'Good boy, that's it ... you've almost got it; give it another try,' Mummy whispers.

But I haven't 'got it' at all, Dory. I can't get in the right position to fit the fucking Isofix in and I'm about to fuck the fucking thing in the road and drive over the fucker while calling it a see-you-next-Tuesday.

'You're so close; don't give up now,' Mummy continues.

Rather than snap a retort back at Mummy, who to her credit is trying to help your fuckwit of a Daddy, I decide to adjust my position from standing out on the road and leaning in, to crouching in the footwell, giving me better visibility and more leverage options.

In case you didn't know what a six-foot adult male looks like squeezed down in the back of a Peugeot trying to install an Isofix, I'll tell you, Dory. He looks like an oversized mutant frog trying to fuck an Isofix.

Sunday, 20 October 2019 – Let's Get Ready To Rumble!

Mummy's grunted expletives have reached a higher level of obscenity than even I thought possible. Imagine it's 'Royal Rumble Night' on the wrestling channel and all the wrestlers are rhinos suffering from ADHD and rabies, and they haven't had an uninterrupted night's sleep in months. To cap it off, they're told that if they lose the match, their whole family (whom they're fond of) will be burnt alive.

And that's only what I have to listen to when Mummy wants to flick her hair out of her face – don't get me started on her tying her shoelaces.

Monday, 21 October 2019 – Next-Door Screams

Our next-door neighbours have a baby girl, and when she screams, I can hear it from our bedroom. Her pitch travels through brick, plasterboard, wallpaper and paint.

She's crying right now, as a matter of fact. It's 11.45 p.m. I look at your Mummy, and she looks at me. We don't say anything – at least, not verbally.

Tuesday, 22 October 2019 – Another False Alarm

You gave us another scare today, kiddo. It was the same story as on the previous two occasions: a lack of movement on your part. Only today, you were lying in an unusual position that caused Mummy's tummy to appear flat; it looked a little bit like Table Mountain. Fortunately, a lovely midwife down at the hospital quickly removed our concerns. You started raving as soon as she strapped the CTG monitor to Mummy.

I wonder how many women go through pregnancy with zero scares, zero complications and zero dramas. I bet the percentage is in single digits. Up to this point, I still think Mummy has had an excellent pregnancy, and she would say the same thing, even taking into account the night when we thought you were in real trouble, because even that turned out to be nothing serious, so we can't record it as a complication; it was more of a self-imposed drama.

Still, for a 'normal' pregnancy we've had several unplanned check-ups and two unscheduled scans. Mummy's iron levels have been a constant hot topic, as has her flatulence.

No more, please.

Wednesday, 23 October 2019 – Failed

While leaving the office at the end of the day and rushing (because I was late) over to the bus stop, I missed a call from Mummy. I returned her call within thirty seconds, only to be told that I had failed the phone test, and that she could have been in labour. Thirty seconds, Dory – that's all it takes to win the award for shittest partner of the year.

As an aside, the reason I ended up running to catch the bus was because I was booking tickets for the new *Star Wars* film.

Thursday, 24 October 2019 – Full Term

Thirty-seven weeks today, kiddo. I'm not sure if it's you or Mummy who is classed as full term, but as of today you will not be born a premature baby. This was the final milestone before labour. Sure, we might have a couple more midwife appointments, and I know we have a discussion coming up next week about the prospect of Mummy having an iron infusion, but hitting week thirty-seven was the one for me. You and Mummy have done such outstanding work, and I'm proud of both of you.

And now we wait.

There are no more planned scans, no more heartbeat monitoring, no more tests. We wait. It sounds crazy – I never thought I would be feeling like this at this stage – but I'm not as excited as I thought I would be. I obviously can't wait to meet you, but I approach the next phase with a mixture of apprehension and anxiety: all through the pregnancy I've worried about my lack of control over external circumstances. Up until now, that fear has remained chiefly in my peripheral vision, always there, but only fleetingly coming into focus. But not any more. The birth approaches and my fear has taken centre stage. I see it in front of me wherever I go and closing my eyes to it only makes my visualisation of it sharper. Try as you might, you can't escape your own mind, Dory.

The two people I hold most dear are about to undergo a traumatic experience, and many potential, if highly unlikely, risks lie ahead – some of which could be fatal to either or both of you. That is just the reality. It's certainly not what I'm focusing on, but I'd be lying if I said I hadn't once or twice in recent days asked myself what would happen if something went tragically wrong.

I will not be telling Mummy any of this. I've told her that everything will be fine, that we will face it all together and that she has everything she needs to get you here safely. Most of that is true; statistics are on our side, Dory, which is something we can all take comfort in. Chances are, everything will be fine. *It will be fine.*

My focus now is looking after Mummy as much as I can, because when labour begins it will be very much the Mummy-and-Dory show. There won't be a lot I can do, but I'm going to be as supportive as I can be, and I'll try and keep Mummy calm and relaxed – if that's even possible.

You're almost there; we're so close to having our family together. Just a little bit further, kiddo.

Sunday, 27 October 2019 – The Clocks Go Back, Possibly Forever

Last night, the clocks went back, meaning I had an extra hour in bed. Mummy turned to me and said, 'That will be the last time in ten years that we get to enjoy that hour uninterrupted.'

I'm sure that's not true – is it? You'll stay in bed for that extra hour. Right, Dory?

Monday, 28 October 2019 – Check, Check Again And Then Recheck Everything

Mummy is meticulous about her packing (not to mention sensitive), and my ability to dismantle her excellent work sends her into a fury; not something we want to be encouraging during labour.

It's for that reason that I'm checking and rechecking everything in Mummy's maternity bag. I need to familiarise myself with where everything 'lives' and train my awareness to be able to retrieve specific items on command. Also, I need to be able to do this without tipping everything out onto the floor.

During this exercise, I'm asked to pack one additional item – Dobble. Dobble is pretty much a spruced-up version of the card game snap. As with most games, the objective is to have fun and also to use concentration and focus in competing against other players to win points. Dobble is a game that demands immaculate attention to detail.

I'm not sure we'll have time for games while Mummy is in labour, especially when she's five centimetres dilated or more. Does she expect just to breathe away the pain so she can concentrate when it's her turn?

I'm thinking of following suit and unplugging the Nintendo so I can get a few hours of *Zelda* in while Mummy watches, encouragingly helping me with the problem-solving aspects of difficult dungeon puzzles. What do you think, Dory?

Now, I want it documented right here that bringing games to the labour ward was Mummy's idea. If the nurses, midwives and doctors take one look at the naïve new parents and think we're fucking idiots for bringing games with us, then that's all on Mummy.

Tuesday, 29 October 2019 – Hunky-Dory

I woke up this morning to find Mummy already wide awake. I asked her if everything was OK, and she said, 'Everything is hunky-dory.'

I don't know why, but that immediately sent me an image of you as a baby with lots of muscles; you were roided up to the nines, Dory – scary shit.

Wednesday, 30 October 2019 – There's A Lot More Screen Time These Days

Every day I look at my phone, waiting for Mummy to call me and say the words: 'I think Dory is coming.'

Thursday, 31 October 2019 – Happy Halloween

Happy Halloween, Dory, you're thirty-eight weeks today. The day has started excellently; Mummy and I have been at the hospital with her consultant who decided to perform an unexpected scan; don't worry – all is well, kiddo.

Because you're packing on a bit of timber these days, the imagery was a lot more defined than anything I've seen on previous scans. She went close up on your heart, and we could see it thumping away – spectacular stuff.

Your estimated weight is 6 lbs 8 oz. We're told that at this stage you'll pile on half a pound each week, on average – meaning if you arrive around your due date, you'll weigh something in the order of 7 lbs 8 oz.

To celebrate the spooky calendar date, I've rolled up my sleeves and given my best effort to decorating Mummy's Dory-bump as a pumpkin. Unfortunately, my artistic incompetence rivals my dancing ability.

At least we have the picture …

November

Friday, 1 November 2019 – You're All But Guaranteed To Be A November Baby

As of today, you are all but guaranteed to be a November-born baby. Even if you are late, Mummy will only be allowed to carry you for up to two weeks after the due date before she's induced. There is a small chance that a long labour with complications could tip you into December, but that's most unlikely.

———

It's 9.00 p.m. on a Friday …
   Is tonight the night?

Saturday, 2 November 2019 – Dory Roulette

Last night wasn't the night, which is good, because this weekend marks the beginning of a fun little game – Dory Roulette. The rules of the game are as follows: I have to stack the weekend up with plans, chores and other important jobs. Then I must systematically work through them one by one, while hoping you don't send Mummy into labour early.

   The first job today is to go and see my physio. You may recall I wrote some months ago about my back not being in great shape. I'm pleased to report that I've seen dramatic improvements. At the end of my appointment, the physio confirms that a follow-up appointment is not required. I've said it before, but there's nothing like the impending birth of your first child to shake you into action.

Time check. It's midday. A quick call to Mummy confirms what I want to hear: no signs of labour.

The afternoon is spent downstairs in the basement beginning Operation Clear-Out. The basement is the last remaining room in the house that we need to finish before we can finally draw a line under our house-renovation project. I know I've been saying that for a while now, but this time I mean it. Maybe.

The basement is to become Daddy's office, and I have a small space reserved for you. You'll have your own desk and your own arts-and-crafts box. It will be fun, but only if Daddy clears the basement out and gets it looking all office-like.

The office furniture has been ordered and is due to be installed next Friday, which I suppose means I'm playing Dory Roulette for a bit longer than the weekend.

Because I'm an overachiever at procrastination when it comes to this type of job, I only manage to sort out one small corner before it's time to call it a day.

Still no signs of labour.

———————

It's now evening, and Mummy and Daddy have friends over from Ireland. We were going to host them but we can't guarantee you won't ruin our plans, so we've gone out for dinner instead.

The meal proceeds without contractions, waters breaking or anything else to suggest Mummy is in labour. We crawl into bed at 11.00 p.m.

It's been a long day, Dory, and both your parents are shattered. Can you please stay put tonight, kiddo?

Goodnight. Daddy loves you.

Sunday, 3 November 2019 – Who Wants To See My Magic Trick?

Morning, Dory. Sleep well? Daddy did but Mummy didn't, which I think means you didn't either, because if you're up and about then Mummy is too.

Not to worry, my day has started phenomenally well. Mummy has discovered that if she coughs, her belly button shoots out at least a centimetre. I cannot emphasise enough how funny I find this.

It's day two of Dory Roulette, and finishing the basement clear-out is on the docket. I've recruited the Matriarch and Granny Smurf to assist. The Matriarch is in charge. She can't lift, but she can point, direct and bark orders. She excels at this type of work even without the added boost of pregnancy hormones, especially when it's Daddy who's taking the orders.

We finish the clear-out by 2.00 p.m. – without Mummy going into labour.

And now we've driven up to Granny Feeder's house to borrow Grandad Tools's van to pick up a bookcase for the basement and to drop off leftover paint tins, tools and any other crap that Mummy doesn't want in the house but doesn't want to chuck out.

Still no signs of labour, Dory. Also, Granny Feeder isn't as impressed as Daddy is with Mummy's new belly-button trick.

It's four o'clock and the bookcase is in the basement. Now we're filling the van up ready for a tip run in the morning – the rubbish mound in our garden is almost big enough to fill Mummy's bra.

Still no sign of you, Dory.

Now it's five o'clock – and call it beginner's luck or natural talent, but I've played Dory Roulette well. How long can my run of good fortune continue? I don't want to take it for granted, so I move straight on to another little job I've been meaning to do – assembling the doors of the wardrobes in the spare room.

These wardrobes remain my biggest fuck-up of the year: there were parts missing, but I paid in cash to a dodgy firm in London and it was all arranged over WhatsApp so I can't take them back; I didn't measure the height correctly, meaning assembly has been ... challenging; and I still need to hang the doors on (which I'm about to attempt now), but they weigh more than a stegosaurus on cheat day.

At least I haven't left it to the end of the day to complete the hardest job. That would be very silly indeed.

Let's see how I get on, Dory.

———————

It's 6.00 p.m. Dory, these fucking, cunting wardrobes can go and fuck themselves. I've hung the doors, and they don't line up. I've seen more accuracy from a blind man trying to hit a bullseye in the wind. Fuck the doors, fuck the wardrobes and fuck any more chores tonight.

It's 7.00 p.m. It may surprise you to learn that I'm in a foul mood now, Dory. I know I asked you this yesterday, but would you mind holding off from making an appearance for another evening?

To cheer myself up, I've asked Mummy to perform a bout of coughing with her belly button exposed. She doesn't disappoint; she excels – and also, she admits that her performance caused her to wet herself again.

Monday, 4 November 2019 – Are We On?

I think it's Monday, but it could be Tuesday. What I do know is that it's night-time, and your Mummy isn't in bed. She's in the bathroom. Well, I assume that's her, unless there's someone else in there throwing up while simultaneously groaning in pain. Is this it, Dory? Are we on?

No.

At least, Mummy doesn't think so. She thinks she's experiencing Braxton Hicks contractions. The timings are irregular and the pains are infrequent – she thinks it's another false alarm, Dory. Nevertheless, it's a good job Mummy made it to the hospital earlier today to finally have her iron infusion.

Neither of us can get back to sleep, so I download a contraction timer. Dare I ask Mummy if she fancies a game of Dobble?

Tuesday, 5 November 2019 – No, Mummy!

A friend from work has brought you a lovely outfit as a present. She's also written a card. In it, she offers me some advice:

Enjoy the cute noises, endless naps and minimal movements – toddlers are fucking savages!

She then proceeds to tell me how her darling little princess punched her in the tit this morning while screaming 'No, Mummy!' in her face.

Wednesday, 6 November 2019 – Daddy's Last Day At Work

Today is my last day at work. I now (hopefully) have a few days to relax until we meet.

Timing is everything, Dory. Ideally, I need you to arrive as close to your due date as possible, but I will allow you to come two or three days early. You're welcome.

There are several reasons why I favour that particular window. I'm gearing up for another round of Dory Roulette, as our office furniture has arrived and I need to install it; I'll also need time to rearrange it at least twice after Mummy has finished relaying her interior-design orders to me. Next up, Grandad Tools is due to fly to Ireland on the fifteenth and we would hate for him to miss out on meeting his second grandchild. Finally – and here comes the most important reason of all – Daddy wants to catch up on watching all the *Star Wars* films ahead of episode nine, which is due out in December. I realise this is a self-centred reason, but there it is.

What are your thoughts? Do you fancy complying? I hope so. Physically we're ready, but mentally I'm not quite there yet ...

Thursday, 7 November 2019 – Mummy's Early-Labour Campaign

It's my first day off, and your mother is already trying to fuck things up for me. In short, she wants to start employing every trick in the book to bring on an early labour. I've been alluding to you all year that she's a psycho (though never in her earshot) and, yet again, she's proved me right.

Anyway, I've taken a rare and brave move against her and said I will not help. She's not happy. One of the myths about how to bring on labour is that having 'an early night', so to speak, will do the trick. I've refused all her efforts in that direction and placed a household-wide ban on anything more intimate than eye contact.

She is not deterred by my non-compliance; her next trick is to move on to a labour myth where I'm not needed – raspberry tea. Or at least, she's bought some with the intention of starting to drink it. Her words to me were: 'I don't need you for this one.'

Which is true, of course; Mummy doesn't need me to drink raspberry tea. But she does need the raspberry tea itself. That one is vital to the entire raspberry-tea-drinking operation. And despite Mummy's acquisition of said raspberry tea, it's gone missing. We don't know where it's gone. It's all very cloak-and-dagger stuff, Dory. No one in the house has the slightest idea where it could be. I think it will go down as one of life's biggest unsolved mysteries.

Friday, 8 November 2019 – Daddy Failed To Consider The Lighting

I want to say thank you for staying put today, Dory. It's been an intense game of Dory Roulette but one we've all played well. I've had time to collect, build and install all of our new office furniture with help from one of Mummy's cousins. I even had time to move it all around again after the Matriarch offloaded her ideas for making the layout 'better'. Told you this would happen, didn't I?

Apparently, Daddy's layout didn't consider the lighting. I was about to remind Mummy that it's a fucking basement that has next to no natural light, and the light it does have comes courtesy of nine evenly dispersed spotlights, so the layout of the furniture is irrelevant to the lighting, but then I remembered … you know … Miss Heidi.

———

It's 11.00 p.m., and I think Mummy's in labour. She keeps grabbing her tummy in pain, and I'm waiting for it to subside or for her to tell me if she thinks it's a Braxton Hicks contraction or a Dory's-coming contraction.

But it is yet another false alarm, Dory. These false alarms are happening more and more, especially over the last couple of days.

In other news, I'm one *Star Wars* film down. It's controversial, but I'm watching them in chronological order. I never thought I'd be that guy, but I guess everything is changing this year.

Saturday, 9 November 2019 – Dear Dory

I'm on tenterhooks waiting for Mummy to go into labour at any second. Every time she makes a noise, a gasp or any sudden movement, I wonder if this is it. I wonder if this is the day we meet. It's so surreal.

I don't know what to do with myself, so I've written you a letter.

Dear Dory,

You will arrive any day now. It could even be today.

I don't have a clue how to perform my new job. I've spent eight months preparing for it, but I still don't have a clue. I've asked questions to parents, I've read books, I've read articles and I've paid for classes. I've spent time with babies and I've fed them – I've even changed a nappy. I've learnt from all of these interactions and experiences, yet I still don't have a clue about parenthood.

I'm somewhat OK with this, though. I'm not scared to take steps into the unknown. Besides, I'm not alone. Some paths in life are marked out clearly – the directions are signposted, and the boundary lines are defined and tangible – you simply cannot go wrong. The parenthood path is different. The lines are fluid and translucent; they ripple and shimmer and compel you to define your own boundaries. It's up to me and Mummy to choose the route – and it's up to you as well, I guess.

This is daunting, but it's also liberating. We can go anywhere we want: left, right, forwards or upwards. Our pace can be quick or leisurely. We control the path. Thinking about becoming a Daddy, and about the world you will be born into, has got me thinking about legacy, and the lessons I want you to learn, so that you're equipped to forge your own path.

I want to share some of what I've learnt. These are lessons I consider to be critical. Maybe they will help you someday. Here goes.

It's OK to fail. One failure in life can teach you more about yourself and the world than three terms in school sitting behind a desk copying notes from a whiteboard. If you're afraid to fail, then you'll never explore opportunities outside your comfort zone. Fail often, learn from it and then fail again in a different way. If you fail often enough at something, eventually you will succeed.

Closely linked to failure is rejection. No one likes to be told they're not good enough: for a partner, for a job, for a place on the team. I will take great pride in every single one of your rejections because it means you had the courage to confront rejection head on – hopefully, with a notepad and a pen. Learn from rejection, and then try again. You might as well fall in love with the word 'no'; after all, you'll spend enough time with it.

Define your own success. Don't allow a car-engine size, a house in a certain postcode or a job title to define what success is for you. We have so many people telling us what it means to be successful, but how can anyone whittle down what success means to something you might read on the back of a pamphlet, when success can only truly be measured and defined by us as individuals – all of whom are different? I would rather you spent your life working a minimum-wage job where you felt proud of your endeavours and found meaning in your efforts, instead of becoming the CEO of a 'fill-in-the-blank' company where you derived little real value or satisfaction for yourself. Only you can decide what success means to you – even I can't tell you that, but I will try and help you to figure it out for yourself.

Learn humility and embed it in your bones. It is in our DNA to act in our own self-interest. No one is truly selfless. Nevertheless, try and see yourself as one cog in the giant machine that is the world. That way, when you see someone else in pain, you'll be in pain too, because you'll care about that other person. This practice doesn't burden you with a responsibility to cure all known diseases. Sometimes, it could mean going up to someone you don't know who looks sad, and asking them if they're OK, or buying them a drink, or maybe encouraging them to just keep swimming. Simple acts of kindness fuel the faith in humankind and they will reward you and make you feel good about yourself. There is zero downside to humility.

But this doesn't mean you have to let people abuse you, or interpret your humility as weakness. You can still help others while maintaining your self-respect. If something doesn't feel right to you, then listen to the voice inside you – you own it – and don't allow others to take control of your choices. If you are struggling with this, or if someone is trying to make you do something you don't want to do, send them my way!

Befriend humour as soon as you can. It will be your best friend. It can comfort you during the dark times, and elevate you during the good. If you look hard enough, you can find humour everywhere, even in the direst of conditions and the most unpromising situations. It's a well that never runs dry, so drink from it as often as you can. If you gift humour to others they will love you for it.

Finally, learn how to learn; and then learn every day until the day you die. Learning is a gift that defies the law of diminishing returns; it has the opposite effect – it compounds the profits. A contract with the quest for knowledge will inspire you every day; it will help you to clamber out of bed (teenage years notwithstanding) and ask why. Ask why to everything – never take anything at face value. Ask. Why is this? Why is that? Ask why all the time, even if it drives your parents insane. Asking why will help you challenge and shape your own opinions and beliefs as they develop and change over time – this is what is meant by growing.

I won't always get things right – it's insane for me to suggest otherwise. I hope you can forgive the many mistakes I will make over the course of your life. Despite the uncertainties that lie ahead, I want you to know that I am as committed to you as rain is to falling from the sky. I'm going to do my best, and I'm going to try and make it fun along the way – and so is your Mummy.

Personal bias aside, I can tell you that you are blessed to have the Mummy you do. If Steve Jobs was destined to build computers and Beethoven was destined to make music, then your Mummy was destined to become a Mummy. She's a natural; she has a gift with children that is unrivalled. They are drawn to her warmth, and they take comfort in her care. It's something that needs to be witnessed to be believed.

Her reputation is causing her fear and anxiety about parenthood. She worries that everyone expects her to be a model Mummy because of the gift she shows in caring for other children. She worries she won't live up to it. This is where you and I come in; we need to remind her that she doesn't have to live up to anyone's expectations, even ours; she just needs to take it moment by moment.

Between the three of us, we'll all learn as we go. Remember this: I don't know what I'm doing, but then if I did, it wouldn't be as much fun, would it?

Good luck on your journey from Mummy's tummy to the outside world. I'm told it's quite traumatic for babies (though I've forgotten my own experience), but try not to worry; you have your parents' everlasting love and affection waiting for you on the other side.

Much love,

Daddy

xxx

Sunday, 10 November 2019 – The Plot Thickens, My Dear Watson

It's taken her three days to notice, but Mummy has discovered that her raspberry tea has gone walkabout. She's not happy and she's holding me accountable. Furthermore, she's also not happy about how she found out that her tea was missing.

Her words to me were as follows: 'Last night, I couldn't sleep because your son or daughter was kicking the shit out of me, and so I thought I would get up and drink some raspberry tea.'

By the way, it's totally obvious that I hid the tea, right? Good. Just checking.

Mummy continues, 'So I went downstairs, opened up the cupboard and noticed it was missing. I thought I was going mad. Then I searched the other cupboards. Still nothing. I even had to turn the big light on.'

Now, I was holding it together while she was detailing her seek-and-capture strategy, but when she admitted to having to resort to such desperate measures as turning the main light on, I couldn't hold it in any longer.

'And I thought, has that little bastard hidden it? No, he wouldn't do that to a nine-month pregnant woman. But I can see now by your laughter that that's exactly what you've done.'

'You forced my hand.'

To be clear, Dory, not only have I put her through the ordeal of having to turn the main kitchen light on, but I'm now trying to avoid any blame coming my way by using manipulation tactics.

'How have I done that?'

'You're attempting to bring on an early labour and I wanted to get the last of the painting done and watch a few *Star Wars* films – your selfishness backed me into a corner and forced me into taking drastic measures.'

'You're a child!'

'That's like saying the sky is blue. Now, how about I go and make us a nice cup of raspberry tea?'

Tuesday, 12 November 2019 – I'm Ready

I'm ready to meet you now. The last few days have been a bit surreal for me as I adjust to not going to work and sorting out the last few bits around the house. I think I've been guiltier of nesting than Mummy has, but now I've done all that and I want to meet my child.

Hurry up, please.

Thursday, 14 November 2019 – Due Date

Mummy is forty weeks today – she's hit her due date. Well done, kiddo. Now please come out and meet your parents.

Friday, 15 November 2019 – One Day Late

Nothing, Dory – not a peep.

Saturday, 16 November – Two Days Late

Still nothing, Dory – and that's a problem. Mummy hasn't felt you move at all today, but she feels bad about potentially wasting the midwives' time by asking them to check her out. But she won't relax until she knows you're OK, so I've said if she wants to get checked out – we need to go in!

I make a quick call to Rebecca, who validates my thoughts: 'Go in and get checked.' She says she would come in herself, but Sean is in New York, and she doesn't have a babysitter for her little girl.

5.00 p.m. Mummy calls the hospital, and they advise her to come in, and to bring an overnight bag just in case – this is a precaution, because Mummy is now two days overdue.

5.20 p.m. After checking the hospital bags a dozen times, we're ready to go. But as we're about to leave I remember two important items that we've forgotten. I run upstairs and grab Ruby and your Dory toy from the bed and pack them in your bag – just in case.

5.30 p.m. We arrive at the labour ward and meet the receptionist, Kate. Kate tells us that in the two years that she's worked here, she's never known the ward to be this busy.

Great.

We manage to get separate seats in the waiting area and begin reading our books. I feel this will be a long night.

5.32 p.m. Kate walks into the middle of the busy waiting room and finds Mummy with a gaze. 'Where's your partner?' Kate says.

I make my presence known.

'Would you both like to follow me?'

I feel a dozen pairs of eyes glaring at the back of my skull, but I'm as confused as anyone as to why Kate has called us through, especially after what she told us a few moments ago.

We follow Kate through a corridor and away from the busy waiting room. Kate turns to Mummy and says, 'Rebecca's been on the phone and asked me to move you somewhere more comfortable where you can make yourself a cup of tea. I hear tea is very special to you.'

It really does pay to know the right people.

The sitting room has a fridge, a kettle, a television and two double-seater sofas – not to mention a couple of medicine balls for the Mummies (or the Daddies) to sit on.

While waiting for Mummy to be seen, I notice a stats chart on the wall. It tells me that the biggest baby born in the hospital in the last twelve months weighed 5.49 kg – that's 12.037 lbs. Now that is what you call a front-bottom ouchie, Dory.

6.48 p.m. Rebecca arrives at the hospital in plain clothes to personally carry out Mummy's checks. Apparently, she managed to get her sister to babysit at short notice. I should also mention that Rebecca is six months pregnant herself.

6.50 p.m. Mummy is wired up for a CTG monitoring. This will tell us if you're OK.

7.20 p.m. The results have come back as satisfactory – you're fine. Mummy and Daddy can relax now. However, we're told that because Mummy is past her due date, she'll need to be induced, but they're busy with the other Mummies (I think everyone got lucky on Valentine's Day) and they don't know when they will be able to fit us in. It's looking likely to be Wednesday – another four days of waiting to meet you.

8.10 p.m. While waiting for a doctor to review Mummy, Rebecca realises that she hasn't checked her blood pressure. She straps Mummy in and lets the machine do its thing.

I realise there's a problem instantly. I can read it on Rebecca's face.

'That's odd,' she says.

What's odd, Dory? What the fuck is odd?

'Let me repeat the test manually; sometimes the machines can be inaccurate.'

Rebecca repeats the test, but the results are the same – the machine was accurate. Mummy's blood pressure is 167/104. This is not normal. Rebecca wants to carry out a few more tests to rule out Mummy having pre-eclampsia.

I don't even know what pre-eclampsia is. I've read about it many times, and it's come up in our NCT classes, but I've never understood exactly what it is.

While waiting for the results, I read up on the condition that Mummy might have. The NHS website says that the exact cause of pre-eclampsia is unknown, but it's thought to occur when there's a problem with the placenta. Sometimes (and this is apparently rare), pre-eclampsia can lead to something called eclampsia (known as a pre-eclamptic fit) where the Mummy will have a seizure. A small percentage of cases can lead to permanent disability or brain damage depending on the severity of the seizure.

I stop reading after that.

Are you OK? Is Mummy OK? Can they treat it?

8.39 p.m. A doctor arrives to perform a scan to check you're OK. He then explains to Mummy that she will need an internal examination to see if we can get things going with a stretch and sweep. Not one single person in the room appreciates my offer to perform this examination myself.

Ahead of the examination, Mummy realises that she's wearing *Minions* underwear.

9.00 p.m. I've just realised that it's exactly eight months to the day since my day of discovery.

9.06 p.m. Rebecca performs a stretch and sweep and becomes the first person other than Mummy to have direct contact with you, Dory. She can feel your head.

On a side note, I should say that I have no idea if these details will fuck you up as an adult. I don't know if you want to know all this, so I apologise if some of it is 'too much information'. But I'm running blind here, Dory, so give your old man a break, all right?

The results of the examination reveal that Mummy is two centimetres dilated. She needs to get to ten centimetres before she can start the eviction process.

9.26 p.m. It's official: Mummy has pre-eclampsia. Not only will she need to be induced, as the only way to cure pre-eclampsia (so Rebecca tells me) is to have the baby and get rid of the placenta, but she must also stay in the hospital until you're here. The induction won't begin tonight, because the labour ward is too busy and the staff don't deem it safe to start another Mummy off into labour.

We both take some time to adjust to the news, and then I help Mummy get settled in for the night. I'm not allowed to stay at the hospital with you both, so I tell her that everything will be fine, kiss you both goodnight and then head home.

11.07 p.m. I'm lying in bed wondering if we'll meet each other tomorrow. I hope to fuck you guys are OK.

Sunday, 17 November 2019 – Three Days Late

8.05 a.m. Mummy calls me and announces that she feels groggy, she's been sick and she didn't get to sleep until 5.00 a.m. She also requests that I come to the hospital armed with chocolate croissants.

11.45 a.m. The induction officially begins. Sophie (the on-shift midwife; Rebecca tells us that she is wonderful) inserts something called a 'Propess' into Mummy. I'm told it contains a synthetic hormone which should soften things up inside, and hopefully get labour started. Sophie becomes the second person to have direct contact with you.

12.02 p.m. I can hear another midwife giving breastfeeding advice to a couple in another room. However, only the man is responding to the midwife. He says things like 'Yes, OK' or 'I understand' every time she imparts some new information. This makes it seem as if he's the one who's breastfeeding. It reminds me of the film *Junior*.

12.05 p.m. I've had a flatulence report from the Matriarch. She says, 'Last night, I had some of the worst category-1s ever. They were pure evil and nasty.'

12.54 p.m. Mummy could be in hospital for a few more days, so I've been given a special piece of paper that allows me to buy another special piece of paper for ten pounds. This in turn will allow me unlimited parking for the next seven days.

Exchanging the first special piece of paper for the second special piece of paper is like going through the twelve labours of Hercules. First, there is only one desk in the entire hospital that can issue the second special piece of paper. Of course, this one desk is nine miles away. Once I eventually reach it, I find it devoid of personnel. However, there is a phone on the desk with a phone number displayed next to it and an instruction to call that number. I've got nothing else to go on, so I might as well comply. Eventually, I speak to security, who tell me I can park free for twenty-four hours and that I didn't need to bother with any bits of paper.

1.15 p.m. I'm on my way back to Mummy when one of the Daddies from our NCT class spots me. He's just had a little boy. The new Mummy edges over ever so slowly and gives me a broad-brushstrokes summary of her labour experience – in short, Dory, it was horrific. It lasted three days and had more drama in it than the complete works of Shakespeare. Still, this news means that six out of eight Mummies from our NCT group have given birth – and all babies and Mummies are doing OK. Let's hope we can soon add you to that club.

2.25 p.m. No signs of contractions, but Mummy's blood pressure has dropped to a less alarming level. She's at 140/91. She celebrates the occasion by setting herself a little challenge. The challenge is for her to be the loudest snorer on the ward. She's winning.

At least she's resting.

7.49 p.m. You've got hiccups. I lay my face on Mummy's tummy so I can feel them. I wonder if this will be the last time I feel them while you're still in Mummy's tummy. I hope so – in the nicest possible way.

9.00 p.m. I'm back at home, Dory, and I'm getting straight into bed, in case I'm called back into hospital in the middle of the night. Once again, I'm wondering how long until we meet: hours or days?

Monday, 18 November – Four Days Late And The Start Of The Longest Night Of My Life

7.05 a.m. I wake to the following message:

> Hey baby, I don't want to wake you, so I'm texting. I'm having tiny contractions, so I'm going to be monitored from now on, and then this afternoon (when they can take us), I will have my waters broken. We could have a baby either today or tomorrow latest. Xxxxx

I get out of bed, shower quickly and eat as much porridge as my stomach will allow me to swallow without throwing up, because I don't know when I'll next eat. I pack you some muslin squares, as we'd forgotten about them.

8.06 a.m. I zigzag through the ward and arrive at Mummy's bed only to find her dozing.

She stirs, and then reports that: 'Contractions have started.'

'How bad?' I ask.

'Not too bad yet, they just hurt my bum a bit.'

Mummy's wired up to the CTG monitor which, as well as your heartbeat, also records when contractions happen. So far, the reading hasn't gone above eighty, but then I make her laugh and that sends the monitor into three digits, before causing Mummy to wet herself. I can now say that I've literally made someone piss themselves laughing.

Is today the day?

A porter arrives to take Mummy to another ward, which turns out to be similar to the previous one, except that the visitor's chair is adjustable and I can lie right back, which gives me the feeling that I've received a flight upgrade.

11.00 a.m. Annoyingly, the contractions have stopped. The upside is that Mummy is able to get some decent sleep for the first time since Saturday night.

Midday. Mummy wakes and almost throws up at the sight of a small plastic cup on her bedside table containing cold tea. 'Can you go and buy me a mug so I can have a decent cup of tea?'

On my way into town, I stumble into a vintage shop that I didn't even know existed. It's out of character for me to go browsing anywhere other than in a bookshop. Anyhow, I walk in and realise that this is Mummy's idea of heaven. It has a seemingly endless number of nooks and crannies where all sorts of vintage delights reside: retro posters, outdated furniture, records, figurines, ornaments from the '50s, '60s and '70s.

I don't know how we've not been here before. I take a quick look around and remember that I've not got Mummy a 'push present' – a gift from the Daddy to the Mummy to acknowledge everything the Mummy goes through to bring a baby into the world. Perhaps I can find something here.

There are two things that Mummy loves more than anything (I'll remind you that you've not been born yet): vintage furniture and Alice in Wonderland. Her thirtieth birthday party was Alice in Wonderland themed.

I'm staring at a handcrafted, upcycled chair that has an Alice in Wonderland quotation on it, not to mention the little lady herself printed on the cushion fabric. I don't believe in fate, but something is at work today; the coincidences are stacked higher than the Eiffel Tower.

I spoke too soon. There's no price tag on the chair, only a tag that reads: 'SOLD'. Damn it. Let's not give up, though, Dory. What does Daddy like to say? Yes, this is just another problem to overcome.

I approach the chap behind the desk and ask if the chair is indeed sold, and if it is, whether there is any way we can contact the buyer and come to an arrangement. I'm not sure what the arrangement looks like, but it ends with me owning the chair. I explain why the gift is important, but he tells me that there is nothing he can do.

'Do you have anything that's even remotely similar to the chair coming into the store any time soon?' I say.

'Funny you should say that; the maker is due to send us another one at some point before Christmas.'

'Wonderful stuff – can you mark it as sold for me right now?'

'I can.'

Ten minutes later, my phone goes off; it's the chairmaker, following up on the order. She asks if the chair is for a Christmas present. I explain that my partner is in the early stages of labour and that this is her push present.

'I will get to work on it immediately, and I'll do my best to have it ready within the next couple of weeks,' she says.

'Perfect.'

Like I said, Dory, something is at play here.

1.32 p.m. I'm back at the hospital, having completed my mission of a mug purchase. The Matriarch is happy with my work in the field. Contractions have not started up again, and the labour ward is still extremely busy, which means Mummy's waters won't be broken until this evening.

1.38 p.m. You won't believe what I'm doing right now – I'm reading the rules of Dobble. I'll never hear the end of it. But we need something to do to pass the time, so Dobble it is.

2.30 p.m. I won at Dobble and Mummy is sulking. This has led to her sending me home to clean the house.

3.00 p.m. Rebecca's been in contact to say that, if we want, she has the opportunity to work an extra shift tomorrow and can come in and look after Mummy. I'm hoping that you'll be here by then, but in case you're not, it will be nice to have a familiar face who works on the labour ward. We accept her offer.

4.00 p.m. I'm still at home. Mummy rings me to say that the labour ward is still too busy, so unless she goes into labour naturally (which is looking more and more unlikely), her waters won't be broken until lunchtime tomorrow – good job we took Rebecca up on her offer.

7.00 p.m. I sit down, having finished my cleaning chores, and think about putting Star Wars on, when I get a call from the Matriarch.

'Change of plan; they're breaking my waters tonight,' she says.

'I'm on my way.'

7.30 p.m. I've lost count of the times I've walked from the car to the labour ward recently, but this is the first time I've done it carrying your baby bag.

7.35 p.m. I arrive, and Mummy introduces me to Hannah, our midwife for tonight. Hannah has been hand-selected by Rebecca, who continues to micromanage proceedings behind the scenes on our behalf. Rebecca assures us we're in good hands – Hannah is one of the best.

7.45 p.m. I'm chairing a video conference between me, Hannah, Mummy and Rebecca, who has called for an update, and also to deliver further instructions to Hannah.

'Hannah, don't be rushing anything; I know it's selfish, but I want to be there for the birth. Take your time,' Rebecca says.

The midwives continue to strategise about how best to ensure that you make your appearance as close as possible to the start of Rebecca's shift. The whole thing is surreal but also hilarious – can you imagine the scene?

Despite her obvious exhaustion, Mummy's in high spirits; calm and relaxed, but also ready to meet you and discover that you're a healthy baby boy or girl.

9.30 p.m. It's almost time for Mummy to have her waters broken (still no signs of anything happening naturally), but before this happens, Mummy puts on a special dressing gown. It's the same one Granny Feeder wore when she gave birth to Mummy.

9.43 p.m. Hannah's about to break Mummy's waters using an amnihook – a tool for that purpose. She asks me to hand it to her, which I think means that Daddy can take ten per cent of the credit for delivering you.

9.44 p.m. Hannah breaks Mummy's waters.

9.47 p.m. Next, Hannah applies a clip directly on to your head, so she can continually monitor your heart rate (more accurately than the CGT machine), which she needs to do because of the pre-eclampsia and the induction process.

Mummy appears to be relaxed.

I pretend to be, but I'm not. Something tells me we're in for a long night. I know I'm about to see the woman I love endure more pain than she's experienced before in her life. This terrifies me. But I'm doing none of the hard work tonight, so I bury those feelings and put on a strong face. 'You've got this,' I tell Mummy.

10.33 p.m. Hannah steps out of the room, and the three of us are alone. Mummy confesses that she is in fact scared as well. 'I'm not looking forward to the pain, and I feel sick,' she says.

But then, in quick succession, two things happen that settle her nerves (temporarily, at least). First, she farts loudly and we each burst into a fit of giggles, sending the growing family of monitors that she's wired up to into a frenzy. Then, as I run around the bed to fetch a sick bowl for her, I bang my head on a lamp, bringing on even more laughter.

11.03 p.m. Mummy reports that she's sore and uncomfortable, that contractions have started up again, and that she needs a wee (even though she's just been for one). A moment later, Hannah returns with unwelcome news.

'I'm afraid you've got a water infection.'

No wonder Mummy needs the toilet, Dory. But, because Mummy is wired to so many machines, any time she needs a wee, Hannah and I have to lift her up and out of the bed so that she can squat over a cardboard bedpan.

Fuck me, Mother Nature doesn't make this easy, does she? I think back to our NCT classes and wonder how much better off we all would be with a few tea lights dotted about the room to brighten the mood.

The going-for-a-wee protocol will remain in place for the duration of the labour.

Mummy's now into her third night in the hospital and active labour is only now about to begin. And she has a water infection. For the first time since my day of discovery, I wonder if I would prefer you to be a boy, so that you're spared the pain that women endure.

11.58 p.m. Despite mild contractions, Mummy hasn't dilated any more; she's still at two centimetres (remember, we need her to be at ten). The next step in the induction is to start Mummy on a synthetic hormone drip to encourage stronger and more frequent contractions.

'Understand that the induction process is an unnatural way to bring on labour,' Hannah says. 'When the contractions begin, they will be intense right from the start. Do you understand?'

'So basically, it's about to fucking hurt?' Mummy says.

Hannah's tone is sympathetic. 'Yes.'

The hormone drip adds to what is already a logistically complex set up. Mummy is now wired up to a contraction monitor on top of her tummy;

a heart-rate monitor on your head that's coming out the front door; a blood-pressure strap on her right arm, inflating and deflating at regular intervals; and a cannula the size of a broom handle in her left hand (which she can't bend) administering the hormone drip.

Strangely, cannulas didn't come up in our NCT class while we were practising birthing positions.

Tuesday, 19 November 2019 – Just Keep Swimming

12.01 a.m. It's Tuesday, 19 November 2019. Is today the day? Before I can give it any more thought, Mummy signals that she's in discomfort. The contractions are getting stronger, and she's struggling to get into a good place mentally. At least this finally means progress, Dory – we're long overdue a bit of progress.

12.27 a.m. Hannah and Daddy have moved Mummy onto her side, which has helped her to get comfortable. Hannah has turned off the lights and Daddy has put Mummy's hypnobirth music on.

The music has worked, Dory. Mummy's breathing instantly changes. She's found a place where her mind is comfortable, and she's there now – in the zone. She's looking strong; her resilience is inspiring.

Women are incredible.

Hannah says that, unless you materialise beforehand, she will re-examine Mummy at 5.00 a.m. to see how far dilated she is. That's a little over four and a half hours away. Come on, kiddo.

1.31 a.m. I've stepped outside to make a coffee and take a deep breath. I'm finding it difficult seeing Mummy go through this, knowing that I don't have the resources or capability to do anything about it. I knew to expect this, but it doesn't make it any easier. I just feel utterly useless.

1.50 a.m. So far, Mummy has refused any type of pain relief, despite experiencing intense contractions for almost two hours now. Hannah suggests gas and air (Entonox) to help with Mummy's breathing. Mummy accepts.

Anything to take the edge off, Dory.

2.03 a.m. What I'm watching is physically painful for Mummy and psychologically discomforting for Daddy; however, it's deeply intimate. It's different from the intimacy that lovers share; it's a broader human intimacy. I feel as though I'm peeking into the heart of the human experience. It's not just my child that's being guided towards the start of a new life; it's a member of the human race. It's a majestic thing to watch – despite everything else that comes with it.

2.05 a.m. Hannah's called away for something, and the moment she leaves the door, Mummy spins over and offers the gas-and-air tube to me. That she has time and space to think about my experience in all of this is beyond me.

'Quick, get on this,' says the most perfect woman in all of existence, Dory.

I take a few deep breaths. After a couple of seconds, I begin to feel light-headed and relaxed. My fingers start to tingle slightly. Now that I've ticked that box, I gently roll Mummy back on her side, hand back the gas and air and whisper in her ear, 'You're doing great, keep going.'

2.25 a.m. Contractions are coming hard and fast now, Dory, yet Mummy doesn't make a sound. She breathes through them every time. I don't understand how this is possible when she's never done this before and she's in that much pain.

I don't say anything. I still feel useless, but I know what my role is now. I need to sit here, remain silent and let Mummy do her thing. If she needs me, she'll ask for me, and I'll be right by her side.

2.45 a.m. While helping Mummy out of bed with Hannah for what feels like the hundredth wee of the night, I somehow end up with a handful of … let's call it 'stuff' (although I think they call it a 'show' in midwifery terms: basically a stretchy blob of blood-streaked mucus) in my hand.

It was a knee-jerk reaction on my part. I was helping Mummy aim for the bedpan when I noticed – and there's no way to sugar-coat this – globules of this stuff about to come spilling out of Mummy and drop onto the floor with a big splat. I didn't want Mummy to worry or get distracted from the great work she's doing. Instinctively, I reached out as the stuff dropped out of Mummy and caught it in the palm of my hand. Neither Hannah nor Mummy saw me do this.

But as I said, it was instinctive – I didn't refer the decision to a committee for a vote on it to see if it was a good one or not. So now Mummy is finishing up her business, with me and Hannah standing on either side of her. I'm secretly holding a handful of Mummy – and I don't have a stack of options as to what to do with it.

Somehow, along with Hannah, I help Mummy hobble back into bed without needing to use my left hand, which is carrying the cargo. Once Mummy is back in bed, I walk to the sink and offload it by discreetly washing my hands.

2.51 a.m. Another midwife has come to relieve Hannah so that she can have a break; she too is an angel. I'm astounded by the level of care these women give to the Mummies. Anyone can go to college and learn the science, biology and medicine of what's entailed in childbirth, but that only partly qualifies you. It's the bedside manner that can't be taught in a classroom; the small details that cement the bond between patient and caregiver: the encouraging half-smiles, the gentle rub of a shoulder, the hushed reminders to the Mummies of how well they're doing.

This isn't at all what I expected. I expected screaming, frantic movements, and nail marks clawed into my arms – but there's been none of that so far.

4.40 a.m. It's twenty minutes before Hannah is due to examine Mummy. Mummy signals that she's had another big contraction, but that this one feels different. She says she feels as though she needs to push.

Is this it, Dory? Am I minutes away from meeting you? Will I soon be holding you in my arms, and will Mummy's pain come to an end?

Hannah tells Mummy to listen to her body; if it's telling her to push, then she should push.

4.50 a.m. Hannah has left the room again, and I seize the opportunity to take a quick selfie while Mummy is having another huge contraction. The world will judge me, and other Mummies might hate me, Dory, but I know your mother; she will be grateful that I took that picture … I hope …

4.59 a.m. The need to push has disappeared, Dory – the contractions have returned to 'normal'. One more minute until Hannah re-examines Mummy. My money is on her being seven to nine centimetres dilated.

5.00 a.m. Hannah re-examines Mummy. It's not the news we wanted, Dory. Mummy's only made it to three centimetres.

How? Mummy has been at this all night, yet she's only progressed one centimetre. My heart splits down the middle for Mummy, who turns to me, and I can read her expression before she says the words: 'Three fucking centimetres?'

Dory, this isn't fair. She's traversed the night brilliantly; she deserves more than this.

I'm reading high empathy levels in Hannah's face. She tries to soften the blow: 'You've done incredibly well; try not to be disheartened. You have to understand that an induction is not a natural process, and it can often take a long time.'

'What happens now?' I say.

'We need to be prepared for the fact that this could still take some time. How do you feel about an epidural?'

5.15 a.m. Mummy reluctantly agrees to the epidural and Hannah hands me an information card and asks me to read it to Mummy; she then leaves the room to go and find the anaesthetist. I scan the card, and it doesn't make for entertaining reading, especially at a time like this. It lists the chances of Mummy experiencing the following: a drop in blood pressure, severe headaches, nerve damage, an epidural abscess, meningitis, blood clots, unconsciousness and severe injury that includes paralysis.

I begin reading to Mummy, but she's still having contractions. She turns to me and says, 'Is there any fucking point?'

She's right. What's the fucking point? Mummy's been in the hospital for almost sixty hours, she's been in pain most the night, she's exhausted and things are not progressing. She's made the decision, so let's get on with it. Having a long list of possible risks read out to her will do nothing for her peace of mind, so I put the card down and lie to Hannah when she comes back into the room; I tell her I've read everything to Mummy.

5.20 a.m. Jane enters our room to perform the epidural. According to Rebecca, if there is one person in the world who we want performing an epidural, it's Jane.

We move Mummy into a seated position over the bed, and she's told to lean forward and relax her shoulders. I start shaking; I'm almost crying. I'm outraged by the injustice of how this labour is progressing for us, despite the lunacy of getting angry at external events beyond my control. That said, I may not have read the risk sheet to Mummy, but I did read it myself. *Come on, Jane.*

Just keep swimming, Mummy.

Just keep swimming, Dory.

Just keep swimming, Daddy.

Jane inserts the enormous, fuck-off needle into her spine and begins administering the epidural while Mummy remains leaning forward with her shoulders relaxed.

Mummy now has yet another tube protruding from her body, attached to yet another machine.

Childbirth – the gift that keeps on giving.

6.20 a.m. Mummy feels more relaxed; she can still feel contractions, but the epidural is doing its job. Hannah tells her that if she went into labour naturally, she thinks Mummy would cope fine with gas and air. This is exactly what Mummy needs to hear right now – once again, I'm amazed at how well the midwives can read their patients.

6.37 a.m. For the first time in over thirty hours, Mummy shuts her eyes for some sleep.

6.50 a.m. Mummy is no longer asleep. Hannah has woken her up to report that your heart rate has dropped. In a blink-and-you-miss-it moment, two other midwives and a doctor are suddenly present in the room (that's in addition to Hannah, Mummy, you and me) watching the monitor that's linked to your heart rate.

Neither Mummy nor I say anything, but nor do we stand on ceremony and try to hide our anxiety; panic is carved across our granite-like faces.

They turn Mummy on her side to see if that does anything. It doesn't. They move her onto her other side. That doesn't work either.

But then it does work – your heart rate normalises.

This is fucking torture.

7.00 a.m. Rebecca arrives at work and reports for duty in room four. Her patient today is a 35-year-old female who's in labour with her first child – she's been through the wringer.

7.40 a.m. Despite contractions continuing, the epidural allows Mummy to sleep.

'Why don't you try and get some sleep in the car?' Rebecca says to me.

I don't want to leave you and Mummy, so Rebecca makes me up a makeshift bed next to you guys. It consists of one thin blanket, one overly large pillow and a hard floor. For the first time in forever, I close my eyes and drift off to sleep.

10.00 a.m. Mummy and I are awake and we're in good spirits, all things considered. I don't know how your mother can be cheery with everything that's going on, but she is.

We've agreed on a plan with Rebecca: another examination will happen at 11.00 a.m. to see if Mummy's further dilated. If progress is good – brilliant, we'll see you in a few hours. If not, we'll begin emergency C-section discussions.

10.30 a.m. I've been to the canteen to eat breakfast and my walk back through the labour ward reveals a different atmosphere to the one I experienced last night. I can hear other Mummies screaming in agony – each scream an affirmation of the strength of their gender, and a reminder of the sacrifices they make so that the human race can continue. I can hear them crying tears of joy as they meet their newborn babies for the first time.

I've been so focused on you and Mummy that I've failed to notice all the other stories that are happening at the same time, all around me.

I cast my attention wide to see what's going on: lots. I hear the heavy footsteps of medical staff thundering in tune to the emergency alarms that are sounding; I hear babies crying and people cheering; I see midwives yawning and a kettle pouring; I see vending machines churning and porters wheeling.

I watch Daddies on their phones, updating their loved ones on the progress so far. A Mummy waddles slowly to the toilet. She's in pain, but she's in love; her baby is here, and her baby is OK. If you look past the screaming and the agony and the tiredness and the chaos, you find something else. Something beautiful.

I experience all of this in under thirty seconds, as I make my way back through the ward.

11.05 a.m. Mummy is five centimetres dilated. It's progress, but it's less progress than we were all hoping for.

How much longer will this go on for, Dory?

To add to the fun, Rebecca has discovered you've got a minor swelling on your head (called a caput), which is sometimes caused by the baby lying in an awkward position. This can prolong labour even more.

Rebecca says our chances of a C-section are now fifty-fifty.

12.20 p.m. A doctor has arrived to examine Mummy. Rebecca gives the doctor a progress report, along with her thoughts on the likelihood of an emergency C-section. The doctor agrees with Rebecca.

1.00 p.m. Another examination – Mummy is six centimetres dilated; still not where we wanted to be.

Everyone in the room is disheartened by the progress (or lack of it).

Rebecca is conflicted as to what she should be advising us to do now. Should she tell Mummy to continue as she is and see if she can get to ten centimetres, in the hope that there won't be any further complications? Or should we call it a day and send Mummy down to theatre for an emergency C-section?

I didn't want you to be delivered by C-section, but, equally, I didn't want Mummy to endure a three-day labour with pre-eclampsia, a urine infection and a full-scale induction that's hobbling along on crutches towards an uncertain conclusion.

Mummy is shattered; I can see it in her eyes.

We agree to give it two more hours.

2.27 p.m. Mummy is sound asleep. If I'm reading the monitor correctly, she's still having regular contractions. Once again, I'm in awe of the advances we've made in medicine – particularly the epidural procedure. There are risks; I'm not saying an epidural is the answer for every Mummy having a baby, but when the circumstances called for it, I'm thankful that the option to have it was there for Mummy.

2.54 p.m. The final examination is in six minutes. Fingers crossed for eight centimetres or more.

3.00 p.m. Rebecca carries out the examination. Seven centimetres dilated.

Not good enough.

Rebecca believes that if Mummy keeps at it, she will eventually get to ten centimetres, but she also thinks, as you are not lying in the best position and progress has been snail's-pace slow, that Mummy will probably require the doctor's help in delivering you, and that instruments will be necessary.

'If I were in your position, knowing what I know, I would rather have a C-section than risk something like a forceps delivery,' Rebecca says.

But Rebecca is conflicted, and her conscience is weighing in on the argument: she's emotionally tied to this delivery because she's a friend of ours; she feels bad for joking with Hannah about delaying the induction process so that she can be the one to deliver you (which we'd all love); she's worried that all of this is affecting her ability to judge what the right treatment is for her patient and friend. I think she's being hard on herself. Her logic and reasoning through every one of her decisions today has been sound.

In the end, Rebecca calls the doctor in for a second opinion as well as seeking counsel from her midwife colleagues.

As far as your parents are concerned, we want you here, and we want you here now – Mummy has had enough; I can read it in her eyes.

How she has any mental or physical strength left is beyond me.

3.15 p.m. The doctor is here. She weighs up the risks of the C-section against carrying on as we are. After she finishes, she asks Mummy for a decision. She takes one look at me, and we both nod.

'I want the section,' Mummy says.

3.45 p.m. I'm in the toilet having one last moment to myself. I'm wearing a full set of scrubs and a sexy pink hairnet. In these final moments before the surgery, I recap the previous eight months. On Saturday, 16 March 2019, I discovered I was going to be a Daddy: an unlikely scenario according to doctors. Then, at ten weeks, we thought we had lost you. This journey has had it all. It's been funny; it's been scary; it's taken twists and turns – it has had everything you look for in a thrilling narrative.

And now I need it to have a happy ending.

I don't care what the stats say about successful C-section procedures, and I don't care how experienced everyone in the operating room is – Dory, I am fucking shitting it! Please, please, please be OK. And please, please, please let Mummy be OK too.

You're on your final length of the pool – there's nowhere else to turn. The finishing line is in sight. One more time, kiddo, what do you say? Just keep swimming.

??.?? p.m. Mummy is carted off to theatre and I follow behind. There are several people in our entourage, though I only recognise Rebecca.

We reach the entrance to the theatre.

Someone in scrubs says, 'Would you like to wait here while we prepare for the procedure?'

'No, he's coming in,' declares Rebecca.

Even I can tell that this isn't open to debate. Once again, her influence has allowed me to sidestep protocol. I enter the theatre with your Mummy as a two-person family. When we leave, it will be as a three-person family.

Any number less than three is not up for discussion.

??.?? p.m. I take my place in the corner of the room and survey my new environment. The first thing I notice is how bright the room is: brighter than any room I recall standing in for a long time. I can't see any shadows.

But I can see machines, lots of machines – and a collection of metal instruments and other accoutrements all laid out like items on a cutlery tray in a workplace canteen.

There are eight other people in the room (not including you, me and Mummy), all scrubbed up and ready for surgery.

This all feels somehow … busy, like rush-hour traffic or the Boxing Day sales. People's movements are quick – perhaps too quick; it almost feels as though they're rushing. Notes are hastily checked, operating instruments are quickly counted, and machines are tugged and wheeled over to Mummy, and then connected to her.

My heart is beating so hard that I wonder if I've somehow got pre-eclampsia myself, despite not having a placenta inside me.

Time passes (I have no idea how much), and eventually I'm asked to take a seat next to Mummy. I take one look into her eyes, and all I can read is fear. I wonder if she can read mine as well. If she can, she might as well be looking in a mirror.

The theatre staff are arguing about who's doing what. It's surreal.

Imagine turning up to work in a kitchen expecting to be on veg prep, but instead, you're assigned pot-wash duty and you're not happy about it; you're so incredibly unimpressed that you choose to voice your dissatisfaction to your colleagues right there and then. But your work, in this scenario, involves major surgery on a woman who has been in the hospital for three days, who hasn't slept and who is shit-scared for the safety of her unborn child and herself – and she's lying there slap-bang in the middle of the ongoing conversation.

I glance at Rebecca; she's livid.

Now a young woman is spraying something on Mummy, asking her to tell her when she can feel the cold. The feedback from Mummy will tell her if the epidural is working in all the right places. Apparently, pain receptors carry a temperature reading to the brain, so if Mummy can't feel the cold spray then she won't feel pain either.

I don't know where to place my hands; there are so many wires in the way that Mummy looks like an android that's been mauled by a pack of wolves.

'Make sure you're touching me; I don't care where,' Mummy says.

I stroke her head, and I promise her everything will be all right. Then I rest my hand on her shoulder and squeeze it lightly to tell her I'm here with her.

'Don't go anywhere,' she says.

'Never,' I say.

She means here; right now, in this moment – but I mean forever, in every moment. This woman, your Mummy, has done humankind proud.

The next thing I know, a makeshift screen is erected over Mummy's tummy. I presume it's there so that neither of your parents can watch the doctors perform the surgery.

It's a strangely isolating feeling – the two of us back here behind the curtain. I think the anaesthetist is on watch behind us somewhere, but I can't be sure.

Mummy says she can feel tugging; she looks terrified.

'But can you feel any pain?' one of the doctors asks gently.

'No,' Mummy replies.

That's normal, then. Mummy will feel movement, but she won't feel pain. This means they have begun the procedure. It won't be long now, Dory.

Mummy is shaking, Dory. I don't know what to say to keep her calm. I'm shaking as well.

'Your insides look really good,' Rebecca jokes; the perfect thing to say at exactly the right time. Mummy smiles and her shaking reduces.

Time passes, Dory. It feels like hours, but it can only be minutes.

'Almost there,' Rebecca says.

Am I ready for this? It's a bit fucking late if I'm not. In a few moments, I won't know who I am, because who I am is about to shift continents as I officially receive my new identity.

I remember the feeling I had the first time I realised I was going to be a Daddy.

One day you'll call me Daddy.

Yes, I'm ready.

I'm crying now, Dory, and so is Mummy. We're staring into each other's eyes, waiting.

Waiting.

Waiting.

Still waiting.

And then I hear it – the sound of you, my newborn baby, crying.

If I took all the chocolate, sugar and honey in the world and mixed them together, their sweetness wouldn't match that of the cry my newborn baby makes as it takes air into its lungs for the first time.

You're here, Dory.

But your cry vanishes as quickly as it arrived – it was a short, sharp cry, not the continued wailing that you see in the movies.

Is everything OK?

But then Rebecca appears by our side. She's carrying a bundle of blankets, and in the centre of it is my world.

She lifts the blanket for me to see you clearly. I turn to Mummy and through the tears and the smiles I whisper four words: 'We have a boy.'

'He's got a willy?'

I nod.

My special little boy. We will have adventures that rival those of any Greek mythical hero: our lightsaber fights will be the stuff of legend, we'll build forts, we'll fight baddies, we'll hide from Mummy, we'll play in the park, we'll go camping. There is so much I want you to see and do. I will devote my life to you. You are loved unconditionally.

'Do you have a name?' Rebecca asks.

'We're still deciding,' Mummy says.

We have two names for a boy, Dory. Mummy prefers one, and I prefer the other; though we love them both.

'Actually, we do have a name,' I say.

I turn to your Mummy. 'After that performance, you can choose any name you want,' I say.

'Are you sure?'

'Of course I'm sure, how can I not be?'

'OK,' she says.

Dory, this will be the last time I call you Dory. I want to say thank you for the last eight months. You have given me such a wonderful experience; one that, as a man, I never imagined I would have. You have taught me a lot about myself, and you have helped me prepare for fatherhood. For that, I will forever be thankful to you, Dory.

Whenever things get tough, whatever life throws at me, I will try to remember the words I've been telling you during the pregnancy. No matter what hardships you face, and no matter what obstacles you find in your way – just keep swimming.

But now it's time to say our goodbyes, and welcome in a new chapter in our lives.

'What's the name, then?' Rebecca presses.

Goodbye, Dory – thanks for everything.

'Arlo,' I say. 'His name is Arlo.'

Your name is Arlo. And your Mummy and Daddy love you to the moon and back.

~~The End~~
The Beginning

Acknowledgements

No one achieves in isolation. I would like to thank a number of people whose help was invaluable to me in writing this book.

I was fortunate enough to work with several brilliant editors. Thanks to Ian McIlroy: your commitment to making the book better than I alone could make it will forever remain an unpayable debt. You are a literary angel. To Lucy Rose: your structural advice on what to cut was invaluable – especially so where you pointed out that I perhaps shouldn't call the mother of my unborn child an idiot for eating undercooked chicken.

To Ross Dickinson, another fantastic editor: your keen insights and impeccable command of the English language filled the many (and I mean many) gaps in my knowledge.

I'd like to thank those people who read an early draft of *Dear Dory,* including Steph Kater, Tom Roberts, Laurel Chalk, Ceri Bate, Haylee Loe, Martin Birse, Marie Hepplewhite, Laura Mutlow, Laura Day, Cara Pritchard, Samantha Arnold, Hazel Lewis and my grandad, Mike Kreffer. The book is better because of your feedback. Special thanks to Jasmine Storr, who not only provided feedback but also came up with the book's title.

To my good friend Jamie Allerton, who ran point on reviewing the book's humour, and for providing the Butlins joke (one of my favourites in the book): I'm thankful that I have a professional stand-up comedian for a friend. Also, thanks for lending me the money for a deposit on my first house.

To Teressa and Adaline at TJM Cover Designs who took charge of book design and layout: working with you was a pleasure.

To Andrew Roberts: thank you for taking charge of narrating the audio format.

To the writers of *Finding Nemo*, Andrew Stanton, Bob Peterson and David Reynolds: I don't know which one of you came up with the line 'Just keep swimming', but know that it got me through some dark moments during the pregnancy. Thank you to Thomas Newman for writing the music to *Finding Dory*. The track 'Shells' will stay with me forever.

Thank you to the midwives, doctors and nurses of Northampton General Hospital. You helped play a part in welcoming a new member to the Kreffer family; words alone cannot express the depth of my gratitude, especially to you, Hannah, for keeping me company during the longest night of my life, and for being an outstanding ambassador for the midwifery community.

Rebecca, if I noted down all the 'thank yous' I owe you there wouldn't be a tree left standing on the planet, so I'll simply say thanks for everything.

Mum, you've always encouraged me to write stories and seek inspiration: thanks for letting me stay up late one school night so I could watch *Return of The Jedi* for the first time.

To my partner, Charlene: thanks for supporting this project. Despite knowing how candidly our relationship would be portrayed you signed off on it, anyway. You are the Mona Lisa of motherhood, not to mention a wonderfully funny pregnant woman to write about, if a little scary at times. And you always support me.

To my son, Arlo: you are everything to me. Thanks for smiling every day, and for trashing the shit out of my Blu-ray shelf while I was busy with the rewrites.

Finally, to any woman who has ever carried a child – hats off to you.

A Note From the Author

I'm a new writer, but I'd love to become an old one!

And by old, I mean someone who gets to release a ton of books over the course of their career. But to do that, I need your help. If you enjoyed *Dear Dory*, please consider heading over to Amazon or Goodreads and leaving a review. Tip: you can copy and paste the same review in both platforms. Reviews are immensely valuable to me, so your help and support is greatly appreciated.

And if you're planning to tell your mates about *Dear Dory*, they can find it on sale at all the big retailers (Amazon, Audible, Apple Books, Google Play, Barnes and Noble – plus many more outlets). It's available in the following formats:

Paperback
Hardback
eBook
Audio
Large print*

*Large print is available in both hardback and paperback editions.

About Tom Kreffer

Tom Kreffer has a degree in film and television and has worked in finance for over ten years. *Dear Dory* is his first book.

He lives in Northampton, England with his family, whom he intends to exploit for many more story opportunities in the years to come.

Say Hello!

My website www.tomkreffer.com
email at tom@tomkreffer.com

www.goodreads.com/tomkreffer
www.twitter.com/tkreffer
www.instagram.com/tom_kreffer
www.facebook.com/officialtomkreffer

Want More?

As a gift to readers of *Dear Dory*, I have excavated some of the entries that didn't make it into the final version of the manuscript. These are entries that I will not be publishing on my website. *Dear Dory: The Deleted Journals* is exclusively for those who took time out of their day to read *Dear Dory* – something for which I'm extremely grateful.

You can download *Dear Dory: The Deleted Journals* from:

www.deardory.co.uk/deleted-journals

Coming 2021

TOM KREFFER

Lightning Source UK Ltd.
Milton Keynes UK
UKHW011918121120
373303UK00010B/789/J